THE

KIRĀTĀRJUNĪYE by BHĀRAVĪ

(With Translations and Annotations)

CANTO VII TO XII

by

KAISHER BAHADUR K. C.

RATNA PUSTAK BHANDAR
BHOTAHITI, KATHMANDU
NEPAL

Publishers :
Ratna Pustak Bhandar
Bhotahiti, Kathmandu
NEPAL

First Published : 1974
1000 Copies

Printed in Nepal at
Jore Ganesh Press Pvt. Ltd.
Balaju Industrial District, Kathmandu.

Dedication

Dedicated to the immortal Nepali poet Bhāravi

—Kaisher Bahadur K. C.

CONTENTS

1. List of Abbreviations:	
2 Editor's Note	1–VI
3. Bio-data of the Editor:	VII
4. Canto VII :	1
5. Canto VIII:	27
6. Canto IX:	61
7. Canto X :	107
8. Canto XI :	140
9. Canto XII :	187
10. References :	219
Bibliography:	219
List of Inscriptions:	220

List of Abbreviations

1. GNI	—	Nepalese Inscriptions in Gupta Characters
2. ISMEO	—	Italian Institute for the Middle and Far East in Rome
3. Five Ms.	—	Pañcha-makāra, viz., **Madya** (wine), **maṃsa** (meat), **maithuna** (copulation,) **mantra** (spell)

Editor's Note

The publication of Bhāravi's inscription of the sixth century A.D. in the English edition of the classical work of the Kirātārjunîye has led to further researches by Śri Hemarāja Baudhopāsaka of the city of Lalitpur to publish in his booklet known as Abhilekha Prakāsh (1969 A.D.) another inscription of the poet dated Samvat 492 (572-573 A.D.) on a broken slab of stone measuring 11.5" X 10" in a bath served with a water-conduit surmounted by the figure of a peacock in the famous locality of Mangal-bazār to the east of Bhimasena and Visvanātha temples. According to Mr. Hemarāja the inscription of Bhāravi was set on the wall of a sunken court, which is normally covered by water. The author discovered it on the occasion of the sithi (Kumāraṣaṣthi) festival on Vikrama Samvat 2015, when the wells and fountains were being cleaned revealing temporarily Bhāravi's inscription in the pit beneath the water-spouts, of which he took a stamping. On examination the script was found to be of the early Licchavi period and the language was a refined Sanskrit. On the basis of Mr. Hemarāja's rubbings Mr. Dhanavajra Bajracārya published the text of Bhāravi's inscription in his compilation of Licchavi inscriptions published by the Tribhuvana University (No. 52). Bhāravi seems to have based himself on the inscription of his mother Vijayavatî contained in the Editor's Introduction to Part I of The Kirātārjuniye so far as his prayer to "Iśah" (Śiva) is concerned. Like the fountain of the village of Hārigāon dedicated to the immortal fame of himself and his grandfather Māna Deva I contained in the Editor's Introduction, the poet has dedicated this fountain to the memory of his parents (Princess Vijayavatî and Vārtta Devalābha) about twenty year's after the first event. What is most interesting in this inscription is the fact that the poet has donated landed property lying south-west of Yūpa-grāma (Licchavi name for what is the locality of Mangal-bazār in the heart of the city of Lalitpur today) to the Gausṭikas (co-operative organisation) yielding a total of fifty Maṇkas (coins of king Māna Deva I) on the assessment of rent at twenty (for each such land). Presently, we are planning to rescue the inscription and publish the result of the stamping with our translation in the Appendix. It is a matter of immense interest to the entire human community that such ancient baths with fountains are functioning in the heart of Nepal with the inscription of the immortal classical poet Bhāravi even to our own day.

Side by side we are happy to reproduce the book review in the Rising Nepal and the Editor's reply about the Sanskrit classic of the Kirātārjunîye, which will speak for themselves. It is equally interesting for the student of human history that Mr. L. Deosa Rai of Kiratā-origin has written the most profound review of the immortal classic of the Kirātārjunîye so far.

Book Review by Mr. L. Deosa Rai

"The book under review is an English translation of the Kirātārjuniye by Kaisher Bahadur K.C., who is a Nepali scholar-administrator-diplomat bundled into one. It, however, contains translation of only six cantos, out of the total of eighteen cantos. It gives a summary of each canto, and then the text, the transliteration of the text in Roman scripts and the English translation. Also, the author has taken pains to add his own notes to almost all stanzas, translations mainly with a view to restoring Bhāravi to his original reading by pointing out, wherever literal intrepretation is inadequate, the origins of the secondary or transferred meanings against the back-ground of the 'materials for the Nepalese history and culture'.

As one among the five well-known Sanskrit Mahākavyas and also as the only work on Bhāravi, the Kirātārjunîye, has been known to the literary world for more than thousand years, but the commentators throughout the century have made of it a medium to propagate their own ideas and beliefs.

This classic work is ranked with those of Kālidās, Bhavabhūti and the like and its author, Bhāravi, has been acclaimed for his 'profundity of thought and diction.'

EDITOR'S NOTE

The translator, Kaisher Bahadur K.C. has prefaced his work by giving reasons for his taking up the tranlsation and has also given an introduction in which he has made an attempt to prove by all available evidences Bhāravi as a Nepali. He has also added a note on the title 'Kirātārjunîye.'

The translator has made commendable attempt to render the great work into readable English prose. By choosing English as the medium of his expression the translator has addressed himself to wider readership, and that way the translator has made a definite contribution towards building up the image of Nepal. The English-knowing people can know by going through this book that "the profoundest poet in the history of Sanskrit literature", Bhāravi, was born and brought up in Nepal and not at Mālawā or Berar in South India as made out by the Indian historians and scholars. In his introductory portion of the book, the translator has quoted the authority of Prof. Gnoli's reading of the Licchavi Inscriptions to prove the birth in Nepal of the celebrated author of the Kirātārjunîye and, to clinch the issue, he has also brought in the authority of the inscription on the slab of stone which bears the name of Bhāravi and which was rescued by the translator himself from the foundation of a house at Hārigāon in Kathmandu, This latter inscription made by the order of Bhāravi himself proves that Bhāravi was the grandson of historically well-recorded king Mānadeva I. But the translator does not stop here. He brings in the whole background of social, political and religious situation and contends that "the inscription of Bhāravi dated Samvat 427 (550 A.D.) lends support to the theory that Mānadeva II mentioned in the inscription of Kevalpur may be identified with Bhāravi.

What is remarkable about this whole book is not the rendering of the classical work into English but the way the learned translator has brought all his erudition to bear upon the main task of building up his central thesis. In the process he has corrected the direction and drift of Bhāravi's original work; in other words, he has cleared up the misleading interpretations of Kirātārjunîye by the most authentic commentator and Sanskrit pandit, Mallināth, of South India, and has put Bhāravi's work in its correct perspective in relation to Space and Time of the poet himself.

All said, however, a few questions remain unanswered. The translator has proved Bhāravi to be a Nepali, but he has put forward only some circumstantial evidences to prove that this Nepali Bhāravi was non other than the same celebrated author of the Kirātārjunîye. And the curiosity still lingers if Bhāravi which finds mention in the inscription of Jina poet Ravikīrti in the Megauti temple (India) is a different person altogether and hence the real poet of the Kirātārjunîye since he is mentioned therein along with the great poet Kālidās.

Another point which the translator has dealt rather inadequately is about the identity of Indra-Kîla. According to him, "the craggy heights of Indra-kîla" appears to be a disguised name of the hillock marked by a Śiva-linga known as Kirātesvara in the Valley of Kathmandu.

The name Indra-kîla which was for the first time mentioned in the Vana Parba of the epic Māhābhārat, has been identified with the present-day Sikkim by the late Māhāmahophādhyāya Har Prasād Śhastri who has done intensive research on the ancient name 'Uttarākhanḍa', as well as by Gurunāth Vidyānidhi Bhattācharya in his preface to the edited version of the Kirātārjunîye in Bengali.

While the translator has given the impression at the end of preface that the book is complete in itself although consisting of only six cantos, the reference to Appendix I throughout the book is rather misleading, inasmuch as no such Appendix is to be found in the book.

The long list of errors at the end of the book of such a value is also undersirable since that is an indication of the magnitude of slips which has occurred in the book and that impinges on the accuracy of this book. The picture of dedicatory of stone could have been reproduced well on art paper and it would have looked better if placed as a frontis-piece facing the preface-page. Otherwise, the book is well produced."

Editor's Reply to the Above

"Thank you for your mature, stimulating and constructive criticism of my English edition of 'The Kirātārjunîye by Bhāravi' in the column of your Book Review of September 14,1973. With reference to some of your unanswered questions I have the pleasure to state as follows :- The climax of the classic of the Kirātārjunîye is depicted in the rock-relief of Mamallapuram (south of the city of Madras), which made Professor H. Goetz conclude that Bhāravi was the court poet of the Pallava King Mahendravarman I (600-630 A.D.). The inscription of Ravikîrti in Meghauti temple is dated 634-635, A.D. in which the Jina poet claims that his work is equal to those of Kālidāsa and Bhāravi. These evidences proved that Bhāravi had become extremely popular in Penninsular India by the second quarter of the 7th century A.D.

On the other hand, the inscription of Bhāravi indicating the water conduit to the temples of Dharamānesvara and Vāsudeva before Anuparama's celebrated pilaster of Hārigāon is dated 550-551 A.D. According to the inscription of Princess Vijayavatî in the gorge of Surya-ghāta (to which we have adequate reference in the body of the Kirātārjunîye), the poet's father Vartta Devalābha had died in 505 A.D. Judging by the poet's personal feelings about his grandfather Māna-Deva I in his inscription, I have reason to feel that the poet was born some time in the last decade of the fifth century and continued on to 560 A.D. when King Gaṇa-deva ascended the throne of Nepal with Bhauma-gupta Gomin of Āvir origin as his Prime minister. This hiatus of about a century will have to be worked out, and we have to consider the evidence of Śivadeva and Amsuvarman's inscription of Cāngu Nārāyaṇa, which seems to be earlier than the inscription of Ravi-Kîrti and the rock-reliefs of Mamallapuram. The inscription of Khuddasvani in the periphery of the temple of Paśupati leave us in no doubt that there was contact between Nepal and South India at the period. The internal evidences of the Kirātārjunîye provide a window on the world of the Kirātas, Yakśas, Kinnaras, Śākyas, Kolis and Sākas of Gold-race origin mentioned in our chronology against the rising tide of the Brāhmannic legends of King Sagara. As the classical work continues from the seventh Canto on to the closing eighteenth Canto, Bhāravi gives us glimpses of the steady development of the lost horizon of our Samyak Society, which culminated in the millennia of King Māna Deva anticipated by Bhāravi's grandmother Vijayasvāmîni in her inscription dedicated to Devî Bhagavatî Vijaya śhree of the village of Palānchowk (vide Plate XVIII. The Judicial Customs of Nepal Part I).

About Indra-kîla I found no evidence of the worship of Indra in the kingdom of Sikkim on my several visits to this ancient country. I have pointed out in the Judicial Customs Plate 28 depicting the image of Indro-nāma-divākara (the Sun of Power under the name of Indra with the icon of Śākyamuni on its crown) dated 480 A.D. how a part of the ancient Koli-grāma acquired the name of Indragriha (Yengāla) in the heart of what is Kāthmandu to-day. We know from our annual festival of Indra-jātra how Indra-parvata, Indra-daha, the image of Indro-nāma-divākara and Indra-griha occupy important places in the circumambulation of the holy places. The Annals of China confirm that Chi-pin (Indra-Pura), judging by their descriptive account of their Embassy, was this country in the fifth century A.D.

The internal evidences of Kirātarjunîye specifically mention Vijayavatî's worship in the gorge of Surya-ghāta, the basreliefs of Śiva Tripurantaka, Virupakṣya, Vishnu as the Midget in Three Vedic Steps, Mahendra-nāga and Kailāṣa in the neighbourhood of Indrakîla where Arjuna practised his penances befores the phallus of Śiva in the wake of the worship of Śākyavardhana. The style and make of the the Linga of Kirātesvara as well as the site and situation described in the Kirātarjunîye leave us in no doubt that Arjuna chose the place for his penances. Finnally the prayers of Arjuna to Pashupati in the scheme of Vyuha (fortress) in Canto XVIII establish that the scene of the immortal classic was very well laid in Paśupati-kṣetra.

For your kind information I wrote the entire introduction to cover the 18 Cantos together with the Appendix, which my publishers are planning to bring out sometime in 1974.

I agree with you that the long list of errors in such a classical work is undesirable. We would do our best to improve matters in the remaining 12 Cantos and the Appendix.

As desired by you I have invited the kind attention of my Publishers so that they may reproduce the picture of the dedicatory slab in art paper."

—Kaisher Bahadur K.C.

THE EDITOR

Bio-data from The International Who's Who (1970-1971)

With further Biographical Entry for the 1974-75 Edition :

Bahadur K.C., Kaisher; Nepalese educationist and diplomatist; born 28 January; 1907, Kathmandu; son of Major Dana Bahadur and Jagat Kumari Khattri Chettri; married Dev Kumari 1923; one son; one daughter; educated St. Paul's Mission School, St. Xavier's College and University College, Calcutta.

Translator and lecturer, Tri-Chandra College 30-32; research, inscriptions and sculpture in Nepal 32-45; Nepalese Resident in Tibet 46-50; Secretary, Ministry of Education,Health and Local Self-government 56-61; Delegate to UN 56-57, UNESCO 60; Amb,. to Peoples's Republic of China, concurrently to Mongolian People's Republic and Burma 61-65, also to Republic of Indonesia and Kingdom of Laos 62-65; Chairman, Nepal Public Service Commission 66; Chief Editor, Civil Service Journal of Nepal: awarded Italian Order of Merit for his discovery of "Materials for the study of Nepalese history and culture"; Order of the Gurkhas (first class) of king Mahendra 62.

Published "Description of the countries and peoples of the world" in Nepali language 35; Ancient and Modern Nepal 53; The Judicial Customs of Nepal, Part I First Edition 58 (revised versions of Parts I and II after a comparative study of the religious systems, culture, manners, customs and social institutions of China and countries of South-East Asia against the background of their ancient forms and history in the overall scheme of the Sumeru-culture complex under the impact of Nirvāṇa, Śaka and Māna Deva Millennias appearing on the fronton of ancient inscriptions, coins and dated image 65); Eroticism in Nepalese art 60; Introduction to Kathmandu and Patan on the visit of Her Majesty Queen Elizabeth II to Nepal 61, Universal value of Nepalese aesthetics Parts I and II 61-62.

Additional information :

The author had to resign from the Chairmanship of the Public Service Commission on January 15, 1970 to bring out the revised and enlarged second edition of the Judicial Customs of Nepal and also to publish an English edition of the immortal Sanskritic classic of The Kirātārjunīye by Bhāravi in three volumes, Nepal and Her Neighbours and Nepal after the Revolution of 1950 with a portrait of peerless king Tribhuvana 1972-1975.

KIRĀTĀRJUNIYE
CANTO VII

CANTO VII

Summary

This Canto consists of forty stanzas, and it opens with a quick trip of the fairies, music-makers, divine horses, and elephants in their spaceship out into the universe from heaven which is beyond the solar system, at the speed of their mind which is faster than the speed of light. As a good astronomer Bhāravi gives us his awesome grasp of creation vis–a–vis the Brāhmannic concept of the Three Worlds, as he unfolds his new visions of creation. Going through the Milky Way— the family of stars to which our solar system belongs, the poet gives us the coherence and grandeur of the universe which are made of star-dusts forged in the burning suns and born in cataclysm. We find from the experience of the heavenly bodies how the action starts from the infinitesimal particles of atoms which scintillate and blow like winds everywhere as the divine elephants roar to the echo. Very much earlier than the Chinese astronomers who were so far believed to be first to detect such explosions in 1054, the poet gives us a new picture of the universe with which the heavenly fairies and mankind had to live in the years ahead. As the fairies prepare to descend on Indrakîla, the poet gives us the impression that the earth is far from the flat, mechanical and cut and dried universe of the Vedic Brāhmins which could be covered by the THREE INCOMPREHENSIBLE STEPS of the Almighty Viṣṇu. On the other hand, the poet gives us the impression that the angels and mankind form part of the vast drama of the universe and that everything is made out of the star-dust forged in the workshop of the Eternal Śiva who wears the garland of the galaxy of stars. Arrived at their destination with their retinue of horses, chariots and elephants, the poet gives us an account of their descent and the encampment of the fairies and music makers in the open space of Kailāsa situated between Mahendranaga and Indrakīla. Thus the poet makes us realise with what awful grandeur the material of our person was produced, and thereby he gives us a new sense of our relationship with Śiva.

श्रीमद्भिः सरथगजैः सुराङ्गनानां गुप्तानामथ सचिवैस्त्रिलोकभर्तुः ।
संमूर्च्छन्नलघुविमानरन्ध्रभिन्नः प्रस्थानं समभिदधे मृदङ्गनादः ॥१॥

Śhreemadbhih sarathagajaih surāñganānāṃ guptānmath sacivai-strilokabhartuh //
sammûrcchannalaghuvimānahrandrabhinnah prsathānaṃ samabhi-dadhe mridanganādah //1//

Translation:

Just at the moment when the heavenly houris and the music-makers accompanied by their magnificent chariots, horses and elephants entered through the wide portals of the spacious chambers of the vimāna belongling to Lord of the Three Worlds, the scene of departure presented a glorious spectacle when the air-vehicle floated through the cosmos to the accompanyment of sound of drums and joyful cheers of the occupants.

सोत्कण्ठैरमरगणैरनुप्रकीर्णान्निर्याय ज्वलितरुचः पुरान्मघोनः ।
रामाणामुपरि विवस्वतः स्थितानां नासेदे चरितगुणत्वमातपत्रैः ॥२॥

Sotkaṇthairamaragaṇairanuprakīrṇanniryāya jvalitarucah purānma-ghonah /
rāmāṇāmupari vivasvatah sthitānāṃ nāsede caritaguṇatvamāta-patraih //2//

Translation:

Though eager to learn about the atmosphere (of the solar system) as the immortals made their exit from the dazzlingly radiant city of Indra (on their journey to earth) they could not learn anything about the nature of the solar atmosphere as they floated over the stratosphere of the sun.

धूतानामभिमुखपातिभिः समीरैरायासादविशदलोचनोत्पलानाम् ।
आनिन्ये मदविहितां श्रियं वधूनामुष्णांशुद्युतिविहितां कपोलरागः ॥३॥

Dhûtānāmabhimukhapātibhih samîrairāyāsādaviśadalocānotpalānāṃ/
āninye madavihitāṃ śriyaṃ vadhûnāmuṣṇāṃṣudyutivihitāṃ kapolarāgah //3//

Translation:

Suffering directly under the current of foreign atmosphere and their winkless eyes rolling in agony, the heat created by the pityless rays of the sun melted the resins of the hair-do of the angels already overcome by excessive drinking to undo the virtues of women.

N. B. Mallinātha's gloss of "Madajanitāṃ" (= generated by intoxication) does not give us the significance of "Vihitāṃ" to describe the effect of heat of the solar system on the angels who had entered the sphere of the sun.

It appears to me that this is not rhetoric but simple statement of facts as it occurred to the poet from a study of contemporary literature and conditions of the lives of the Licchavis who had a very wide experience of travelling. Evidently, it was not unnatural during the age of the itenerant Licchavis to carry with them on their travels, not only talismen to protect them, but also drinks and drugs to overcome the hazards of the journey. Unlike the Italian astronomer Galileo Galicei (1564—1642) who had to suffer martyrdom for his new ideas, the essence of Bhāravi's work is wrapped in a covering of satire and irony. We will see in the next stanza how the poet satirises the prevailing concept of the sun travelling in the sky in his chariot driven by seven white horses.

तिष्ठद्भिः कथमपि देवतानुभावादाकृष्टैः प्रजविभिरायतं तुरङ्गैः ।
नेमीनामसति विवर्तनै रथौघैरासेदे नभसि विमानवत्प्रवृत्तिः ॥४॥

Tiṣṭhatbhih kathamapi devatānubhāvādākriṣtaih prajavibhirāyataṃ turañgaih /
Nemînāmasati vivartanai rathaughairāsede nabhasi vimānavat-pravrittih //4//

Translation:

How certainly the felly (ring) of the wheel of the sun's chariot carried far in the sky by the brisk and apocalytic horses stood steadfast in the sky and achieved the characteristics of the air-vehicles in response to the Divine injunctions !

N. B. Mallinātha's gloss of "Viyati" (= bird in the sky) do not carry Bhāravi's sense of "Nabhasi" (sky or atmosphere).

कान्तानां कृतपुलकः स्तनाङ्गरागे वक्त्रेषु च्युततिलकेषु मौक्तिकाभः ।
संपेदे श्रमसलिलोद्गमो विभूषां रम्याणां विकृतिरपि श्रियं तनोति ॥५॥

Kāntānāṃ kritapulakah stanāñgarāge vakreṣu cyutatilakeṣu mauktikābhah /
saṃpede śramasalilodgamo vibhûṣāṃ ramyāṇāṃ vikritirapi śriyaṃ tanoti //5(//

Translation:

Their breasts tense with the strain of the change of atmosphere and the make-up of their faces and bodies swept away by the pearly drops of sweat added to the ornament of the heavenly houris. O! how the undoing of the make-up adds to the beauty of the fair.

राजद्भिः पथि मरुतामभिन्नरूपैरुल्कार्चिः स्फुटगतिभिर्ध्वजाङ्कुशानाम् ।
तेजोभिः कनकनिकाषराजिगौरैरायामः क्रियत इव स्म सातिरेकः ॥६॥

Rājadbhiḣ pathi marutāmabhinnarûpairulkārcih sphuṭagatibhirdhvajāñkuśānāṃ /
tejobhih kanakanikāsarājigaurairāyāmah kriyata iva sma sātirekaḣ //6//

Translation:

While making a quick trip through the interminable and wide paths of the sky lit up by the unusual bursts of fiery phenomen (super suns), the rays changed colour from white and violet to purple like the pinion of gold in a whetstone.

N. B. This stanza gives us indications of how Bhāravi detected the explosion of super-stars in the universe long before the Chinese astronomers had noticed it in 1054. Later, we can explain Bhāravi's ideas of explosions with this stanza to guide us.

रामाणामवजितमाल्यसौकुमार्ये संप्राप्ते वपुषि सहत्वमातपस्य ।
गन्धर्वैरधिगतविस्मयैः प्रतीये कल्याणी विधिषु विचित्रताविधातुः ॥७॥

Rāmāṇāmavajitamālyasaukumārye saṃprāpte vapuṣi sahatvamātapasya /
gandharvairadhigatavismayaih pratîye kalyānī vidhiṣu vicitratāvidhātuh //7//

Translation:

On finding how the delicate and flower-like bodies of the handsome fairies became acclamatised to the heat and bustle of the unwonted journey, the music-makers were most astonished to learn how God fulfils himself by the synthesis of the antithesis of the Two-in-one (Kalyāṇî =Ardhanārîśvara) in his most inscrutable workshop of creation.

N. B. This is as good as telling us the truth about the action of the infinitesimal particles of atoms with their negative and positive charges holding together to form the hydrogen atom which is the simplest of elements. It is next to nothing —a plus and a minus holding each other—yet it is the basis of everything. It is marvellous that the poet explains this scientific idea by his concept of the Two-in-one (Kalyāṇî). To-day radio telescopes and space probes have discovered the protons and electrons scintillating and blowing like winds everywhere through the galaxies to form the universe.

सिन्दूरैः कृतरुचयः सहेमकक्ष्याः स्त्रोतोभिस्त्रिदशगजा मदं क्षरन्तः ।
सादृश्यं ययुरुणांशुरागभिन्नैर्वर्षद्भिः स्फुरितशतह्रदैः पयोदैः ॥८॥

Sindụraih kritarucayah sahemakakṣyāh strotobhistridaśagajā madaṃ kṣarantah /
sādriśyaṃ yayuruṇāṃśurāgabhinnairvarṣadbhih sphuritasatahradaih payodaih //8//

Translation:

The sight of the well-caparisoned divine elephant decked with golden girth and glowing with red resins of vermillion as well as seating and discharging its ochre and semen from the different organs of its body consequent upon the heat generated by the disc of the sun– could be likened, for example, to the terrestrial scene of the sunbeam falling aslant over the rain-bearing clouds charged with dazzling play of lightenings to the rumble of thunder.

N. B. The poet is giving us the sense experience of the divine elephant which seems to be flying in the air-vehicle through the solar system on their way to the Milky Way. The air-vehicles have begun their journey from the radiant heaven of Indra and are now flying through the solar system, where the poet wants to give us the sense experiences of the divine elephant (Airāvata). According to modern scientists, a quick trip out in the universe at the speed of light— 299,338 kilometres a second— will help us to consider how inconceivably huge is the stage on which creations unfolds, and how there are different atmospheres on the journey. At that speed, we pass the moon in a mere 1.3 seconds and in five hours we are out of the solar system if we begin our journey from the earth. But it is four years later before we reach the nearest star in the Milky Way. In any case, this is the first vision of an astronomer of the new visions of the Universe.

अत्यर्थं दुरुपसदादुपेत्य दूरं पर्यन्तादहिममयूखमण्डलस्य ।
आशानामुपरचितामिवैकवेणीं रम्योर्मिं त्रिदशनदीं ययुर्बलानि ॥९॥

Atyartham durupasadādupetya dûram paryantādahimamayukha-maṇdalasya /
āśānāmuparacitāmivaikaveṇîṃ ramyormiṃ tridaśanadîṃ yayurbalāni //9//

Translation:

Drifting far and away from the oppressively hot atmosphere of the solar system, which decimated and sapped their physical vitality, the retinue of Indra were thrilled to see the scintillating water of the divine river of the three hundred thirty–three million gods of the sky as one continuous current of light (star-dusts blowing through the air in the milky way).

N. B. Mallinātha's identification of the Divine river of the three hundred and thirty–three million gods of the sky with river Mandākinî is ridiculous. The fairies, music-makers, elephants, horses and chariots are flying in their air-vehicles from the radiant city of Indra into the solar system and they are out in the wide galactic plains of the Milky Way. It appears to me that the astronomical observations of Bhāravi in the middle of the sixth century is breath-taking.

आमत्तभ्रमरकुलाकुलानि धुन्वन्नुध्दूतग्रथितरजांसि पङ्कजानि ।
कान्तानां गगननदीतरङ्गशीतः संतापं विरमयति स्म मातरिश्वा ॥१०॥

Āmattabhramarakulākulāni dhunwannuddhûtagrathitarajāmsi pañkajāni /
kāntānāṃ gagananadîtarañgaśîtah saṇtāpaṃ viramayati sma mātariśvā //10//

Translation:

Like the budding lotuses waking up to the pollen dusts stirred by the vibration of the humming hosts of intoxicated black bees, the changing climate of the galactic plains created by the cold clouds (particles of atoms) blowing across the River of the Sky (Milky way) acted as balms to soothe the ladies from the oppressive heat (generated under the sun's hot atmosphere).

N. B. I find in this stanza a reference to the ancient cult of "Bhriñgāreśvara" (GNI LXII and LXXVIII) where the vibration of the hum of the intoxicated black-bees on the lotuses was acceped as the sole factor in the nuptial of the earth and the sky. This is Bhāravi's exposition of the scientific formation of the spell of Oṃ maṇi padme hum (= O I am in the hum of the jewel in the Lotus) to explain the stupendous drama of creation. The antiquity of the cult of Bhriñgāreśvara can be traced to the introduction of the astro-psychic scheme of Kālacakra after the record of the Piprahavā-Buddhist vase epitaph.

संभिन्नैरिभतुरगावगाहनेन प्राप्योर्वीरनुपदवीं विमानपङ्क्तीः ।
तत्पूर्वं प्रतिविदधे सुरापगाया वप्रान्तस्खलितस्खलनं पयोभिः ॥११॥

Saṃbhinnairibhaturagāvagāhanena prāpyorvîranupadavîṃ vimāna-paṅktîh /
tatpûrvaṃ pratividadhe surāpagāyā vaprāntaskhalitaskhalanaṃ payobhih //11//

Translation:

As the array of cosmic-crafts bearing the Divine horses and elephants floated separately along the undulating and unending shores of the Milky Way, all of them felt the commotion of the tumultuous cosmic clouds pertaining to the geodosic dome (of the universe) in accordance with nature's laws.

N. B. Mallinātha's gloss of "vivertanaṃ" (= revolving or whirling round) does not convey Bhāravi's "skhalana" (= mutual rubbing together and trembling by contact with the cosmic phenomenon) to describe the enormous dark particles of atoms blowing along the galactic shores of the Milky Way. It appears to me that the onomatopoetic expression "Vaprāntaskhalitaskhalana" precisely describe the dynamic and volatile state of elemental gases in the Mysterious workshop of Almighty Śiva who is conceived as wearing a garland of constellations. Judged by modern scientific standards this description does not appear to be an extravagant rhetoric, but the result of the poet's keen observation of the solar system vis-a-vis the star-bespangled Milky Way which was interpreted by ancient astronomers as the river of the gods in the sky.

क्रान्तानां ग्रहचरितात्पथो रथानामक्षाग्रक्षतसुरवेश्मवेदिकानाम् ।
निःसङ्गं प्रधिभिरुपाददे विवृत्तिः संपीडक्षुभितजलेषु तोयदेषु ॥१२॥

Krāntānāṃ grahacaritātpatho rathānāmakṣāgrakṣatasuraveśmave-dikānāṃ /
nihsaṅgaṃ, pradhibhirupādade vivrittih saṃpîdakṣubhitajaleṣu toyadeṣu //12//

Translation:

As they emerged from the planetary orbits of the solar system (comprised by the nine planets), the axis of their air-vehicles found themselves in the enormous dark clouds of dusts blowing across the vast regions between stars, where the swirling granules acted as catylists to compress and impart motion to the independently drifting particles of dusts scintillating in space.

तप्तानामुपदधिरे विषाणभिन्नाः प्रह्लादं सुरकरिणां घनाः क्षरन्तः ।
युक्तानां खलु महतां परोपकारे कल्याणी भवति रुजत्स्वपि प्रवृत्तिः ॥१३॥

Taptānamupadadhire viṣāṇabhinnāh prahlādaṃ surakariṇāṃ ghanāh kṣarantah /
yuktānāṃ khalu mahatāṃ paropakāre Kalyāṇî bhavati rujatsvapi pravrittih //13//

Translation:

Like the pillar under the impact of the blows of Prahlāda (to produce Narasiṃha or the Man–Lion Incarnation of Viṣnu to defeat Hiraṇya-Kaśyapa) the dense mass of dusts (swirling through space) disintegrated by the splitting impact of the sharp tusks of the divine elephant. With the great object and aim of helping creative activities by the synthesis of antithesis of nature Kalyāṇî (Ardhanārîśvara) finally acts as a catalyst, though through painful processes.

N. B. One can clearly read in this stanza a reference to the basrelief of Narasiṃha (Man-lion) contained in the Judicial Customs of Nepal Part I Plate V. According to the legend of Padmapurāna, Prahlāda was the son of Hiraṇya-Kaśyapa (Kaśyapa or Buddha Kaśyapa of the Gold country) who did not believe in the cult of Viṣnu against the deep faith of his son who held that his Brāhmannic god was omnipotent, omnipresent and omniscient. Hiranya-Kaśyapa in a fit of anger asked his son to prove his thesis by producing his omnipotent Viṣṇu from the pillar of the hall they were sitting. At this Prahlāda struck the pillar with his fist, whereupon Viṣṇu emerged from the pillar in the form of Man-Lion to tear his father with his nails, killed Hiranya-Kaśyapa and placed Prahlāda on the throne, after which he ruled his subject according to the laws of the Brāhmannic Revelations. We have pointed out in our Judicial Customs of Nepal Part I how the figure of Hiraṇya-Kaśyapa on the laps of the Man-Lion is the figure of a Buddha who may be easily identified with Buddha Kaśyapa. In such a religious context Bhāravi's introduction to Kalyāṇî (Ardhanārîśvara) to explain the synthesis of the anti-thesis of creation in the scheme of their own traditional cosmic theories and their faith in Strî-iśvara seem to be marvellous indeed.

संवाता मुहुरनिलेन नीयमाने दिव्यस्त्रीजघनवरांशुके विवृत्तिम् ।
पर्यस्यत्पृथुमणिमेखलांशुजालं संजज्ञे युतकमिवान्तरीयमूर्वोः ॥१४॥

Saṃvātā muhuranilena nîyamāne divyastrijaghanavarāṃśuke vivrittiṃ /
paryasyatprithumaṇimekhalāmśujālaṃ saṃjagñe yutakamivāntarîayamûrvoh //14//

Translation:

Moving with the elemental atmosphere (of the enormous dark clouds of dusts swirling through space) the spark of white light (generated by the heavy impact of the sharp tusk of the Divine Elephant) climbed up the skirts of the Divine Ladies in a burst of radiance until it touched their gem-studded hip-belts and activated their genetic impulses (for the synthesis of antithesis). Then the spark of light rose with dazzling luminosity to transform the ocean across the intermediate space (of the galactic paths of the Milky Way) for the genesis (of planets, planetary atmosphere and stars) and get the business of life going.

अप्यार्द्रीकृततिलकास्तुषारपातैः प्रह्लादं शमितपरिश्रमा दिशन्तः ।
कान्तानां बहुमतिमाययुः पयोदा नाल्पीयान्बहुसुकृतं हिनस्ति दोषः ॥१५॥

Apyārdrîkritatilakāstuṣārapātaih prahlādaṃ śamitapariśramā diśantah /
kāntānāṃ bahumatimāyayuh payodā nālpiyānbahusukritaṃ hinasti doṣah //15//

Translation:

The equation of the (expanding) heat acting on the compressed granules of vapour, though it undid the make-up of beauty on their ruffled faces, made the Divine ladies happy. On balance small faults are created in the mighty maze of nature as catalysts to contribute to the ultimate and all-round good end (in the workshop of the Almighty Śiva).

N.B. Mallinātha's gloss of "Pratyārdrikrita (= cleaned or purified) become meaningless if we do not restore the poet to his original of "Apyārdrikrita" in the scientific sense of shower of ice-granules (tuṣārapātaih) losing contraction by contacting with the heat generated by the bodies of the Divine Ladies to convert itself into vapour, as the cosmonauts travel in their space-crafts along the galactic plains of the Milky Way. The poet tries to show how the workshop of the Almighty Śiva works through the images of the Divine Ladies, Music-makers, elephants and horses in their strange journey from the Paradise of Indra over the solar system on to the vast regions between the atmosphere of the Milky Way and our Planet, where, according to modern scientists, enormous dark clouds of dusts blow across the galactic plains. We have pointed out in our Judicial Customs of Nepal Part I how the ancient astro-physicists and astronomers had sought and theorised about the cosmic forms in the inter-stellar Milky Way right from the period of the historical Buddhas. Reading about the experiences of the modern cosmonauts on their mystical journey to the moon, it gives me pleasure to translate Bhāravi, whose observations seem true to "the kindred spirit of Heaven and Home."

यातस्य ग्रथिततरङ्गसैकताभे विच्छेदं विपयसि वारिवाहजाले ।
आतेनुस्त्रिदशवधूजनाङ्गभाजां संधानं सुरधनुषः प्रभा मणीनाम् ॥१६॥

Yātasya grathitatarañgasaikatābhe vicchedaṃ vipayasi vārivāhajāle /
ātenustridasavadhûjanāñgabhājāṃ saṇdhānaṃ suradhanuṣah prabhā maṇînāṃ //16//

Translation:

While flying along the clouds of inter-stellarx dusts (with negative and positive charges) brightened (lit) by the net work of elemental gases as catalysts (vipayasi) to give the appearance of scintillating masses of water, the resulting burst of vari-coloured radiance reflected on the bejewelled bodies of the wives of the three hundred and thirtythree million gods with the unique experiment of the rainbows.

संसिद्धावितिकरणीयसंनिबद्धैरालापैः पिपतिषतां विलङ्घ्य वीथीं ।
आसेदे दशशतलोचनध्वजिन्या जीमूतैरपिहितसानुरिन्द्रकीलः ॥१७॥

Saṃsiddhāvitikaraṇîyasaṃnivaddhairālāpaih pipatisatāṃ vilañghya vithîṃ /
āsede daśaśatalocanadhvajinyā jîmûtairapihitasānurindrakîlah //17//

Translation:

With success of their mission in view after their adventure in space, the retinue bearing the standard of the god with thousand eyes (Indra) began talking loudly among themselves as their space-crafts safely entered the orbit of the earth and prepared to descend along the path of the birds on the mountain of Indrakîla, which was shrouded in the dense atmosphere of light, air and water to support life.

N. B. Many ancient poets have written fantastic stories about the adventure of men and gods in the "Vimānas" (air-vehicles') and also related the story of king Jîmûta-vāhana in Kathāsaritsāgara (Ocean of stories). According to the play known as "Nāgānanda" he was the son of the benevolent and pious king Jimutaketu, who was the king of the Vidyādharas. When his kinsmen attacked his father's kingdom, he pursuaded his father to surrender his throne and repair with him to the Malaya mountains to lead a holy life. One day he met a serpent, who was to be offered to Garuda as his daily meal and he offered himself to take his place. The story is told very pathetically how he induced Garuda to give up his practice of devouring the serpents by his generous and touching arguments.

However, what Mallinātha explains away as examples of Bhāravi's rhetoric can, in recent years, be understood by recourse to experimental science. The poet does not betray his weakness for such legends. On the other hand, his accounts of the adventure of the Divine ladies and their retinue through the Solar System, Milky Way and their reentry into the orbit of the earth show the poet's powerful observation of nature in the wake of such early cosmologists, evolutionists and astronomers like, for examples Buddha Kanakamuni, Kapilamuni and Buddha Kaśyapa mentioned in our Judicial Customs of Nepal Part I. Their descent to the earth's orbit is similar to the account given to me by the cosmonauts when the entered the earth's orbit after their adventure in space. The scene of landing in the following stanza appears to be most realistic by modern standards, which is what makes the world of the Licchavis so very well advanced materially and morally.

आकीर्णा मुखनलिनैर्विलासिनीनामुद्धूतस्फुटविशदातपत्रफेना ।
सा तूर्यध्वनितगभीरमानदन्ति भूभर्तुः शिरसि नभोनदीव रेजे ॥१८॥

Ākîrnā mukhanalinairvilāsinîmuddhûtasphuṭaviśadātapatraphenā /
sā tûryadhvanitagabhîraānadanti bhûbhartuh śirasi nabhonadiva reje //18//

Translation:

The scene of landing of the pleasure-seeking divine women. with their tense looks in the dense atmosphere under the opening white umbrellas, presented a spectacle as bright as the descent of the river of the sky (Milky-way) over the crest of mount Indrakîla as they landed to the resounding roar of the air-vehicle which resembled the sound of long trumpets.

N. B. Mallinātha's gloss of "Apatanti" (=approaching or coming down) do not convey Bhāravi's expression of "Anadanti" (=to the resounding roar all around). The Divine ladies, unlike the fairies of fairy tales, do not seem to have wings, so that they could alight whereever they liked. They are alighting from the spacecraft by the aid of white umbrellas that are opening up to parachute them to the crests of Indrakîla while the space craft is circling with a resounding roar in the sky. The poet conceives that the descent of the Divine Ladies under the cover of their white umbrellas looked like the descent of the Milky Way itself on the summit of Mount Indrakîla. It is remarkable that the scene reminds me of mass parachute jumping in modern air operations and exercises.

सेतुत्वं दधति पयोमुचां विताने संरम्भादभिपततो रथाञ्जवेन ।
आनिन्युर्नियमितरश्मिभुग्नघोणाः कृच्छ्रेण क्षितिमवनामिनस्तुरङ्गाः ॥१९॥

Setutvaṃ dadhati payomucāṃ vitāne saṃrambhādabhipatato rathāñjavena //
āninyurniyamitaraśmibhugnaghonāh kricchreṇa kṣitimavanāminasturangāh //19//

Translation:

As the chariots glided down (plummeted or rolled down) the ramps (bridges) of watercharged clouds under the powerful attraction (gravity of the earth), the Divine charioteers had difficulties in raining in and balancing the necks and noses of the champing and chafing steeds when they descended from their air-vehicles of the magnetic fields (of Indrakîla).

माहेन्द्रं नगमभितः करेणुवर्याः पर्यन्तस्थितजलदा दिवः पतन्तः ।
सादृश्यं निलयननिष्प्रकम्पपक्षैराजग्मुर्जलनिधिशायिभिर्नगेन्द्रैः ॥२०॥

Māhendraṃ nagamabhitah kareṇuvaryh paryantasthitajaladā divah patantah /
sādriśyaṃ nilayananiṣprakampapakṣairā jagmur jalanidhiśhāibhirnagendraih //20//

Translation:

Like, for example, the fall of the flying mountains emerging from the bed of the ocean (when their wings were clipped by the thunderbolt of Indra) the pick of elephants glided to a halt by the bank of a river right in front of mount Indrakîla.

उत्सङ्गे समविषमे समं महाद्रेः क्रान्तानां वियदभिपातलाघवेन ।
आमूलादुपनदि सैकतेषु लेभे सामग्र्यं खुरपदवी तुरङ्गमाणाम् ॥२१॥

Utsange samaviṣame samaṃ mahādreh krāntānāṃ viyadabhipātalāghavena /
āmûlādupanadi saikateṣu lebhe sāmagryaṃ khurapadavı turañgamānām //21//

Translation:

Accustomed to flying unobstructed in the rarefied atmosphere of the sky in all the perfection (of their air-vehicles), the Divine horses sighed at the sight of the ups and downs of the gigantic mountains as their hoofs touched the boulder-strewn ground on the bank of the rivulet at its base (base of mount Indrakîla).

N. B. Mallinâtha's gloss of "sāmagriṃ" (= collection or assemblage of materials) do not convey Bhāravi's sense of "Sāmagryam" (=in all the perfection of being borne or flying unobstructed in the rarefied atmosphere of the sky). The commentator has not taken note of the fact that the apocalyptic horses drawing the divine chariots have landed from their air-vehicles by the bank of a river strewn with uneven boulders at the base of mount Indrakîla. What the poet means to say is that the entire atmosphere of the earth was a new experience for the retinue from the radiant city of Indra of flying through the sky unobstructed and in all the comfort of their Vimānas.

सध्वानं निपतितनिर्झरासु मन्द्रैः संमूर्च्छन्प्रतिनिनदैरधित्यकासु ।
उद्ग्रीवैर्घनरवशङ्कया मयूरैः सोत्कण्ठं ध्वनिरुपशुश्रुवे रथानाम् ॥२२॥

Sadhvānaṃ nipatitanirjharāsu mandraih saṃmûrcchanpratininadairadhityakāsu /
udgrîvairghanaravaśankayā mayûraih sotkaṇṭhaṃ dhvanirupaśuśruve rathānām //22//

Translation:

The screech and thud of the wheels of the chariots adding to the deep rumble of the waterfalls reawakened the peacocks to the all too familiar thunder of the clouds, with the result that they made reciprocal response with their darting necks and feathers.

संभिन्नामविरलपातिभिर्मयूखैर्नीलानां भृशमुपमेखलं मणीनाम् ।
विच्छिन्नामिव वनिता नभोन्तराले वप्राम्भःश्रुतिमवलोकयम्बभूवु : ॥२३॥

Saṃbhinnāmaviralapātibhirmayûkhairnîlānāṃ bhriśamupamekhalaṃ maṇînām /
vicchinnāmiva vanitā nabhontarāle vaprāmbhah srutimavalokaya-ṃbabhûbuh //23//

Translation:

The Divine ladies were thrilled and enthralled by the sight of the torrent of waterfall, which scattered itself into vari-coloured gems giving the illusion of lady's chastity-belt sparkling with gems as it cascaded and sprayed in the intermediate space.

आसन्नद्विपपदवीमदानिलाय क्रुध्यन्तो धियमवमत्य धूर्गतानाम् ।
सव्याजं निजकरिणीभिरात्तचित्ताः प्रस्थानं सुरकरिणः कथंचिदीषुः ॥२४॥

Āsannadivipapadavîmadānilāya krudhyanto dhiyamavamattya dhûrgatānām /
savyājaṃ nijakariṇîbhirāttacittaḣ prasthānaṃ surakariṇaḣ kathaṃ-cidîṣuh //24//

Translation:

Distracted by their passion for she-elephants, the Divine elephants in their rut seemed to be harbouring clandestine feeling, and they riled in furious mood unmindful of the elephant-goad, when their Mahouts guided them into the paths of the wild-elephants for Khedah in the virgin forests.

नीरन्ध्रं पथिषु रजो रथाङ्गधूतं पर्यस्यन्नवसलिलारुणं वहन्ती ।
आतेने वनगहनानि वाहिनी सा घर्मान्तक्षुभितजलेव जह्नुकन्या ॥२५॥

Nîrandhraṃ pathiṣu rajo rathāñgadhûtaṃ paryasyannavasalilāruṇaṃ vahantî /

ātene vanagahanāni vāhinî sā gharmāntakşubhitajaleva Janhukanyā //25//

Translation:

Like the daughter of Jahnu (river) at the end of the sultry season of summer the clear water of the rivulets took on the maroon colour of the dusty road as the wheels of the chariot with their creaking yoke-pins dragged themselves strirring dusts through the primeval forest-paths.

N. B. Mallinātha's gloss of "rathāñganunnaṃ (=propelled by the wheels which formed part of the chariot) calculated to explain the theory of Amarkoṣa do not give us the idea of the creaking yoke-pins of the wheels, as the chariots dragged themselves through the path of the forest scattering dusts and colouring the water with the colour of the road. The chariots were dragged by horses and there is no question of the wheels moving by their own propulsion. "Rathāñgadhûtam" refer to the creaking yoke-pins of the chariot. Here the poet describes how the river took on the maroon colour of dusts stirred by the screeching wheels of the chariots (as if they were in spate at the end of summer) when the chariots churned through the dusty road. The poet is describing the experiences of the Heavenly Houris, music-makers, charioteers, mahouts, elephants and horses from the radiant paradise of Indra as they alighted in the atmosphere of our work--a-day earth.

संभोगक्षमगहनामथोपगङ्गं बिभ्राणां ज्वलितमणीनि सैकतानि ।
अध्यूषुश्च्युतकुसुमाचितां सहायावृत्रारेरविरलशाद्वलां धरित्रीम् ॥२६॥

Saṃbhogakṣamagahanāmathopagañgaṃ vibhrāṇāṃ jvalitamaṇîni saikatāni /
adyhûṣuścyutakusumācitāṃ sahāyāvritrāreraviralaśādvalāṃ dharitrîm //26//

Translation:

At last the music-makers and divine ladies of the dispeller of darkness (Indra) found a balmy holiday paradise by the bank of the river against the setting of a fertile and lushy corner of the earth with the lure of vari-coloured lights and feasts of flowers for their enjoyment and sports of love.

N. B. It is remarkable that Bhāravi refers to the Vedic king of gods as "Vritrāri" the killer of the demon Vritrāsura who is supposed to be personification of darkness in the Vedic myths.

भूभर्तुः समधिकमादधे तदोर्व्याः श्रीमत्तां हरिसखवाहिनीनिवेशः ।
संसक्तौ किमसुलभं महोदयानामुच्छ्रायं नयति यदृच्छयापि योगः ॥२७॥

Bhûbhartuḥ samadhikamādahde tadorvyāḥ srimattāṃ harisakhavāhinîniveśaḣ /
saṃsaktau kimasulabhaṃ mahodayānāmucchrāyaṃ nayati yadrichayāni yogah //27//

Translation:

The phalanxes comprised by the caravans of Indra pitched a fantastic group of tents amid the majestic sweep of mountains for their lodging. O! what is beyond the reach of those who make common efforts for their extravaganza !! For, even nature and fortune combine to help the efforts of brave and ambitious people.

सामोदाः कुसुमतरुश्रियोविविक्ताः संपत्तिः किसलयशालिनीलतानाम् ।
साफल्यं ययुरमराङ्गनोपभुक्ताः सा लक्ष्मीरुपकुरुते हि या परेषाम् ॥२८॥

Sāmodāh kusumataruśriyoviviktāh sampattiḣ kisalayaśālinîlatānāṃ /
sāphalyaṃ yayuramarāñganopabhuktāḣ sā lakṣmirupakurute hi yā pareṣām //28//

Translation:

They were delighted by the balmy breath of flowers and trees and by the lovely arbours sprouting with creepers; and the entire atmosphere found fulfilment on account of its enjoyment by the immortal ladies. For, indeed, handsome is that hansome does.

N. B. Mallinātha's gloss of Yayā" (= by the act of) does not convey Bhāravi's positive sense of "hi" (indeclinable used to express strict reasoning) and "Yā" (whose meanings are variously modified by the poet according to the noun with which it is connected). More because the word "lakṣmî" in Nepalese inscriptions is used to denote "beauty", handsomeness and purposefulness (e. g. lakṣmîvatkāraitva bahvana mihaśubhaṃ G.N.I. III. l. 2). I do not see any reference here to the propagation of the Bhāgavata cult of Nārāyaṇa and his consort Lakṣmî as it being hinted by Mallinātha.

क्लान्तोऽपि त्रिदशवधूजनः पुरस्ताल्लीनाहिश्वसनविलोलपल्लवानाम् ।
सेव्यानां हतविनयैरिवावृतानां संपर्कं परिहरति स्म चन्दनानाम् ॥२९॥

Klāntoऽpi tridaśavadhûjanah purastāllînāhiśvasanavilolapallavānām sevyānāṃ hatavinayairivābritānāṃ saṃparkaṃ pariharati sma candanānām //29//

Translation:

(In their first night on earth) the wives of the three hundred and thirty three million gods of the sky were entertained with cool amenities of lush green herbs, which were served under the coating of sweet smelling sandal-wood to allay their fatigues, though it was done in contravention of the rules of medical practices.

N. B. Mallinātha's gloss of "Śvasita" (=breathing, respiring or panting) does not give Bhāravi's idea of "śvasana" (=sniffiing or breathing the balmy blight of drugs to induce sleep in their first night on earth). Melancholia or manic depressive illness is the most common disorder in the Himālayan journeys and sniffing green drugs (marijuana) was, perhaps, done under the coating of sweet-smelling sandal-wood. Evidently this was contra-indicated in the vinayas (rules) of medical books.

उत्सृष्टध्वजकुथकङ्कटा धरित्रीमानीता विदितनयैः श्रमं विनेतुम् ।
आक्षिप्तद्रुमगहना युगान्तवातैः पर्यस्ता गिरय इव द्विपा विरेजुः ॥३०॥

Utsriṣṭadhvajakuthakañkaṭā dharitrîmānîtā viditanayaiḣ śramaṃ vinetuṃ /
ākṣiptadrumagahanā yugāntavātaih paryastā giraya iva dvipā virejuh //30//

Translation:

As they (the Mahouts) laid themselves down for rest on mattresses (at the end of a long day) after taking off the banners and the elephant goads, the herds of elephants left to forage in the forests of the mountain (Indrakîla) presented a totally uprooted spectacle as if it were hit by the deadly squall of wind at the end of the cycle known as "Yuga" (an age of the world comprising the four cycles of Satya or the Golden Age consisting of 1,728,000, Tretā consisting of 1,296,000, Dvāpara consisting 864,000 and Kali consisting of 432,000 years of men. All the four Yugas comprise one Mahāyuga consisting of 4,320,000 years).

N. B. According to Bhagavadgîtā (Celestial Song Canto 4 stanza 8) Visṇu incarnates himself from cycle to cycle to save his faithfuls from the physical and moral degradation in each cycle. In such a context Bhāravi's use of the expression of "Yugāntavātaiḣ" (= the squall of wind to spoil the earth at the end of such cycle) to describe the spoliation of the forests in the mountain of Indrakîla at the end of the yoke (age) seems to relegate the entire concepts as a very paltry idea of foraging and spoliation of the forests by the herds of elephants.

प्रस्थानश्रमजनितां विहाय निद्रामामुक्ते गजपतिना सदानपङ्के ।
शय्यान्ते कुलमलिनां क्षणं निलीनं संरम्भच्युतमिव श्रृङ्खलं चकाशे ॥३१॥

Prasthānaśramajanitāṃ vihāya nidrāmāmukte gajapatinā sadānapañke /
śayyānte kulamalināṃ kṣaṇaṃ nilînaṃ saṃrambhacyutamivə śriñkhalaṃ cakāse //31//

Translation:

When sleep induced by the fatigue of the journey deserted them with the following dawn, the Mahouts, already accustomed to the smell of the ruttish elephants, waked up suddenly sat at the end of their beds with the clang of bright chains calculated to secure the feet of chafing elephants.

N. B. Mallinātha's gloss of "vilînam" (= sticking to) to describe the elephants of the Khedah-camp do not give us the idea of the transformation implied by the poet's expression of "nilînam" (= encompassed, surrounded or destroyed). It appears that the wild elephants of our planet had attacked the divine elephants with the result that they were clanging their chains in all their fury.

आयस्तः सुरसरिदोघरुद्धवर्त्मा संप्राप्तुं वनगजदानगन्धि रोधः ।
मूर्धानं निहितशिताङ्कुशं विधुन्वन्यन्तारं न विगणयांचकार नागः ॥३२॥

Āyastah surasaridogharuddhavartmā saṃprāptuṃ vanagajadānagandhi rodhah /
mûrdhānaṃ nihitaśitāñkuśaṃ vidhunvanyantāraṃ na vigaṇayāncakāra nāgah //32//

Translation:

Sniffing the scent of the ochre of wild elephants on the other side of the river and obstructed (impeded) by the current of the river to overtake (their enemies), the elephants did not mind the stunning and sharp thrusts of the elephant-goads of their Mahouts in their fury.

N. B. Now we get a clear picture of what has happened in the camp on the previous night. Such scenes are common in the Khedah of elephants. Elephants are sensitive animals and I have personally been witness to such scenes.

आरोढुः समवनतस्य पीतशेषे साशङ्कं पयसि समीरिते करेण ।
संमार्जन्नरुणमदस्रुती कपोलौ सस्यन्दे मद इव शीकरः करेणोः ॥३३॥

Ārodhuh samavanatasya pîtaśeṣe sāśañkaṃ payasi samîrite kareṇa / saṃmārjannaruṇamadasrutî kapolau saṣyande mada iva śîkarah kareṇoh //33//

Translation:

Goaded by the mahouts to the brink of the river, the elephants (of the Khedah) approached the water with suspicion fearing lest it was defiled by their wild enemies; and they finally stooped to draw the water in their trunks and spray it on their temples washing their ochre as if to incarnadine the river with its intoxicating smell and scarlet colour.

आघ्राय क्षणमतितृष्यताऽतिरोषादुत्तीरं निहितविवृत्तलोचनेन ।
संपृक्तं वनकरिणां मदाम्बुसेकैर्नाचेमे हिममपि वारि वारणेन ॥३४॥

Āghrāya kṣaṇamatitriṣyatāऽtirosāduttiraṃ nihitavivrittalocanena / saṃpriktaṃ vanakariṇāṃ madāmvusekairnāceme himamapi vāri vāraṇena //34//

Translation:

Though extremely thirsty at the moment, the elephants smelt but refused to drink the cold water muddied by the ochre of their enemies, and they fixed their wild stare in extreme anger on the other side of the river spoiling for a fight.

N. B. Mallinātha's gloss of "api" (=also, even if vide Canto I; stanza 28) does not convey the poet's sense of extreme provocaton or anger of the domestic elephants meant by the "ati" (= extremely or excessively). We have seen how the elephants were attacked by wild elephants in the previous night so that all of them were very angry in the morning and spoiling for a fight. The poet is describing the habit of the elephants of Khedah. It appears to me that both Mallinātha and Govinda Śharmā have missed the point.

प्रश्च्योतन्मदसुरभीणिनिम्नगायाः क्रीडन्तो गजपतयः पयांसि कृत्वा ।
किंजल्कव्यवहिततामत्रदानलेखैरुत्तेरुः सरसिजगन्धिभिः कपोलैः ॥३५॥

Praścyotanmadasurabhîṇinimnagāyāh krîdanto gajapatayah payāṃsi kritvā /
kiṃjalkavyavahitatāmradānalekhairutteruh sarasijagandhibhih kapaolaih //35//

Translation:

While sporting in a buff of the river (Kauśikî) littered with the ochre of wild elephants, the owners (Mahouts) washed away the aromatic hair-dressing composed of a mixture of pollens and red resin of copper and they emerged with the smell of the wild elephants of their heads.

आकीर्णं बलरजसा घनारुणेन प्रक्षोभैः सपदि तरङ्गितं तटेषु ।
मातङ्गोन्मथितसरोजरेणुपिङ्गं कौशेयं वसनमिवाम्बु निर्बभासे ॥३६॥

Ākîrṇaṃ valarajasā ghanāruṇena praksobhaih sapadi tarañgitaṃ taṭeṣu /
mātañgonmathitasarojareṇupiñgaṃ Kauśeyaṃ vasanamivāmbu nirvabhāse //36//

Translation:

The water bearing the colour of deep crimson cosmetics of the army of swimmers and the ripples dyed in the saffron colour of the mud stirred from the shore by the tread of elephants appeared like the purple attire of river Kauśikî.

N. B. Mallinātha's gloss of "māngistam" (= red colour) totally lose sight of the geographical situation of river Kauśikî and the colour of the country meant by the world "Kauśeyam" (= silken currents of river Kauśikî). The scene is a Khedah in the dense forests by the bank of Kauśikî, where the divine elephants have been attacked by their wild enemies. The Mahouts wake with the clangs of chain of the angry elephants, and all proceed to the bank of river Kauśikî to find that the wild elephants have crossed the river. So, they stop by one of the buffs of the river to have their morning ablutions. The poet describes how the washing of the pigment from the body of the retinue of bathers have dyed the silken currents of the river in crimson colour, while the saffron coloured mud stirred by the tread of the elephants from the bank of the river has combined to impart a purplish colour to the silken attire of Kauśikî. By restoring Bhāravi to his original of "Kauśeyam" (= silken garment of Kauśikî) we get the true geographical connotation and colour of the scene. This could be a typical scene of the Khedah of elephants to our own day.

श्रीमद्भिर्नियमितकंधरापरान्तैः संसक्तैरगुरुवनेषु साङ्गहारम् ।
संप्रापे विसृतमदाम्बुभिर्गजेन्द्रैः प्रस्यन्दिप्रचलितगण्डशैलशोभा ॥३७॥

Śrimadbhirniyamitakaṇdharāparāntaih saṃsaktairaguruvanesu sāṅgahāraṃ /
saṃprāpe visritamadāmvubhirgajendraih prasyandipracalitagaṇda-śailasobhā //37//

Translation:

As the tuskers pulled out of the buff after being ornately bedecked with the aromatic garland of the trees and shrubs of "aguru" (aquilaria agallocha) and properly caparisoned in the latter part of the day for further adventure, their temples covered over with ochre presented a customarily moving spectacle similar to the grandeur of the blue mountains girdled by river Gaṇdakiî

N. B. Mallinātha's gloss of "nisrita" (= extending or spreading or being attached to) appears to have misled Śri Govinda Śharma in translating this stanza into Nepali. The poet describes how the ruttish tuskers with their foreheads oozing with ochre, garlanded with aromatic aquilaria agaloccha and properly caparisoned, looked like the blue mountains of Gaṇdakî watered by the tributaries of the river, which is a common sight. More because, a badly mutilated Licchavi inscription in the temple of Gorakhnāth in the village of Gorkhā describes the region with the expression "Gaṇdakî nagamālikā". In such a context, stanzas 36 and 23 of this Canto, when they are restored to their original, give us a true picture of the great drama. The Inscription of King Māna-deva also speaks of his campaigns beyond river Gaṇḍakî. We have pointed out in our 'Judicial Customs of Nepal' how the rivers and mountains of Nepal find mention in the "Annals of China" and the literature of the ancient world.

निःशेषं प्रशमितरेणु वारणानां स्रोतोभिर्मदजलमुज्झतामजस्रम् ।
आमोदं व्यवहितभूरिपुष्पगन्धं भिन्नैलासुरभिमुवाह गन्धवाहः ॥३८॥

Niḥśeṣaṃ praśamitareṇu vāraṇānāṃ srotobhirmadajalamujjhatāma-jasraṃ /
āmodaṃ vyavahitabhûripuṣpagandhaṃ bhînnailāsurabhimuvāha gandhavāhah //38//

Translation:

The breeze, already balmy with the ochre of ruttish elephants in full blaze of their decorations, was surpassed by the scent of a variety of Puṣpagandha (= sorghum vulgare = जुनेलो) and the fragrance of "ailā" (= elettaria cardamomum = एनाइनो इलायची or अलैंची) to add to the pleasure of smell.

N. B. Mallinātha's gloss of "Puṣpagandhok (= smell of a variety of flowers) overlooks the specific botanical species meant by Bhāravi's expression of "Puṣpagandham" (= sorghum vulgare= जुनेलो). Similarly, "Ailā" is not just a variety of creepers but the fruit of plants of the genera Elettaria and Amomum, with a distinct aromatic odour, belonging to the family of Zingiberaceae, which abound in the Kauśikī region of Nepal. It appears that these botanical species were as famous in the time of Bhāravi as they are, as articles of trade to our own day. Nepal had "Alaici kothi" in Patna to trade in cardamomum till the time of the Rānās.

सादृश्यं दधति गभीरमेघघोषैरुन्निद्रक्षुभितमृगाधिपश्रुतानि ।
आतेनुश्चकितचकोरनीलकण्ठान्कच्छान्तानमरमहेभबंहितानि ॥३९॥

Sādriśyaṃ dadhati gabhîrameghaghośairunnidrakṣubhitamrigādhi-paśrutāni / ātenuścakitacakoranîlakaṇṭhānkachāntānamaramahebhavriṃ-hitāni //39//

Translation:

The night prowling king of beasts were disturbed and awakened angrily from their midday siesta in their lair to hear the trumpetings of the Divine elephants resembling, for example, the deep thunder of the clouds, which also attracted the attention of the Brāhmî-ducks and peacocks in the sheltered islands (Veṇṭhadîpo) on the banks (of river Kauśikî).

N. B. This is a typical scene of Khedah or Big hunting in the intra-montane region of Nepal.

शाखावसक्तकमनीयपरिच्छदानामध्वश्रमातुरवधूजनसेवितानाम् ।
जज्ञे निवेशनविभागपरिष्कृतानां लक्ष्मीः पुरोपवनजावनपादपानाम् ॥४०॥

śākhāvasaktakamanîyaparicchadānāmadhwaśramāturavadhûjanasevi-tānāṃ / jagñe niveśanavibhāgapariṣkritānāṃ lakṣmih puropavanajāvanapā-dapānaṃ //40//

Translation:

The Department responsible for putting up lodgings had acted with speed in advance to provide an enclosure in the midst of the forest with the aid of branches and flowers, which was roofed by colourful tent-clothes and beautifully furnished quarters served by a bevy of busy and beautiful ladies.

N. B. The metre is Vasanta-tilakā to describe the sports of the kings of the Kirātas in their Ganarājyas (confederation of People's Republics). On reading these stanzas, we get an idea of how well-organi-nised were the kingdoms of the Kirātas in their own scheme of Gaṇarājyas.

The end of Canto VII.

KIRĀTĀRJUNIYE
CANTO VIII

CANTO VIII

Summary

This Canto consists of fifty seven stanzas. We have here a descriptive account of the arena laid out by the advanced party of canto followers and furnishers for aquatic and floral sports of the Divine ladies and music makers. This Canto seems to be influenced by the scenes of the seduction of Śākyamuni by the daughters of Māra and by the Buddha-carita (Life of Śākyamuni Buddha) composed by the celebrated Kauśik poet Aśvaghoṣa in the Court of Emperor Kaniṣhka and also Lalita-vistara (sports of Buddha) composed by Lalita. Judging by the accounts of the courts of the Huns and Āvirs contained in the Annals of China and European kings of the period, I have reason to feel that their peripatetic organisations seemed to be based on the nomadic lives of the Kirātas and the Yakṣas. This scene could be taken as an example of the moving courts of Kirāta, Yakṣa, Śaka, Kuṣāna, Licchavi, Ābhîra and Hunnic kings, who were constantly on their adventure. Now my readers will see how Bhāravi describes the scene:

अथ स्वमायाकृतमन्दिरोज्ज्वलं ज्ज्वलन्मणिव्योमसदां सदातनम् ।
सुरांगना गोपतिचापगोपुरं पुरं वनानां विजिहीर्षया जहुः ॥१॥

Atha swamāyākritamandirojjvalaṃ jjvalanmaṇivyomasadāṃ sadātanaṃ/
surāṇganā gopaticāpagopuraṃ puraṃ vanānāṃ vijihîrṣayā jahuḥ//1//

Translation:

Then (with the setting up of the camp in the heart of the forest after their own desire) the wives of the gods left the radiant and fortified camp, which was made on the pattern of traditional and permanent pagoda temples and entered the forest through the tall, rainbow arches accompanied by the music makers for their floral sports.

N.B. The metre in this Canto is Vaṃśastha.

Mallinātha's gloss of "sanātanam" (=eternal, perpetual) do not explain Bhāravi's idea of the pattern of the temporary buildings of the camp after the ever happy pagoda style of architecture meant by the expression "sadātanam" (=ever happy). No architectural structure could be eternal and ever-lasting.

यथायथं ताः सहिता नभश्चरैः प्रभाभिरुद्दीपितशैलवीरुधः ।
वनं विशन्त्यो वनजायतेक्षणाः क्षणद्युतीनां दधुरेकरूपताम् ॥२॥

Yathāyathaṃ tāḣ sahitā nabhaścaraiḣ prabhābhiruddîpitaśaila-vîrudhah /
vanaṃ viśantyo vanajāyatekṣaṇāḣ kṣaṇadyutînāṃ dadhure-karupatāṃ //2//

Translation:

Living as the Divine ladies did in regular order amid the atmosphere of the shrubby mountains and forests under the illumination of cumulus clouds, their lotus-like eyes winked and became one with the vivid flashes of lightnings.

N.B. Mallinātha's gloss of "rudbhāsita" (= moistened with brightness) does not give Bhāravi's idea of the illuminating properties of the bright cumulus clouds with stratified appearance floating on the shrub covered mountains and forests meant by the expression "uddîpita", which in Sanskritic rhetoric also refers to the excitement of aesthetic pleasure.

According to Brāhmannic legends the gods and goddesses became winkless and deathless after drining the nectar. What Bhāravi seems to suggest in a spirit of satire is that the mortal associations of the mountains and the earth made the immortal ladies wink, and that they acquired the habit of the mortals. (Vide our translation of the first stanza of Māna-deva's inscription of Chāñgu Nārāyaṇa in the Appendix.)

निवृत्तवृत्तोरुपयोधरक्लमः प्रवृत्तनिर्ह्रादिविभूषणारवः ।
नितम्बिनीनां भृशमादधे धृतिं नभःप्रयाणादवनौ परिक्रमः ॥३॥

Nivrittavrittorupayodharaklamaḣ pravrittanirhādivibhûṣaṇāravaḣ / nitamvinînāṃ bhriśamādadhe dhritiṃ nabhahprayānādavanau parikramah //3//

Translation:

Awakened to the mundane realities of earth with their round breasts and ornate attire with the jingling of the anklets in their feet after the fatigue of the long journey in space, the women with handsome hips and large sloping buttocks found it more pleasant to walk round the forests than flying through the sky.

घनानि कामं कुसुमानि विभ्रतः करप्रचेयान्यपहाय शाखिनः ।
पुरोऽभिसस्रे सुरसुन्दरीजनैर्यथोत्तरेच्छा हि गुणेषु कामिनः ॥४॥

Ghanāni kāmaṃ kusumāni vibhrātaḣ karapraceyānyapahāya śākhinaḣ /
puro (ʃ) bhisasre surasundarîjanairyathottarecchā hi guṇeṣu kāminah //4//

Translation:

As the heavenly beauties moved along laying aside the branches within their arms' reach in the improvised arbour dense with budding flowers, they discovered that the longing for time and place in the scheme of mundane society by men and women under the inspiration of the god of love was the main factor for progress and transformation of nature after their own desire.

तनूरलक्तारुणपाणिपल्लवाः स्फुरन्नखांशूत्करमञ्जरीभृतः ।
विलासिनीबाहुलता वनालयो विलेपनामोदहृताः सिषेविरे ॥५॥

Tanuralaktāruṇapāṇipallavāh sphurannakhāṃśutkaramañjarîbhritah /
vilāsinîvāhulatā vanālayo vilepanāmodahritāḣ siṣevire //5//

Translation:

Their red-resin painted palms resembling rosy petals with manicured nails as sprouts on the lithe and creeper-like arms, the cosmetic-covered bodies of pleasure-seeking women walking in the forests attracted the wild bees with their smell.

निपीयमानस्तवका शिलीमुखैरशोकयष्टिश्चलबालपल्लवा ।
विडम्बयन्ती ददृशे वधूजनैरमन्ददष्टौष्ठकरावधूननम् ॥६॥

Nipîyamānastavakā śilîmukhairaśokayaṣtiścalavālapallavā /
vidamvayantî dadriśe vadhûjanairamandadaṣtauṣṭakarāvadhunanaṃ //6//

Translation:

As the black-bees nibbled away the coating of the fresh and tender sprouts, the ladies exhibited their ecstacy by the display of their trembling lips in immitation of the branch of Aśoka tree (saraca indica) bowing down to receive their kiss.

N.B. The Aśoka tree is saraca-indica. We do not find here the convention of Sanskritic poets to the effect that the Aśoka trees put forth red-blossom when they are struck by the feet of ladies decked with jingling anklets (e.g. Kumārasaṃbhava 3. 26: Raghuvaṃśa 8. 62: Meghadûta 78)

करौ धुनाना नवपल्लवाकृती वृथा कृथा मानिनि मा परिश्रमम् ।
उपेयुषी कल्पलताभिशङ्कया कथं न्वितस्त्रस्यति षट्पदावलिः ॥७॥

Karau dhunānā navapallavākritî vrithā krithā mānini mā pariśramaṃ /
upeyuṣî kalpalatābhiśañkayā kathaṃ nvitastrasyati ṣaṭpadāvaliḣ //7//

Translation:

In vain, O proud lady with your look as fresh and fair as a bud (blossom)! you are shaking your hands to ward off the bees. How, on earth, could you cast away the bees who are swarming on you with the image of the creeper of Indra's paradise before them ?

N.B. Evidently a mortal lady is having a dialogue with the Heavenly nymph.

जहीहि कोपं दयितोऽनुगम्यतां पुरानुशेते तव चञ्चलं मनः ।
इति प्रियं कांचिदुपैतुमिच्छतीं पुरोऽनुनिन्ये निपुणः सखीजनः ॥८॥

Jahîhi kopaṃ dayito(ʃ)nugamyatāṃ purānuśete tava cañcalaṃ manaḣ /
iti priyaṃ Kāñcidupaitumicchatîṃ puro(ʃ)nuninye nipuṇaḣ sakhîjanaḣ //8//

Translation:

"Excuse me, O dear lady from Indra's paradise ! you appear to give yourself away and lie down in the heat of passion of your fickle mind"– so a lady friend advised– "Give up your vanity and follow the behaviour pattern of the accomplished courtesans of Kāñcî and look before you leap in matters of love."

N.B. The Licchavi inscriptions of Nepal speak very highly of the accomplishments of the women of Kāñcî e.g. "aṅgaśriyā parigato jitakāmarupaḣ Kāñcîgunāḍhyavanitabhir upāsyamānaḣ" (G.N.I. LXXXI 16 stanza 16). Judging from the inscription of king Rāmadeva (G.N.I. XVII) dated Saṃvat 469 (547 A.D.) mentioning the donation of Khuḍḍasvāmi, the south Indian people seem to be very well established in Nepal during the period of Bhāravi (Vide Judicial Customs of Nepal Part I on Khuddasvāmi, and also Nepal's international contacts in the scheme of Kirāta-gaṇa-rājyas and Buddhistic Janapadas). Kāñcî is identified with what is Tamil Nadu in Madra today.

समुन्नतैः काशदुकूलशालिभिः परिक्वणत्सारसपङ्क्तिमेखलैः ।
प्रतीरदेशैः स्वकलत्रचारुभिर्विभूषिताः कुञ्जसमुद्रयोषितः ॥९॥

Samunnataiḣ kāśadakûlaśālibhiḣ parikkaṇatsārasapañktimekhalaiḣ /
pratîradeśaih svakalatracārubhirvibhûṣitāḣ kuñjasamudrayoṣitah //9//

Translation:

O! the ladies (from Kāñcî) hail from coastal countries abutting upon the junction of the river (Cauvery) and the ocean, where, with the unending flocks of sea-gulls and other birds (of non-migrating variety) on the sea-shore, the orchards are evergreen with silken Kāśa (saccharum spontaneum used for making mats and roofs) and where the happy husbands live with their charming wives amid a scene lavished by prodigally grain all the year round.

N.B. Mallinātha's explanation of "svakalatracārubhi (=charming women wearing their own silken loins) do not appear to be satisfactory, though "kalatra" in stanza 17 of this canto seems to yield meaning. Here Bhāravi seems to be describing the life of the men and women of Kāñci, which is one of the seven famous cities of ancient India. Hsüan–Tsang describes Kāñcipura as the last seaport of Dravida Country for Ceylon. As a widely travelled man Bhāravi gives a factural description of the coastal countries of south India. It is remarkable that the ladies of different countries of the then known earth have met the Heavenly houris from the paradise of Indra, who do not seem to be acquainted with shame and sorrow and the conditions of life on earth. Living as they have done like Eve in the Garden of Eden, the Heavenly houris in stanza 8 give themselves up for a free for all the philandering gods. We have seen how Indra is great philanderer. The ladies on earth are teaching the nymphs how to behave themselves and learn their feminine etiquette from the women of Kāñcî. This appears to be a very interesting dialogue of the women of ancient world.

विदूरपातेन भिदामुपेयुषश्च्युताः प्रवाहादभितः प्रसारिणः ।
प्रियाङ्कशीताः शुचिमौक्तिकत्विषो वनप्रहासा इव वारिबिन्दवः ॥१०॥

Vidûrapātena bhidāmupeyuṣaścyutāh pravāhādabhitah prasāriṇah /
priyāñkaśîtāh śucimauktikatviṣo vanaprahāsā iva vārivindavah //10//

Translation:

Coming as they do from a distant coastal country distinguished for constant current and flow of rivers under an equable climate, the fleeting raindrops cheer the gardens and the orchards like the white light of pearls embracing its darling wearers.

कान्ताजनं प्रेमगुरूकृतादरं निरीक्षमाणा इव नम्रमूर्तयः ।
स्थिरद्विरेफाञ्जनशारितोदरैर्विकासिभिः पुष्पविलोचनैर्लताः ॥११॥

Kāntājanaṃ premagurûkritādaraṃ nirîksamāṇā iva namramûrtayah /
sthiradvirephāñjanaśāritodaraivikāsibhih puṣpavilocanairlatāh //11//

Translation:

Looking on the polite creepers with the eyes of black-bees humming on the flowers and growing and developing in the stable and constant climate of the coastal country (of Kāñci,), which is flowing with milk and honey, these lovely women have become the models of politeness and grace as it were.

N.B. Mallinātha's glosses of "sakhijanaṃ" (= lady friends) and "visāribhih" (=spreading out or strengthening their stomachs) do not give Bhāravi's factual description of the beautiful and graceful women (kāntājanam) of Kāñci, who have developed their polite behaviour pattern and civilised breeding from the glorious atomosphere (vikāsibhih) of the country flowing with milk and honey, amid which they have grown. During my travel in these countries. I was personally impressed by the polite upbringing of the healthy ladies of Kāñci whose supple bodies and civilised behaviour distinguished them as the models of beauty and grace. No doubt, the equable climate and the constant yield of the fields all the year round in these coastal countries contributed much to the moulding of the character of these happy people.

उपेयुषीणां बृहतीरधित्यका मनांसि जन्हुः सुरराजयोषिताम् ।
कपोलकाषैः करिणां मदारुणैरुपाहितश्यामरुचश्च चन्दनाः ॥१२॥

Upeyuşînāṃ vrihatĭradhityakā manāṃsi jahruh surarājayositāṃ/
kapolakāşaih kariṅāṃ madāruṅairupāhitaśyāmarucaśca candanāh //12/

Translation:

The sight of the glamorous ladies of the coastal countries with their hair teasingly tumbled and curled over their heads and cheeks and warmly scented by the shampoo of sandalpaste resembling the maroon tint of the ochre streaming down the dark temples of ruttish elephants, enthralled the divine ladies (from Indra's paradise).

N.B. It would be useful to study the development of hair-style of the statues of Yaksis unearthed in the excavation of Kapilavastu and of the image of Devî Bhagavatî Vijaya Shrêê in Judicial Customs of Nepal Part I (Plate XVIII) to appreciate what Bhāravi is saying.

स्वगोचरे सत्यपि चित्तहारिणा विलोभ्यमानाः प्रसवेन शाखिनाम् ।
नभश्चराणामुपकर्तुमिच्छतां प्रियाणि चक्रुः प्रणयेन योषितः ॥१३॥

Svagocare satypi cittahāriṅā vilobhyamānāh prasavena śākhināṃ /
nabhaścarāṅāmupakartumicchatāṃ priyāṅi cakruḣ praṅayena yoşitaḣ //13//

Translation:

Accomplished, indeed, to win the hearts of men by their lithe form and feature, the ladies knew how to be ravishing by silhoutte combination of their dress and tender flowers. Eager to please the divine music makers, they made themselves expert in the dramatic art of acting (and dancing to the temple of their music).

प्रयच्छतोच्चैः कुसुमानि मानिनी विपक्षगोत्रं दयितेन लम्भिता ।
न किंचिदूचे चरणेन केवलं लिलेख वाष्पाकुललोचना भुवम् ॥१४॥

Prayacchtoccaih kusumāni māninî vipakş agotraṃ dayitena lambhitā/
na kincidûce caraṅena kevalaṃ lilekha vāşpākulalocanā bhuvam//14//

Translation:

Already distinguished by their high-flown flowery style of offering the flowers of love, these proud ladies, when they were asked about their "Gotra" affiliations (pedigree) did not reply, but they wrote with the toes of their feet on the floor with their eyes brimful of tears.

प्रियेऽपरा यच्छति वाचमुन्मुखी निबद्धदृष्टिः शिथिलाकुलोच्चया ।
समादधे नांशुकमाहितं वृथा विवेद पुष्पेषु न पाणिपल्लवम् ॥१५॥

Priye(ऽ)parā yacchati vācamunmukhî nivaddhadrişţih sithilākulo-ccayā /
samādadhe nāṃšukamāhitaṃ vrithā viveda puşpeşu na pāṅi-pallavaṃ //15//

Translation:

The true lover gives her consent without a word (voluntarily) but with concentration in her steadfast eyes and by stripping herself to the scintillation of the buckles of her chastity belt. Other sacraments do not bind the lovers. Why cast a slur on the flower of love ? It is not so much the vow of fidelity, when the palms are joined (with the three sanctions of plighted troth before the sacred five at the altar of marriage), but the capacity of women to make love that gives her the pride of birth and position.

N.B. It appears to me that these stanzas are written to justify the adventure of king Māna-deva and Vijayasvāminî.

सलीलमासक्तवनान्तभूषणं समासजन्त्या कुसुमावतंसकम् ।
स्तनोपपीडं नुनुदे नितम्बिना घनेन कश्चिज्जघनेन कान्तया ॥१६॥

Salîlamāsaktavanāntabhûşaṅaṃ samāsajantyā kusumāvataṃsakaṃ /
stanopapîdaṃ nunude nitamvinā ghanena kašcijjaghanean kāntayā //16//

Translation:

Costumed in iridescent barks and leafs of the wild and exotic forests and dangling ear-pendants of flowers to match, and crazy for sensual pleasures, some unabashed ladies with beautiful hips and well-proportioned buttocks feigned to reel under thorny compliments of teasing their bare breasts by their friends calculated to inflict pain and excite them.

N.B. Mallinātha's gloss of "latānta" =creepers and sprouts) could not be used for their dress by the ladies. "Latā" is symbolic of "warm embrace" which does not convey the sense of pain. The poet seems to be influenced by Vātsyāyana's Kāmasûtra to describe the painful foreplay of love before coitus. Under the circumstances the expression "vanāntabhûṣaṇam" refer to the costume of thorny barks of the forests.

कलत्रभारेण विलोलनीविना गलद्दुकूलस्तनशालिनोरसा ।
बलिव्यपायस्फुटरोमराजिना निरायतत्वादुदरेण ताम्यता ॥१७॥

Kalatrabhāreṅa vilolanîvinā galaddukûlastanaśālinorasā/
valivyapāyasphuṭaromarājinā nirāyatatvādudareṅa tāmyatā//17//

Translation:

Their robust and prolific physical frame clad in skimpy silken bathing trunks and their heavy breasts swinging as the attributes of their sex, the fair ladies made ingenuous sensual display by their bottoms within the enclosure of the improvised playground in an attitude of laissezfare and complete abandon.

N.B. The description of the sports of men and women of the period of Bhāravi remind us of the bathing-clubs or even the clubs of the nudes in advanced countries of our own day. No doubt the age of the Kirātas, Buddhas and the Licchavis seem to be very much obsessed by sex.

विलम्बमानाकुलकेशपाशया कयाचिदाविष्कृतबाहुमूलया ।
तरुप्रसूनान्यपदिश्य सादरं मनोधिनाथस्य मनः समाददे ॥१८॥

Vilamvamānākulakešapāšayāā kayācidāviskritavāhumûlayā/
taruprasûnānyapadišya sādaraṃ manodhināthasya manah samādade//18//

Translation:

Teasingly curling up the long locks of their hair to reveal the beauty of their feature, some of the ladies artfully revealed their form from the tangled roots of the trees in order to attract the mind of their beloved men in a polite way.

व्यपोहितुं लोचनतो मुखानिलैरपारयन्तं किल पुष्पजं रजः ।
पयोधरेणोरसि काचिदुन्मनाः प्रियं जघानोन्नतपीवरस्तनी ॥१६॥

Vyapohituṃ locanto mukhānilairapārayantaṃ kila puṣpajaṃ rajah /
payodharoṅorasi kācidunmanāh priyaṃ jaghanonnatapîvarastanî//19//

Translation:

In their crazy sport of love some of the ladies with bare and heaving breasts pretended their inability to blow off the pollens of flowers by their breath made palatable with the cosmetics of their lips, so that they delibrately slapped their friends in order to arouse their impluses of love by wile, guile and coquettish play of eyes.

इमान्यमूनीत्यपवर्जिते शनैर्यथाभिरामं कुसुमाग्रपल्लवे ।
विहाय निःसारतयेव भूरुहः पदं वनश्रीर्वनितासु संदधे ॥२०॥

Imānyamûnîtyapavarjite šanairyathābhirāmaṃ kusumāgrapallave/
vihāya hiṅsāratayeva bhûruhaḣpadaṃ vanašhrêêrvanitāsu saṃdadhe//20//

Translation:

Seemingly oblivious to the invidious distinction of who is who, these men and women slowly and steadily locked their legs like the root of a tree by natural selection, while on surface they added to the beauty of the forest by sprouting like variagated twigs and flowers.

प्रवालभङ्गारुणपाणिपल्लवः परागपाण्डूकृतपीवरस्तनः
महीरुहः पुष्पसुगन्धिराददे वपुर्गुणोच्छ्रायमिवाङ्गनाजनः ॥२१॥

Pravālabhañgāruṅapāṅipallavah parāgapāṅdûkritapǰvarastanah / mahîruhah puspasugandhirādade vapurguṅocchrāymivānganā-janah//21//

Translation:

Their delicate palms rendered crimson by the crushing of the sprouts and flowers and their sinous breasts tinted white by the shower of pollen-dusts, the pretty ladies found the silhouttes of their physical frames enhanced by the double attraction of natural scene and scent of the forest.

वरोरुभिर्वारणहस्तपीवरैश्चिराय खिन्नान्नवपल्लवश्रियः ।
समेऽपि यातुं चरणाननीश्वरान्मदादिव प्रस्खलतः पदे पदे ॥२२॥

Varorubhirvārańahastapîvaraiściräya khinnānnavapallavaśṛyaḣ/ same(ʃ)pi yātuṃ carańānanśîvarānmadādiva praskhalatah pade pade//22//

Translation:

Victims of langour (in the atmosphere of our earth) for want of exercise of the elephant-trunk like thighs of their budding youths as in the frivolous conditions of Indra's paradise for a long time, they (the divine ladies) fidgeted higgedly piggedly like drankards even in the broad and level ground of the buff.

N.B. Mallinātha feels that this and the following four stanzas represent the comparative observation of the prominent persons of Guild Organisation on the behaviour pattern of the Divine Ladies and our women on earth.

विसारिकाञ्चीमणिरश्मिलब्धया मनोहरोच्छ्रायनितम्बशोभया ।
स्थितानि जित्वा नवसैकतद्युतिं श्रमातिरिक्तैर्जघनानि गौरवैः ॥२३॥

VisāriKāñcîmanirašmilavdhayā manoharocchrāyanitamvašobhayā/ sthitāni jitvā navasnikatadyutiṃ šramātiriktairjaghanānigauravaih //23//

Translation:

Displaying with effect the silhoutte of their beautiful bodies with slender hips and sloping buttocks under the sparkling jewels (pearls and corals) to beat the simmer of fresh sands on the buff, the women (of Kāñcî)proved by their victorious appearance (at the beach) that beauty and elegance was a matter of style and accessories.

N.B. Evidently this is a beauty parade of women from countries as far apart as Kāñcî in Madias and Tusāra in Central Asia. We have already pointed out how the Chinese pilgrim Hsūan-tsang mentions Kāñcipûram as the last seaport of the Dravida country, from where he reached Ceylon in three days of sea voyage. This country was ruled by the Cholas and Pallavas, of which Hsuan-tsang roughly specifies the area. The Madras University archaeologists have now established on the basis of their Excavation of ancient Buddhistic monuments mentioned by Hsūan-tsang that Kāñcî (pûram) lies sixty kilometers to the east of the city of Madras.

समुच्छ्वसत्पङ्कजकोशकोमलैरुपाहितश्रीण्युपनीवि नाभिभिः ।
दधन्ति मध्येषु बलीविभङ्गिषु स्तनातिभारादुदराणि नम्रताम् ॥२४॥

Samucchvasatpaṅkajakošakomalairupāhitašrîṇyupanîvi nābhibhih/
dadhanti madhyeṣu valîvibhaṅgisu stanātibhārādudarāṅi namratām //24//

Translation:

Some of the ladies teasingly gathered the folds of their lotus-chrysalis soft apron in their waist-line to expose the attraction of their navel and show with effect the beauty of their dangling breasts above their supple belly by their crazy style and accesssories.

समानकान्तीनि तुषारभूषणैः सरोरुहैरस्फुटपत्रपङक्तिभिः ।
चितानि घर्माम्बुकणैः समन्ततो मुखान्यनुत्फुल्लविलोचनानि च ॥२५॥

Samānakāntîni tuṣārabhûṣaṅaih saroruhairasphutapattrapañktibhih/
citāni gharmāmbukaṅaih samantatomukhānyanutphullavilocanāni ca//25//

Translation:

As they appeared in the beauty parade on the beach with their glamorous faces and sparkling eyes like rows of budding lotuses in the pond, all the beautiful ladies appeared alike whether they hailed from the perpetually warm and steaming coastal region of the south or from the snow-bound region of Central Asia.

N.B. It appears that both Mallinātha and Govinda Sharma have lost the scene of the beauty parade of ladies in the beach with their distinctive fashions from countries as far apart as "Tuṣāra" or in other words the insular regions of Central Asia in the north to the sultry land of perpetual summer, namely Kāñcî, which steams in heat.

The Chinese pilgrim Hsuan-tsang describes the country of Tusāra (=**a** country of frost, snow, mist and vapour) which has many corrupt versions in Chinese language. Ancient western geographers mention the country as Tokhara. It was supposed to correspond to what is today Bokhara and Badakshan. Judging by the accounts of the Chinese pilgrims it was properly not the name of a country but of great tribes of nomadic and urban peoples occupying a certain large territory of Central Asia. What is of real interest here is how Bhāravi puts up the parade of earthly women via-a-vis the houris from Indra's paradise.

विनिर्यतीनां परिखेदमन्थरं सुराङ्गनानामनुसानुवर्त्मनः ।।
सविस्मयं रूपयतो नभश्चरान्विवेश तत्पूर्वमिवेक्षणादरः ।।२६।।

Viniryattnāṃ parikhedamantharaṃ surāñganānāmanusānuvartmanah/
savismayaṃ rûpayato nabhaščarānviveša tatpûrvamivekṣaṅā-
darah//26//

Translation:

The divine music-makers were surprised to find the dull and subdued face of the divine ladies and their form in a state of fatigue visa-vis the glamour and grace of the terrestrial beauties on the beach; and they learnt to look upon the latter with respect ever afterwards.

N.B. Mallinātha's "gurukheda" (=great lassitude) does not give the poet's idea of "parikhedamantharaṃ" to describe the feeling of fatigue with their own dull feature and form vis-a-vis the glamour and grace of the terrestrial women in the beauty parade on the beach. Thus if Mallinātha slurs over his own gloss,Govinda errs by mistranslating the entire stanza. It is remarkable that this is, perhaps, the earliest description of beauty parade on the beach before taking part in the aquatic sports.

अथ स्फुरन्मीनविधूतपङ्कजा विपङ्कतीरस्खलितोर्मिसंहतिः ।
पयोऽवगाढुं कलहंसनादिनी समाजुहावेव वधूः सुरापगा ॥२७॥

Atha sphuranmînavidhûtapañkajā vipaṅkatîraskhalitormisaṃhatih/
payo (ऽ) vagādhuṃ kalahaṃsanādinī samājuhāveva vadhuh surāpagā//27//

Translation:

Then (after the parade of beauties) as all members of the party assembled themselves on the broad dust-free shore of the river dinning with the songs of a variety of ducks, they were delighted to see the clear water disturbed by the fishes playing in the river.

प्रशान्तघर्माभिभवः शनैर्विवान्विलासिनीभ्यः परिमृष्टपङ्कजः ।
ददौ भुजालम्बमिवात्तशीकरस्तरङ्गमालान्तरगोचरोऽनिलः ॥२८॥

Prašāntagharmābhibhavah šanairvivānvilāsinîbhyah parimristạpañkajaḣ/
dadau bhuǰālambamivattašîkarastarañgamalāntaragocaro(ऽ)-nilaḣ//28//

Translation:

Where was the sting of cold in the water of the buff when the pleasure seeking ladies created ripples by the strokes of their arms on the calm surface, where the wind itself appeared to lend its helping hand in widening the circle with its balmy breath blowing through the lotuses.

गतैः सहावैः कलहंसविभ्रमं कलत्रभारैः पुलिनं नितम्बिभिः ।
मुखैः सरोजानि च दीर्घलोचनैः सुरस्त्रियः साम्यगुणान्निरासिरे ॥२९॥

Gataih sahāvaih kalahaṃsavibhramaṃ kalatrabhāraih pulinaṃ nitambibhiḣ/
mukhaiḣ sarojāni ca dîrghalocanaih surastriyaḣ sāmyaguṅānnirāsiré//29//

Translation:

Swimming deftly with the easy style (gait) of the swarm of gander and goose for their own pleasure, where was the heaviness of the contour of heavy bottoms and breasts as the (exclusive) wives of the gods dipped and emerged (on the surface of water) with happy faces and longing looks to surpass the beauty of the scene in a community bathing ?

N.B. Mallinātha's gloss of "kalaṃsavikramaṃ" (=with the prowess of the flocks of ducks and drakes) does not give us the meandering and sporting gait of the aquatic birds implied by the poet's original of "vibhramaṃ (=roaming–going about or whirling).

विभिन्नपर्यन्तगमीनपङक्तयः पुरोऽवगाढाः सखिभिर्मरुत्वतः ।
कथञ्चिदापः सुरसुन्दरीजनैः सभीतिभिस्तत्प्रथमं प्रपेदिरे ॥३०॥

Vibhinnaparyantagamīnapañktayaḣ puro (ऽ) vagādhāḥ sakhibhirmarutvataḣ/
kathañcidāpaḣ surasundarîjanaih sabhītibhistatprathamaṃ prapedire//30//

Translation:

As the divine beauties encountered a variety of unfamiliar aquatic animals in the deep water, they reformed themselves and somehow managed to follow in the wake of the Gandharavas (the music-makers) for (of being attacked by crocodyles etc).

N.B. Mallinātha's gloss "vigādhāḣ" (= plunging into or diving) does not express the poet's idea of "avagadha' (=following in the wake of). So far all the swimmers are swimming independently.

As they encounter unfamiliar aquatic animals in the deep the ladies particularly are afraid and follow in the wake of their male partners and swim collectively.

विगाढमात्रे रमणीभिरम्भसि प्रयत्नसंवाहितपीवरोरुभिः ।
विभिद्यमाना विससार सारसानुदस्य तीरेषु तरङ्गसंहतिः ॥३१॥

Vigādhamātre ramaṅîbhirambhasi prayatnasaṃvāhitapîvarorubhiḣ/
vibhidyamānā visasāra sārasānudasya tīreṣu tarañgasamhatih //31//

Translation:

Those of the ladies (who could not swim and take to deep water) just entered the shallows knee-deep and sported skillfully with their heavy things to bestir muddy ripples and send them with catcalls in immitation of the sounds of the cranes and storks on the shore (in order to kid the swimmers).

शिलाघनैर्नाकसदामुरःस्थलैर्बृहन्निवेशैश्च वधूपयोधरैः ।
तटान्तनीतेन विभिन्नवीचिना रुषेव भेजे कलुषत्वमम्भसा ॥३२॥

Śilāghanairnākasadāmurahsthalairvrihannivešaišca vadhûpayodharaih/
taṭāntanîtena vibhinnavīcinā ruṣeva bheje kaluṣatvamambhasā //32//

Translation:

The muddy water sent rippling with the current of the river from the shore acted as a blight on the swimmers of Indra's paradise and stone-hard chests of the Gandharvas (music-makers) came into contact with the soft contour of the breasts of the timid and spent beauties.

N.B. Mallinātha's gloss of "taṭābhinitena" (=carried to the shore) upsets the entire setting of the swimming scene. We get a very clear picture by restoring the poet to his original of "taṭāntanitena" (=the muddied water sent rippling through the many currents of the river by the bathers on the beach along with catcalls in immitation of the non-swimming variety of birds like storks and cranes). Evidently the expert swimmers in deep water are clinging together and the bathers on the beach are trying to tease them with catcalls and by stirring mud from the beach and directing them to the swimmers.

विधूतकेशाः परिलोडितस्रजः सुराङ्गनानामवलुप्तचन्दनाः ।
अतिप्रसङ्गाद्विहितागसो मुहुः प्रकम्पमीयुः सभया इवोर्मयः ॥३३॥

Vidhûtakešāh pariloditasrajah surāñganānāmavaluptacandanāh/
atiprasañgādvihitāgaso muhuh prakampamîyuh sabhayā
ivormayah//33//

Translation:

The very sight and close contact with the divine ladies,–who had their locks of hair tousy and loose (due to washing out of the exotic shampoos) with their crown of flowers disturbed and shaken, their sandal paste washed out and their body and face totally bereft of aids and perfume,– made the water itself tremble as if in fear.

N.B. Mallinātha's glosses of "lolita" (=shaking or trembling) and "pravilupta" (= cleared of or rubbed off) are very poor subtitutes for "loḍita" (= shaken or loose) and "avalupta" (=washed out) respectively.

विपक्षचित्तोन्मथना नखव्रणास्तिरोहिता विभ्रममण्डनेन ये ।
हृतस्य शेषानिव कुङ्कुमस्य तान्विकत्थनीयान्दधुरन्यथा स्त्रियः ॥३४॥

Vipakṣacittonmathanā nakhavraṇāstirohitā vibhramamāndanen ye/
hritasya šešāniva kuñkumasya tānvikatthanîyāndadhuranyathā
striyah//34//

Translation:

The disturbing marks of open and bleeding scratches of nails inflicted by the libertines over stark bodies stripped of all beauty aids, though hastily covered by the application of perfumed Kuñkuma (crocus sativus),– rather exposed the ladies beyond their capacity of hiding their shame by spinning yarns among their friends to the regret of happy family members.

N.B. Kuñkuma is crocus sativus obtainable from Kashmir, Bokhara (Bālhika) and Iran. Among the Sanskritic poets of his period, Bhāravi stands alone în his ability to isolate human emotion and relate it to the realities of life in the scheme of Gaṅarājyas (federation of tribal republics). He did not have to search for words; they came to him as if drawn by the irresistible magnetic attraction of international contacts during the period of the Kirātas he has undertaken to describe.

सरोजपत्रे परिलीनषट्पदे विशालदृष्टेः स्विदमू विलोचने ।
शिरोरुहाः स्विन्नतपक्ष्मसंततेर्द्विरेफवृन्दं नु निशब्दनिश्चलम् ॥३५॥

Sarojapatre parilînaṣatpade višāladriṣteḣ svidamū vilocane/
široruhāh svinnatapakṣmasaŋtaterdvirephavrindaṃ nu nišavdaniš-calam//35//

Translation:

O what a wonder ! to judge the ladies by their wide-open and longing eyes looking with undivided attention on the bees enmeshed in the calyx of the lotus over the stems (rising out of the muddy soil), their silence of bliss was louder than the hum of the dying bees (in his state of orgasm within the mess of petals).

N.B. Mallinātha's glosses of "Nu" (=either, or) used disjunctively from "vilînaṣṭpade" (=bees busy in sucking the juice) and "vilola-driṣṭe" (=trembling or unsteady eyes) totally miss the trend and context of "parilīna" (enamoured bees enmeshed in the bliss of sucking the juice) and "višāladriste" (=wide and wondering eyes) calculated to describe the wonder of the ladies in observing the dying hum of the bees in the bliss of sucking the juice in the calyx of the lotus buds, where their silence was louder in their expression than their speech.

The explanation of Mallinātha would be out of context with stanza 27 where the poet says that true love resides in attributes and not in the metabolism of matter. On the last analysis Bhāravi explains the theory of the "JEWEL in the Lotus" in and through the examples of the "hum of dying bees in the calyx of lotus." It is remarkable that the Jewel and the Lotus is the symbol of the astropsychic scheme of death known as "Kālacakra" after the Piprahava-Buddhist vase inscription.

अगूढहासस्फुटदन्तकेसरं मुखं स्विदेतद्विकचं नु पङ्कजम् ।
इति प्रलीनां नलिनीवने सखीं विदांबभूवुः सुचिरेण योषितः ॥३६॥

Agûdhahāsasphuṭadantakesaraṃ mukhaṃ svidetadvikacaṃ nu pañkajam/
iti pralīnāṃ naliniîvane sakhîṃ vidāmvabhûbuh sucireṅa yoṣitah //36//

Translation:

Now the ladies burst into open laughter by exposing the saffron of their teeth or was their face a foil to the expanding lotus bud (nelumbo nucifera)? It was while sporting in the pond abounding in lotuses with their girl friends of earth that the divine ladies had the consciousness of the infra-sound of the humming and loving bees in the mess of petals.

N.B. Mallinātha's gloss of "vikasannu" (=doubtfully blowing as if) does not express Bhāravi's idea "vikacan" (=expanding as lotus bud) and "nu" (which is an indeclinable particle used by the poet with interrogative force and implying some doubt or uncertainty.)

V. S. Apte quotes Bhāravi to show how "nu" is very often compounded with the interrogative pronoun and its derivatives in the sense of 'possibly indeed'. It is only by restoring the poet to his original that we get the idea that the Divine ladies laughed by exposing the saffron of their teeth as a foil to the budding lotus still trembling with the infra-sound of humming in its mess of love. It was not from the heaven of Indra that the divine nymphs learnt the language of love and God. The Poet seems to be explaining the concept of the "Jewel in the Lotus" through the examples of the bees in the lotus petals humming their silent–sound of ecstatic death. Can we compare it to the Swan Song of the western world?

The poet seems to be very sensitive to the sound-waves-which permeate the atmosphere from the infra-sound of the bees to the natural thunder-claps, astral explosions, space-craft flights, earthquakes and high wind. It is only lately that the scientists of advanced countries have begun to pay more attention to infra-sound– waves so low in frequency (usually 6 to 19 cycles per second) that they fall below the threshold of human hearing. Once generated such infra-sound can travel vast distances, and that the throbbling feeling engendered by the intense emissions can endanger our life by causing friction among our internal organs. With the advancement of science, eminent scientists are planning a more comprehensive study of the relationship between infra-sound level and aberrant human behaviour. And if it does turn out that infra-sound can affect people's moods, the implications of the theory of the "bees or jewels in the lotus", as it is being expounded by Bhāravi, could be widespread.

प्रियेण संग्रथ्य विपक्षसंनिधावुपाहितां वक्षसि पीवरस्तने ।
स्रजं न काचिद्विजहौ जलाविलां वसन्ति हि प्रेम्णिगुणा न वस्तुनि ॥३७॥

Priyeṇa saṃgrathya vipakṣasaṃnidhāvupāhitāṃ vakṣasi pîvarastane/
srajaṃ na kācidvijahau jalāvilāṃ vasanti hi premṇi guṇā na vastuni//37//

Translation:

While taking part in the aquatic sports in the buff some of the ladies did not reject the chaplets offered by their lovers to deck their wide breasts in the presence of their husbands. For, love resides in attributes rather than in the metabolism of matter.

असंशयन्यस्तमुपान्तरक्ततां यदेव रोद्धुं रमणीभिरञ्जनम् ।
हृतेऽपि तस्मिन्सलिलेन शुक्लतां निरास रागो नयनेषु न श्रियम् ॥३८॥

Asaṃśayamnyastamupāntaraktatāṃ yadeva roddhuṃ ramaṇîbhirañjanam/
hrite (ऽ)pi tasminsalilena śuklatāṃ nirāsa rāgo nayaneṣu na śriyam//38//

Translation:

Though the water, no doubt, washed away the rosy unguent applied by the ladies in the bath as beauty aids by exposing their white pupils, yet it could not totally deprive them of the attraction of their dancing eyes, which appeared all the more attractive unadorned.

द्युतिं वहन्तो वनितावतंसका हृताः प्रलोभादिव वेगिभिर्जलैः ।
उपप्लुतास्तत्क्षणशोचनीयतां च्युताधिकाराः सचिवा इवाययुः ॥३९॥

Dyutiṃ vahanto vanitāvataṃsakā hritāḣ pralobhādiva vegibhirjalaiḣ/
upaplutāstatksaṇasocanîyatāṃ cyutādhikārāḣ sacivā ivāyayuḣ//39//

Translation:

Finding themselves stripped of the ornament of their beauty aids by the strong current of water out of sheer jealousy and malice as it were, the bevy of fair ladies seemed to be reduced on that instant to pitiable plights like secretaries (ministers) overthrown from their power.

विपत्रलेखा निरलक्तकाधरा हृताञ्जनाक्षीरपि विभ्रतीः श्रियः ।
निरीक्ष्य रामा बुबुधे नभश्चरैरलंकृतं तद्वपुषैव मण्डनम् ॥४०॥

Vipattralekhā niralaktakādharā hritāñjanākṣîrapi vibhratîh śriyaḣ/
nirîkṣa rāmā vuvudhe nabhaścarairalaṇkritaṃ tadvapuṣaiva maṇ-danam//40//

Translation:

The music-makers of Indra's paradise were most impressed and awakened to the unadorned beauty and majesty of human figure when they saw the ladies the more attractive, bright and spritely, though the current of water had washed away the beauty marks on their forehead, the rouge (paint) on their lips and the ointment of their eyes.

N.B. Mallinātha's glosses of "nirañjanākṣi" (=eyes lacking unguent) do not convey the idea of washing out of the beauty aids meant by the poet's original of "hritāñjanākṣî" (=eyes deprived of unguents).

तथा न पूर्वं कृतभूषणादरः प्रियानुरागेण विलासिनीजनः ।
यथा जलार्द्रो नखमण्डनश्रिया ददाह दृष्टीः प्रतिपक्षयोषिताम् ॥४१॥

Tathā na pûrvaṃ kritabhûsaṇādaraḣ priyānurāgena vilāsinîjanaḣ/
yathā jalārdro nakhamaṇdanaśriyā dadāha dristî pratipakṣayoṣi-tāṃ//41//

Translation:

Even as the merry wives did not mind stripping themselves of their ornaments and garments at the outset (of swimming) for the joy of life, so also they took the marks of scratches of the finger-nails of their lovers (on their breasts) as decorations in a sporting spirit by common consent.

N.B. Mallinātha's gloss of "vipakṣa" (=hostile, adverse, opposed) does not seem to take note of the permissive nature of the Samyak Society described by Bhāravi (see Canto XVII. 43). By restoring the poet to his original of "pratipakṣa" (=the opposing side of the party in voting) we get the idea of the most creative phase of the society in Kirātagaṇarājyas which had made conscious efforts in human history to achieve an unsurpassable national ideal of human nobility and religious vision by discussions and of deciding the issue by voting. It is a pity that these expressions of a democratic society had degenerated under the social conditions of Mallinātha to a professional Brāhmannic formula signifying the opposite of what the poet had implied.

शुभाननाः साम्बुरुहेषु भीरवो विलोलहाराश्चलफेनपंक्तिषु ।
नितान्तगौर्यो हृतकुङ्कुमेष्वलं न लेभिरे ताः परभागमूर्मिषु ।।४२।।

Śubhānanāḣ sāmvuruheṣu bhîravo vilolahārāścalaphenapaṇktiṣu/
nitāntagauryo hritakumkumeṣvalaṃ na lebhire tāḣ parabhāga-mûrmiṣu//42//

Translation:

The rows of the flakes of foam moving down with the current of the river could not, however, wash away the aromatic resins of Kuṃkuma (crocus sativus =केसर), with which the fair bodies of the beautiful eyed and timid ladies were besmeared (before bathing), and detract anything from its fragrant properties and tint.

ह्रदाम्भसि व्यस्तवधूकराहते रवं मृदङ्गध्वनिधीरमुज्झति ।
मुहुस्तनैस्तालसमं समाददे मनोरमं नृत्यमिव प्रवेपितम् ।।४३।।

Hradāmbhasi vyastavadhûkarāhate ravaṃ mridangadhvanidhîramu-jjhati/
muhu stanaistālasamaṃ samādade manoramaṃ nrityamiva pravepitam//43//

Translation:

Hit (agitated or disturbed) by the alternating (double) strokes of the hands of the swimming ladies, the water of the pool responded with the deep sound of drum while their breasts kept tempi to the music as if the entire atmosphere trembled for the dance of the beauties.

श्रियाहसद्भिः कमलानि सस्मितैरलंकृताम्बुः प्रतिमागतैर्मुखैः ।
कृतानुकूल्या सुरराजयोषितां प्रसादसाफल्यमवाप जाह्नवी ।।४४।।

Sriyā hasadbhiḣ kamalāni sasmitairalaṃkritāmbuḣ pratimāgatairmu-haiḣ/
kritanukûlyā surarājayoṣitām prasādsāphalyamavāpa jāhnavî//44//

Translation:

The river found its fulfilment (reward) in having created the heavenly atomosphere for aquatic sports as its water mirrored the gracefully smiling faces (of the houris of Indra's paradise) like lotuses in bloom.

परिस्फुरन्मीनविघट्टितोरवः सुराङ्गनास्त्रासविलोलदृष्टयः ।
उपाययुः कम्पितपाणिपल्लवाः सखीजनस्यापि विलोकनीयताम् ।।४५।।

Parisphuranmînavighaṭṭitoravaḣ surānganāstrāsaviloladriṣṭayaḣ/
upāyayuḣ kampitapāṇipallavāḣ sakhîjanasyāpi vilokanîyatām//45//

Translation:

As the shoals of fishes touched their thighs by reacting to the vibration of the unfamiliar sound (of the strokes of the swimmers in the pool of water), the divine ladies with their timid looks and trembling hands offered themselves as sights (became the objects of wonder) even for their terrestrial friends.

भयादिवाश्लिष्य झषाहतेऽम्भसि प्रियं मुदानन्दयति स्म मानिनी ।
अकृत्रिमप्रेमरसाहितैर्मनो हरन्ति रामाः कृतकैरपीहितैः ।।४६।।

Bhayādivāśliṣya jhaṣāhate(ऽ)mbhasi priyaṃ mudānandayati sma māninî/
akritrimapremarasāhitairmano haranti rāmāh kritakairapîhitaiḣ//46//

Translation:

The proud ladies derived their pleasure from unwonted experience of venturing and swimming in the water infested by the leaping

(Himalayan) trouts and crocodyles, though they simulated fear by embracing their lovers. With their appetite for attracting men's minds by artificial acting for a change, beautiful women have a way of teasing (kidding) by their strange behaviour to the terror and chagrin of their male partners.

तिरोहितान्तानि नितान्तमाकुलैरपां विहारादलकैः प्रसारिभिः ।
ययुर्वधूनां वदनानि तुल्यतां द्विरेफवृन्दान्तरितैः सरोरुहैः ॥४७॥

Tirohitāntāni nitāntamākulairapāṃ vihārātalakaih prasāribhih/
yayurvadhûnāṃ vadanāni tulyatāṃ dvirephavrindāntaritai sororuhaih //47//

Translation:

The bevy of ladies sporting themselves in a spirtit of abandon with their tousy hair in the deeply disturbed water (and with even strokes of their breasts as they swam)— presented a spectacle of harmony (of community bathing) like hosts of lotuses covered over with bees.

N.B. Mallinātha's gloss of "vigāha" (=plunging into, diving or bathing) does not give the idea of the pleasure of community swimming meant by the word "vihārāt" (diversion for pleasure) where their tousled hair dishevelled in the water made them look alike like the lotuses covered over with the busy bees (vide Canto IV stanza 15). What the poet means to say is that the ladies from countries as far apart as Central Asia and South India had lost the individual style of hair-dressing and they all looked alike in body and mind and hair–style as they swam. By restoring the poet to his original of "vihārat" we get a panoramic view of the water-sports of the ladies of community swimming in a spirit of abandon.

करौ धुनाना नवपल्लवाकृती पयस्यगाधे किल जातसंभ्रमा ।
सखीषु निर्वाच्यमधार्ष्ट्यदूषितं प्रियाङ्गसंश्लेषमवाप मानिनी ॥४८॥

Karau dhunānā navapallavākritî payasyagādhe kila jātasaṃbhramā/
sakhîṣu nirvācyamadhārṣtyadûṣitaṃ priyāñgasaṃśleṣamavāpa māninî//48//

Translation:

With their hands trembling like fresh sprouts, and swimming with unsteady strokes in the(dangerously) deep water for fear of drowning, the proud women did not mind obscene language of their friends when they clung to the bodies of their male-friends. For, common danger and fear develop community interest and a sense of equality where passion and love provide the motive for union.

प्रियैः सलीलं करवारिवारितः प्रवृद्धनिःश्वासविकम्पिताधरः ।
सविभ्रमाधूतकराग्रपल्लवो यथार्थतामाप विलासिनीजनः ॥४९॥

Priyaiḥ salîlaṃ karavārivaritaḥ pravriddhaniḥśvāsavikampitādharaḥ/
savibhramādhûtakarāgrapallavo yathārthatāmāpavilāsinîjanaḥ//49//

Translation:

As their lovers rush in a burst of motion splashing water by the wild strokes of their arms to impede the progress of the ladies in a restless spirit of passion, the response of the merry ladies with their heaving breath, trembling lips and play of their hands prove that they are voluptuous and wanton ladies.

N.B. Mallinātha's gloss of "vikampitastanah (=heaving or unsteaady breast) seems to be a poor substitute for the poet's original of "vikampitashara" (=trembling lips).

उदस्य धैर्यं दयितेन सादरं प्रसादितायाः करवारिवारितम् ।
मुखं निमीलन्नयनं नतभ्रुवः श्रियं सपत्नीवदनादिवाददे ॥५०॥

Udasya dhairyaṃ dayitena sādaraṃ prasāditāyāḥ karavārivāritaṃ/
mukhaṃ nimiannayanaṃ natabhruvah śriyaṃ sapatnîvadanādivādade//50//

Translation:

Turning aside with patience and grace in response to the courtship of being singled out by the splashes of water, the pairs swam side by side touching lips, eyes closed and eye-brows arched as if they were men and wives in their sport of love.

विहस्य पाणौ विधृते धृताम्भसि प्रियेण वध्वा मदनार्द्रचेतसः ।
सखीव काञ्ची पयसा घनीकृता बभार वीतोच्चयबन्धमंशुकम् ॥५१॥

Vihasya pānau vidhrite dhritāmbhasi priyeṇa vaddhwā madanār-dracetasah/
sakhîva Kañcî payasā ghanîkritā vabhāra vîtoccayavandhamaṃ-śukam//51//

Translation:

Holding the water splashed by their beloved in the palm of their hands in restless spirit of sports accompanied by loud laughter, the bodies of ladies heated by passion slackened the dazzling buckle of their hip-belt (calculated to fasten their swimming trunk) made tough by the water, and they made efforts to hold the ends together after the style of their accomplished companion from (the coastal country of) Kāñcî.

N.B. The repeated mention of the accomplishment of the ladies from Kāncî as models of grace by Bhāravi appears to be very significant. Professor H. Goetz mentions the influence of Bhāravi on the kingdom of the Pallavas from the last quarter of the 6th to the seventh century, so much so that he makes Bhāravi a court poet of king Mahendravarman I (c. 600–630) on the basis, perhaps, of poet Ravikîrti's claim of equality with Kālidāsa and Bhāravi in his inscription of Megauti temple of Aihole on Mahaprabha river in Karnātak in 634/5 A.D. Ravikîrti was a court poet of king Pulakesin II. Then, too, Goetz speaks about the huge rock relief at Māmallapuram "alternately called the Descent of the Ganga", or "Arjuna's Penance', in fact, an illustration of Bhāravi's Kirātārjunîye, describing the encounter of Arjuna, the great hero of Mahābhārata, and of Śiva disguised as a primitive jungle hunter, a Kirāta" and how Śiva revealed himself. All these facts tend to the conclusion that there was a deep contact between Nepal and South India. No doubt king Mahendravarman was greatly influenced by the pleasures of life described by Bhāravi with a deep appreciation of the charm and culture of south Indian people at this transitional period of human history. (vide Five thousand years of Indian art by H. Goetz in "Art of the World" series.

निरञ्जने साचिविलोकितं दृशावयावकं वेपथुरोष्ठपल्लवम् ।
नतभ्रुवो मण्डयति स्म विग्रहे बलिक्रिया चातिलकं तदास्पदम् ॥५२॥

Nirañjane sācivilokitaṃ driśāvayāvakaṃ vepathuroṣṭapallavam/ natabhruvo maṇḍayati sma vigrahe valikriyā cātilakaṃ tadāspadam//52//

Translation:

Deprived of the beauty aids of collyrium pencilling her askant eye-brows and the rosy resins of lac in her trembling lips as well as the red beauty spot on her forehead, the beauty of her youthful and dimpled face, the silhoutte of her graceful form and figure remained to speak for adornment.

निमीलदाकेकरलोलचक्षुषां प्रियोपकण्ठं कृतगात्रवेपथुः ।
निमज्जतीनां श्वसितोद्धतस्तनः श्रमो नु तासां मदनो नु पप्रथे ॥५२॥

Nimîladākekaralolacakṣuṣām priyopakanthaṃ kritagātravepathuḣ/ nimajjatînāṃ śvasitoddhatastanaḣ śramo nu tāsāṃ madano nu paprathe//53//

Translation:

Her lascivous half-closed eyes looking askant and her body trembling in the act of diving very close to her lover, she gasped to expose her prolific breast. Did she do it in state of fatigue or for romance along the path blazed by the god of love?

प्रियेण सिक्ता चरमं विपक्षतश्चुकोप काचिन्न तुतोष सान्त्वनैः ।
जनस्य रूढप्रणयस्य चेतसि किमप्यमर्षोऽनुनये भृशायते ॥५४॥

Priyeṇa siktā caramaṃ vipakṣataścukopa kācinna tutoṣa sāntvanaiḣ/ janasya rûdhapraṇayasya cetasi kimapyamarṣo (ऽ)nunaye vriśāyate//54//

Translation:

Some of the ladies, who had grown up in an atmosphere of conventional morality, took offence at being splashed on the sly by the opposite number of their sex. They could not be consoled.

On the other hand, pacification added to the flame of their fury. (How could reason prevail on minds obsessed by the religious injunction of fidelity enjoined on them by scriptures?)

N.B. Mallinātha's gloss of "rûdhapraṇayasya cetasaḣ" (= under the consciousness of the convention of swimming) seems to be poor substitute for the poet's original of "rûdhapraṇayasya cetasi" to describe the "mental attitude of women obsessed by the religious injunctions of scriptures relating to oaths taken by them in their marriage before the baptism of fire with the water of oblation" calculated to seal the marriage contract.

All this reminds me of the feeling of queen Rājyavatî, when she prepared herself for self-immolation with king Dharmma-deva under the precepts of five-moralities with the result that Māna-deva had to use his influence to intervene and stop her from performing the cruel practice. As the grandson of "Bhoginî" Vijayasvāminî and Māna-deva, the poet's satire on the principles and practices of such conjugal rules seems to be all too apparent.

इत्थं विहृत्य वनिताभिरुदस्यमानं
पीनस्तनोरुजघनस्थलशालिनीभिः ।
उत्सङ्गितोर्मिचयलङ्घिततीरदेश-
मौत्सुक्यनुन्नमिव वारि पुरः प्रतस्थे ॥५५॥

Itthaṃ vihritya vanitābhirudasyamānaṃ
pînastanorujaghanasthalaśālinibhiḣ/
utsañgitormicayalañghitatîradeśa-
mautsukyanunnamiva vāri puraḣ pratasthe//55//

Translation:

At the conclusion of the aquatic sports the swimmers did not show signs of fatigue, and they headed for the shore with agile and effortless strokes of their plump round breasts and thighs (at the end of the long day). Buffeting the current of water with deft strokes (of swimming) they reached the beach in anticipation of going ahead in their career of pleasure (in the evening and far into the night).

N.B. Mallinātha's gloss of "utsarpitormi" (=rolling or swelling bellows of water upwards) does not take note of the art of swimming; and such an exercise ordinarily generates fatigue. By restoring the poet to his original of "utsañgitormi" surfing and swimming with the current) by deft and agile strokes of their breasts and thighs they made common cause between the deep water and the shore as expert swimmers. For Bhāravi's use of the word "utsarpita" please see Canto II Stanza 1.

तीरान्तरेषु मिथुनानि रथाङ्गनाम्नां
नीत्वा विलोलितसरोजवनश्रियस्ताः ।
संरेजिरे सुरसरिज्जलधौतहारा–
स्तारावितानतरला इव यामवत्यः ॥५६॥

Tîrāntareṣu mithunāni rathāñganāmnaṃ
nîtvā vilolitasarojavanaśriyastāḣ/
saṃrejire surasarijjaladhautahārā-
stārāvitānataralā iva yāmavatyaḣ//56//

Translation:

As the glimmering twiligt of the evening advanced over the charming forest of lotuses and seperated the pairs of ruddy ducks on opposite banks (of the river), the ladies washed by the water of "surasarita" sparkled in their jewelries like the twinkling garland of stars in the canopy of sky at night.

संक्रान्तचन्दनरसाहितवर्णभेदं
विच्छिन्नभूषणमणिप्रकरांशुचित्रम् ।
बद्धोर्मि नाकवनितापरिभुक्तमुक्तं
सिन्धोर्बभार सलिलं शयनीयलक्ष्मीम् ॥५७॥

Saṃkrāntacandanarasāhitavarṇabhedaṃ
vicchinnabhûṣanamaṇiprakarāmśucitraṃ/
vaddhormi nākavanitāparibhuktamuktaṃ
sindhorbabhāra salilaṃ śayanîyalakṣmîṃ//57//

Translation:

After having their feel of "nirvāṇa" (emancipation or self-abnegation) in and through the practical experience of aquatic sports in the river, the divine wives of Indra's paradise together with the terrestrial ladies presented a multitudinous picture of unity in diversity for the radianat beauty and romance of night-life, as and when they scintillated in the multi-coloured gems with the beauty aid of sandal-paste which obliterated their distinction of colour, creed and caste.

The end of Canto VIII.

KIRĀTĀRJUNIYE
CANTO IX

CANTO IX

Summary

This Canto consists of seventy-eight stanzas.

It opens with a superb description of sunset followed by moonrise over the Himālayas accompanied by "Pānagauṣṭthis" (community drinking parties) with faithful accounts of amorous advances and sexual intimacies among the ladies and gentlemen from Indra's paradise and from different parts of the world in the Disneyland of the Kirāta-gana-rājya. The Licchavi inscriptions of Nepal mention a number of Gausṭhika organisations, which seem to cover a wide range of human activities. These Guilds (Goṭis-Gauṣṭthikas) seem to be organised on the basis of the Eighteen Artisan Corporations (sāstādasaprakritin) vide GNI XII line 7) of the Buddhistic Janapadas (Republican states). We have given a detailed account in our Judicial Customs of Nepal Part I how Virûḍhaka attacked Kapilavastu and how the Śākyas assembled in the Mote Hall of their capital to discuss and decide whether they should capitulate and open the gate of the city or offer their resistance. Dr Fuhrer has given an account of the seventeen square stupas containing Buddhist vases recording, in the earliest Brāhmî scripts and Prākrit language, the names of the eighteen Śākyas, including Mahānāma, who fell fighting, while the excavation of Kapilavastu has yielded positive proof of the arson that followed the attack.

Speaking about the Śākyan constitution Professor Rhys Davids writes that the administration and the judicial business of the clan was carried on in public assembly, at which young and old were alike present in their common Mote Hall of Kapilavastu. From the accounts of the classical historians and from the discovery of the early symbols and vestiges associated with the worship of Śirî-mā devî and Śākyavardhana as well as the coin of Wima Kadphises with the image of horned Paśupati in the excavation of Kapilavastu, there could be little doubt that the Śākyas and Kolîs had borrowed their worship, symbols and scripts as well as their political concept of General Assembly, a council of elders and an elected head of state from the Indus-valley Republics.

After the defeat and dispersal of the ancient aristocracy of the Śākyas and Kolîs, the Kirātas, Yakṣas and Kinnaras appear to have inherited the democratic tradition of the Buddhistic Janapadas and founded a most powerful confederation of People's Republics under the military rule of Senāpatis (Military governors) comprised by Skanda, Pāñcika and Vaiśravana on the traditional roots of Pharo and Kuvera, which became universal with the rise of the military cult of Tobatsu Bishamon in East Asia. We have already discussed how the works of brave men were assessed by voting in the senate under the term "Puraskrita" (treating with honour).

But there is no record to show how the vote was taken and for what period such military governors were being elected, though the system of voting was called "Chhandas" (=free will or one's own choice along with other meaning of the word in Vedic and metrical sense),decisions arrived at through voting was known as"Chhandasya" rival parties were known as Dvaṇdas (=contending or disputing parties along with a host of meanings associated with the word) and party rivalry was known as Vyutkramaṇa (=standing in opposition or in contrary or inverted order). According to the grammarian Pānini, who writes about the non-monarchical states of the Himālayas and Central Asia, party members are called Vargya (=belonging to a particular group of like-minded persons) and Pakṣaḥ (=a wing or party in general.) The Chinese pilgrim Hsuan-tsang makes Pānini a native of Salātura of the city of Gāndhāra, who met Śiva and got the God's help to write his treatise on etymology 500 years after Nirvāṇa, which, according to Chinese calculation occured in 900 B.C. Professor G. Tucci has now established that the Nirvāṇa of Śākyamuni occured in 483 B.C. All this is very interesting for establishing the period of the Kirātas of whom Bhāravi is writing about.

The Licchavi Inscriptions of Nepal show that each village was ruled by the elected elders of Five men known as "Pahancos" (=Pañcamaṇdali or Pañcas) and that each village was divided into a number of wards known as "Goṣṭhis" (Guṭhis). Members of each Goṣṭhi (ward) assembled and chose representatives who had to qualify for its membership according to its needs. Even among the elected members, only people, who were conversant with committee work, honest and pure of mind and conducted themselves in accordance of the principles and practices of Kāraṇapûjā, were invested with the power and authority to deal with the affairs of Gosṭhis. Those, who had submitted accounts for the year or were guilty of illicit transactions and crimes were disqualified from continuing as members of the Guild.

Unlike the Brāhmannic society based upon the role of kinship and caste hierarchy, the inter-ethnic and inter-cultural contact situation described by Bhāravi in this Canto proves that the Samyak Society, in terms of democratic polity, was a classless society, where government by discussion and popular participation seem to be organised from the rock-bottom level of Goṣṭhis (wards). As a legacy of the Samyak Society of yore, the Samyak Ceremony is held once in every twelve years to our own day. But the majority of the members of the Goṣṭhis (Ghuthis), which by subscriptions pays the expenses for organising the festival of Samyak Sambuddhas from the recognised Eighteen Vihāras is now confined to the dwingling community of Vandayas (Bānrās) and Gubhājus (priests) of the Udās communities. But the impact of the evils of Brāhmannic caste-system has so distorted the original concept of Samyak Society that the Rānās took advantage of its weakness to destroy the organisation during the administration of Prime-minister Chandra Shumshere. It is against the background of such a degeneration, it would be well to return to Bhāravi to see what the Gauṣṭhis were like during the Kirāta and the Licchavi periods of our history. However, it is remarkable that the organisation of Goṭis of the Buddhistic period has survived with us as Guṭhis through the Sanskritic phase of Goṣṭhi, of which Bhāravi gives such a glowing account.

The metre in this Canto is Svāgatā.

वीक्ष रन्तुमनसः सुरनारीरात्तचित्रपरिधानविभूषाः ।
तत्प्रियार्थमिव यातुमथास्तं भानुमानुपपयोधि ललम्बे ॥१॥

Vīkṣya rantumanasaḥ suranārīrāttacitraparidhānavibhuṣāḥ/
tatpriyārthamiva yātumathāstaṃ bhānumānupapayodhi lalaṃbe//1//

Translation:

Then (at the conclusion of aquatic sports) the sun, on seeing the Divine ladies attired in gorgeous dresses according to the illustrations of pornographic paintings and with their minds set on sensual pleasures with their mates,– hastily proceeded towards the sea with a view to compliment the lovers.

मध्यमोपलनिभे लसदंशावेकतश्च्युतिमुपेयुषि भानौ ।
द्यौरुवाह परिवृत्तिविलोलां हारयष्टिमिव वासरलक्ष्मीम् ॥२॥

Madhyamopalanibhe lasadaṃśāvekataścyutimupeyuṣi bhānau/
dyauruvāha parivrittivilolām hārayaṣṭimiva vāsaralakṣmîṃ//2//

Translation:

Past the prime of his midday glow the declining sun half-sunk in the dusk with a divided (and truncated) form became part of the stupendous drama of nature like the chief diamond amid a garland of gems in the canopy of night-sky.

अंशुपाणिभिरतीव पिपासुः पद्मजं मधु भृशं रसयित्वा ।
क्षीबतामिव गतः क्षितिमेष्यंल्लोहितं वपुरवाप पतङ्गः ॥३॥

Aṃśupāṇibhiratîva pipāsuh padmajaṃ madhu bhriśaṃ rasayitvā/
kṣîbatāmiva gataḥ kṣitimeṣyaṃllohitaṃ vapuravāpa patañgaḥ//3//

Translation:

Thirsting extremely for the intoxicating drops of honey inherent in the lotus the sun went red with the plasma of rays like the social drinkers tiddly with its sip and taste, as he went sliding down the night sky.

N.B. Mallinātha's gloss of "ruvāha" (=bore himself or dragged with the burden) does not give Bhāravi's idea of "avāpa" (=looked like or assumed the form).

गम्यतामुपगते नयनानां लोहितायति सहस्रमरीचौ ।
आससाद विरहय्य धरित्रीं चक्रवाकमिथुनान्यभितापः ॥४॥

Gamyatāmupagate nayanānāṃ lohitāyati sahaśramarîcau/
āsasāda virahayya dharitrîṃ cakravākamithunānyabhitāpaḣ//4//

Translation:

The sun presented a mellow and shallow vision to the eyes, as its thousand rays deserted the supporter of life (earth) to the growing sorrow and disenchantment of the pair of Brāhmî-ducks (ruddy goose) that seperate with nightfall.

N.B. Mallinātha's gloss of "cakravākahridayānyasasāda" (=the heart of ruddy goose achieved extreme affliction) does not give Bhāravi's observation of the extreme agitation of the pair of the Brāhmannic ducks (ruddy goose) at having to fast with the red glow of the setting sun implied by the poet's original of "cakravākamithunānyabhitāpah".

Unable to account for the practical observation of the poet, which challenged the most fundamental theories of the Vedic Three Worlds covered by the Three Incomprehensible Steps of Almighty Vişhṇu, Mallinātha's glosses make our confusion worst confounded.

मुक्तमूललघुरुज्झितपूर्वः पश्चिमे नभसि संभृतसान्द्रः ।
सामि मज्जति रवौ न विरेजे खिन्नजिह्म इव रश्मिसमूहः ॥५॥

Muktamûlalaghurujjhitapûrvaḣ paścime nabhasi saṃbhritasāndraḣ/
sāmi majjati ravau na vireje khinnajihma iva raśmisamûhaḣ//5//

Translation:

As the sun spun from its axis in the east and became half-submerged in the western horizon (sky) the waning rays collected themselves like poor and decimated dependents lacking lustre.

कान्तदूत्य इव कुङ्कुमताम्राः सायमण्डलमभि त्वरयन्त्यः ।
सादरं ददृशिरे वनिताभिः सौधजालपतिता रविभासः ॥६॥

Kāntadûtya iva kuñkûmatāmrāh sāyamaṇdalamabhi tvarayantyaḣ/
sādaraṃ dadriśire vanitābhiḣ saudhajālapatitā ravibhāsaḣ//6//

Translation:

The fair ladies welcomed, like their messenger of love, the copper-coloured rays entering the network of their bags containing aromatic beauty aids of Kuñkuma (crocus sativus or safiron paste obtained from Kashmir) as the speedy harbinger of their bonanza.

अग्रसानुषु नितान्तपिशङ्गैर्भूरुहान्मृदुकरैरवलम्ब्य ।
अस्तशैलगहनं नु विवस्वानाविवेश जलधिं नु महीं नु ॥७॥

Agrasānuṣu nitāntapiśañgairbhûruhānmridukarairavalambya/
astaśailagahanaṃ nu vivasvānāviveśa jaladhiṃ nu mahîṃ nu//7//

Translation:

Did the sun go down spreading his soft chrysolite arms of its forward rays to embrace the shady sadness of the trees behind the Mount of the setting-sun or did he sink in the ocean or hid himself behind (the shadows of) the earth?

N.B. It is remarkable how the poet expresses his doubt about the account of the setting sun from ladies coming from the south Indian ports of Kāñcî (in what is Madras today) and from the mountainous countries with his own assessment of the situation, which is very modern.

आकुलश्चलपतत्रिकुलानामारवैरनुदितौषसरागः ।
आययावहरिदश्वविपाण्डुस्तुल्यतां दिनमुखेन दिनान्तः ॥८॥

Ākulaścalapatartikulānāmāravairanuditauṣasarāgaḣ/
āyayāvaharidaśvavipāṇḍustulyatāṃ dinamukhena dinānta ḣ//8//

Translation:

As the evening matins of the flocks of birds filled the air to bid farewell to the sun who was setting on this side of our earth to rise on the other side, its chrysolite rays at the end of the day was akin to that of the morning.

आस्थितः स्थगितवारिदपङ्क्त्या संध्यया गगनपश्चिमभागः ।
सोर्मिविद्रुमवितानविभङ्गैः रञ्जितस्य जलधेः श्रियमूहेः ॥९॥

Āsthitaḣ sthagitavaridapañktyā sandhyayā gaganapaścimabhāgaḣ/
sormividrumavitānavibhañgaiḣ rañjitasya jaladheḣ śriyamûheḣ//9//

Translation:

The rainless and dry clouds scintillating with the rosy tint of twilight under the canopy of western sky assumed the beauty and texture of dark blue waves of the ocean broken by the collection of red coral reefs (coral islands).

N.B. Mallinātha's gloss of "vibhāsā" (=light or lustre) totally misses the poet's comparative study of the rosy clouds under the canopy of the sky and the dark blue waves of the ocean broken by the coral reefs meant by the word "vibhañgaiḣ". Personally, I have been highly impressed by the like scene of coral islands breaking the monotony of the dark blue waves of the ocean. No doubt, Bhāravi was an experienced traveller.

प्राञ्जलावपि जने नतमूर्ध्नि प्रेम तत्प्रवणचेतसि हित्वा ।
संध्ययानुविदधे विरमन्त्या चापलेन सुजनेतरमैत्री ॥१०॥

prāñjalāvapi jane ṇatamûrdhni prema tatpravaṇacetasi hitvā/
sandhyayānuvidadhe viramantyā cāpalena sujanetaramaitrî//10//

Translation:

Though some people offered their prayers with folded palms and their heads bowed down in the dusk to the rejection of their tempestuous passion of love, yet the glimmering twilight of sunset was in the nature of befriending an evil companion.

औषसातपभयादपलीनं वासरच्छविविरामपटीयः ।
संनिपत्य शनकैरिव निम्नादन्धकारमुदवाप समानि ॥११॥

Auṣasātapabhayādapalînaṃ vāsaracchavivirāmapaṭîyaḣ/
saṃnipatya śanakairiva nimnādandhakāramudavāpa samāni//11//

Translation:

By contrast with the glittering light of the dawn of day that imparts, with its warmth, clear vision and distinction to everything, the glimmering landscape gradually faded away with the dusk of the evening while the pall of night levelled down all distinctions.

एकतामिव गतस्य विवेकः कस्यचिन्न महतोऽप्युपलेभे ।
भास्वता निदधिरे भुवनानामात्मनीव पतितेन विशेषाः ॥१२॥

Yekatāmiva gatasya vivekaḣ kasyacinna mahato(ऽ)pyupalebhe/
bhāsvatā nidadhire bhuvaanāmātmanîva patitena viśesāḣ//12//

Translation:

With the fading of the mountains and landscapes from our vision after sunset, we lose our sense of perspective, and with it we also lose our sense of discrimination with the result that the inhabitants of the world (consisting either of the three worlds according to the Brāhmannic concept or the fourteen worlds of Buddhistic cosmology) achieve a special unity (in diversity).

इच्छतां सह वधूभिरभेदं यामिनीविरहिणां विहगानाम् ।
आपुरेव मिथुनानि वियोगं लङ्घ्यते न खलु कालनियोगः ॥१३॥

Icchatāṃ saha vadhûbhirabhedaṃ yāminîvirahiṇāṃ vihagānāṃ/
āpureva mithunāni viyogaṃ lañghyate na khalu kālaniyogaḣ//13//

Translation:

Though some wives pining for their husbands were unwilling to part, they had to separate like the pair of ruddy goose. Indeed, it is impossible to transgress the fortuitous combination of circumstances in the great scheme of wheel of time.

N.B. It would be difficult to agree with Mallinātha that "Kālaniyoga" means here the decree of Fate or Destiny. Evidently, Bhāravi here satirises the theory of Vaiseśika who regarded time as one of the nine elements and with the Brāhmins who identified Time with their god of death Yama or Destiny.

यच्छति प्रतिमुखं दयितायै वाचमन्तिकगतेऽपि शकुन्तौ ।
नीयते स्म नतिमुज्झितहर्षं पङ्कजं मुखमिवाम्बुरुहिण्या ॥१४॥

Yacchati pratimukhaṃ dayitāyai vācamantikagate(ऽ)pi śakuntau/
nîyate sma natimujjhitaharṣaṃ pañkajaṃ mukhaṃivāmvuruhiṇyā//14//

Translation:

The group of lotuses hung down and closed their petals in sympathy at the sad plight of the pair of Brāhmi ducks who could not consummate their love, except by sending their pitiable call, though they lived so close to each other and were eager to mate.

रञ्जिता नु विविधास्तरुशैला नामितं नु गगनं स्थगितं नु ।
पूरिता नु विषमेषु धरित्री संहृता न ककुभस्तिमिरेण ॥१५॥

Rañjitā nu vividhāstaruśailā namitaṃ nu gaganaṃ sthagitaṃ nu/
pûritā nu viṣameṣu dharitrî saṃhritā nu kukubhastimireṇa//15//

Translation

Have the myriad tress and the mountains been tinged by the iridescent glimmer of twilight ? Has the entire canopy of the sky been enveloped by the pall of night? Has the uneven surface of the earth been levelled down and filled up? Or has all the cardinal compass points of the universe been obliterated?

(O! what an experience of the advancing pall of darkness! No doubt this stanza reminds us of the poetry of Keats.)

रात्रिरागमलिनानि विकासं पङ्कजानि रहयन्ति विहाय ।
स्पष्टतारकमियाय नभः श्रीर्वस्तुमिच्छति निरापदि सर्वः ॥१६॥

Rātrirāgamalināni vikāsaṃ pañkajāni rahayanti vihāya/
spaṣṭatārakamiyāya nabhaḣ śrirvastuṃicchati nirāpadi sarvaḣ//16//

Translation:

O! how the glimmering landscape fades from sight with the advancing shades of night! The stars shine in a clear sky which is free from dust. Indeed, the solemn atmosphere affords peace and tranquillity to all.

व्यानशे शशधरेण विमुक्तः केतकी कुसुमकेसरपाण्डुः ।
चूर्णमुष्टिरिव लम्भितकान्तिर्वासवस्य दिशमंशुसमूहः ॥१७॥

Vyānase śaśadhareṇa vimuktaḣ ketakîkusumakesarapāṇduḣ/
cûrṇamuṣṭiriva lambhitakāntirvāsavasya diśamaṃśusamûhaḣ//17//

Translation:

Now the moon released her pale white beams of the colour of the saffron of Ketaki flower (Agave Americana=सुन केवडा) to embrace the cardinal compass points of Indra, which appeared like a fist releasing from its hard grip the white dusts of camphor (cinnamomum camphora).

उज्झती शुचमिवाऽथ तमिस्रामन्तिके व्रजति तारकनाथे ।
दिक्प्रसादगुणमण्डनमूहे रश्मिहासविशदं मुखमैन्द्री ॥१८॥

Ujjhatî sucamiva(ऽ)tha tamisrāmantike vrajati tārakanāthe/
dikprasādaguṇamaṇdanamûhe raśmihāsavisadaṃ mukhamaindrî//18//

Translation:

Then rising gradually from the east with her face beaming with the smile of clear radiance, which had the properties of dispelling the inert and besetting pall of darkness, the moon brightened the borders of the night from close quarters.

N.B. Mallinātha's glosses of "āśu (=swiftly, quickly or directly) does not give the connection of this stanza with stanza 17 meant by the indeclinable particle "atha" (=Then, here or now). I do not see how far the word "antikaṃ" (=nearness, proximity or vicinity) is an improvement on the poet's original of "antike" (=first cousin or satellite closest to earth) and "(tārakarāje" (=lord of the planets) for Bhāravi's original of "tārakanāthe" (=leader of the stars in illuminating earth from close quarters as her first sister). We have already seen Bhāravi has given us his awesome grasp of the universe in the quick trip of the fairies in their air-vehicles through the solar system, where the planets are ruled by the sun, on to the Milky Way. As an astronomer the poet tells us here that the moon, as the closest sister of our planet, illumines the earth with the unique properties of her beams which dispel the darkness from the surface of the earth and illuminates her comparatively more than the twinkling stars which are so far away.

नीलनीरजनिभे हिमगौरं शैलरुद्धवपुषः सितरश्मेः ।
खे रराज निपतत्करजालं वारिधेः पयसि गाङ्गमिवाम्भः ॥१६॥

Nîlanîrajanibhe himagauraṃ śailaruddhavapusaḥ sitaraśmeḥ/
khe rarāja nipatatkarajālaṃ vāridheḥ payasi gāñgamivāṃbhaḥ//19//

Translation:

Emerging from the surrounding glens of the snow-mountains the net work of rays of the moon brightened the lotus-blue sky like the water of river meeting the ocean at its confluence.

N.B. It is remarkable that Bhāravi uses the pre-Aryan language of Gāñga (=river). The Licchavi inscriptions of Nepal have a number of such words as Khoñg and Kiañg. Because of the topographical nomenclature of pre-Aryan Finno-Dravid language, such words as Gāñg (as in the Gāñges), Khoñg (as in Mekong river of Indo-China) Kiañg (as in Yangstekiang of China) and Sikang in Northeast frontier province to describe the rivers. All these probably meant just what they meant in the Licchavi inscriptions as survivals from the historical past of the language of the Kirātas and the Yakṣas.

द्यां निरुन्धदभिनीलघनाभं ध्वान्तमुद्यतकरेण पुरस्तात् ।
क्षिप्यमाणमसितेतरभासा शंभुनेव गजचर्म चकासे ॥२०॥

Dyāṃ nirundhadabhinîlaghanābhaṃ dhvāntamudyatakareṇa purastāt/
kṣipyamāṇamasitetarabhāsā Śaṃbhuneva gajacarma cakāse//20//

Translation:

The dense pall of night thrown off by the forward arms of the moon hung up in the empty space of the pin-dark sky like the black lump of elephant's skin thrown off by Śaṃbhu sportingly (exposing his snow-white form and figure) .

N.B. Mallinātha's glosses of "atinîla" (=extremely dark) and "kari-carma" (=elephant's skin) seem to be poor substitutes for Bhāravi's original of "abhinîla" (=dense pall of night) and "gaja-carma" (=elephant's skin worn by Śambhu). Evidently Bhāravi disputes the ideas contained in such works as Nîlamatapurāna saying that Śambhu took up the sun and moon in his hands to light his path when he fought the demon of darkness known as Jalodbhava. Here Bhāravi seems to be giving his assessment of the dark eṃpty space under the canopy of sky lit up by the rays of the stars, compared to which the slow action of the reflected and illusive rays of the moon could be perceptible. Unlike poet Kālidāsa, who hypostatizes the time nature of Śaṃbhu by the sun and the moon in his introductory stanza of the drama of Sakuntalā, Bhāravi gives the results of his own observation of the night sky which is most modern. (Vide The Judicial Customs of Nepal Note *146)

अन्तिकान्तिकगतेन्दुविसृष्टे जिह्मतां त्यजति दीधितिजाले ।
निःसृतस्तिमिरभारनिरोधादुच्छ्वसन्निव रराज दिगन्तः ॥२१॥

Antikāntikagatenduvisriṣṭe jihmatāṃ tyajati dîdhitijāle/
niḣsritastiṃirabhāranirodhāranirodhāducchvasanniva rarāja digantaḣ//21//

Translation:

The landscape emerged again from the oppressive pall of darkness like the dying man recovering his breath from his stupor as the moon poured her network of elusive beams (on earth) from close quarters.

N.B. Mallinātha's gloss of "jahati" (=leaving or abandoning), though done for the sake of alliteration, seems to be a poor substitute for the poet's original of "tyajati" (=giving up or renouncing or getting rid of the stupor).

लेखया विमलविद्रुमभासा संततं तिमिरमिन्दुरुदासे ।
द्रंष्ट्रया कनकभङ्गपिशङ्ग्या मण्डलं भुव इवादिवराहः ॥२२॥

Lekhayā vimalavidrumabhāsā saṇtataṃ timiramindurudāse/
draṃṣṭrayā kanakabhañgapisañgyā maṇdalaṃ bhuva ivādivarāhaḣ//22//

Translation:

The moon with her pencils of clear and coral-coloured rays lifted the pall of darkness like the primordial Man-Boar Incarnation of Viṣhnu tearing the ball of earth after a tussle with Hiraṇyākṣa who held her in his golden embrace in the cosmic water.

N.B. Mallinātha's gloss of "kanaka-ṭañka (=a stone-cutter's chisel of gold or hatchet or axe of gold) does not yield Bhāravi's exposition of the myth of Hiraṇyākṣa meant by the word "kanaka-bhañga" (=tearing away the earth from the golden embrace of the gold eyed demon Hiraṇyāksa who may be identifiedawith Buddha Kanakamuni.

We have elaborately worked out the myth of the Man-boar Incarnation of Viṣṇu in our Judicial Customs of Nepal Part I Chapter XVI (Plate XXXI). A sacred place of ablution at the confluence of rivers Kauśikî and Kokā known as Varāhakṣetra in the district of Morang is famous for the worship of Varāha in Nepal.

From Vedic myths of the Man—boar incarnation apart, the Himālayan god Śaṃbhu or Śiva-vairocana as the light-maker has found its echo in the Buddhistic and Brāhmannic myths. In the dim past the Himālayan mountain Sumeru was supposed to be axis-mundi, where dwelt Śaṃbhu— the light-maker, who took in his hands the sun and moon to brighten the battle-grounds of the gods in their fight against the demon known as Jalodbhava (born from the cosmic water) who created darkness by his magical powers to confound his adversaries and defeat them. The Casket of emperor Kaniṣhka reproduces the same idea in the person of Buddha Vairocana flanked by the Bodhisattvas Sûryaprabha (light of the sun) and Candra-prabha (light of the moon). With the conquests of Kushāṇas, this idea appears to have found its way to the Fung Hsin temple of Lungmen and the Shanci provincial Museum of China. On my journey to and from Lhasa in Tibet, I was most impressed by the frescoes of Kumbum monastery, where Śaṃbhu and his consort Bhimā-devî were represented as carrying in their hands the sun and moon to brighten the battlefields of the gods in their fight against the creator of darkness Jalodbhava. It is equally remarkable that the Chinese pilgrim Hsûan-tsang mentions the popularity of the cult of Maheśvara (Śaṃbhu) and his consort Bhimādevî in many parts of Central Asia. In such a wide context, Bhāravi's exposition of the myths of Śambhu and Varāha appear to give form texture to the historical devleopment of the concept from Buddha Kanaka-muni down to the period of the Licchavis.

दीपयन्नथ नभः किरणौघैः कुङ्कुमारुणपयोधरगौरः ।
हेमकुम्भ इव पूर्वपयोधेरुन्ममज्ज शनकैस्तुहिनांशुः ॥२३॥

Dîpayannatha nabhaḣ kiraṇaughaiḣ kuñkumāruṇapayodharagauraḣ/
hemakumbha iva pûrvapayodherunmamañja śanakaistuhināṃśuḣ//23//

Translation:

Then rimming the floating clouds on the summits of the Himālayan mountain with her Kuñkuma (resins of saffron used for painting lips) crimson lips and illuminating the azure sky with her refulgence, the moon emerged like a golden goblet on the eastern sea.

उद्गतेन्दुमविभिन्नतमिस्रां पश्यति स्म रजनीमवितृप्तः ।
व्यंशुकस्फुटमुखीमतिजिह्मां व्रीडया नववधूमिव लोकः ॥२४॥

Udgatendumavibhinnatamisrāṃ paśyati sma rajanîmavitriptaḣ/
vyaṃśukasphutamukhîmatijihmāṃ vridayā navavadhûmiva lokaḣ//24//

Translation:

As the moon climbed up with her elusive rays in the night-sky, people of the world gazed upon her as a new bride, who was still trying to hide her face behind the veil with her charming guile.

न प्रसादमुचितं गमिता द्यौर्नोद्धृतं तिमिरमद्रिवनेभ्यः ।
दिङ्मुखेसु न च धाम विकीर्णं भूषितैश्च रजनी हिमभासा ॥२५॥

Na prasādamucitaṃ gamitā dyaurnoddhritaṃ timiramdrivanebhyaḣ/
diñmukheṣu na ca dhāma vikîrṇaṃ bhuṣitaiṣca rajanî himabhāsā//25//

Translation

The reflected rays of the moon could not brighten the canvas between the earth and the sky nor cou.d her glimmering light give form and feature to the outline of the mountains and forests of the landscape nor was the spectrum of her rays adequate to lit up the four cardinal compass corners. Nevertheless, the moon was an adornment to the night (which was a thing of beauty and a joy for ever).

N.B. Mallinātha's gloss of "bhûṣitaiva" (=as if she was an adornment to the night) does not denote the antithesis meant by the use of the indeclinable particle "ca" (=Nevertheless or on the other hand). By restoring the poet to his original we get the poet's collosal vision of the universe, where the moon with her reflected and elusive light is a useless thing in God's stupendous scheme of creation, though she serves His purposs as a thing of beauty.

मानिनी जनविलोचनपातानुष्णवाष्पकलुषान्प्रतिगृहन् ।
मन्दमन्दमुदितः प्रययौ खं भीतभीत इव शीतमयूखः ॥२६॥

Māninîjanavilocanapātānuṣṇavāṣpakaluṣānpratigrihṇan/
mandamandamuditaḣ prayayau khaṃ bhîtabhîta iva śîtamayû-khaḣ//26//

Translation:

Like the mirrors dimmed by the hot tears and trembling to receive the images of proud and jealous women in their crisis of love, the timid moon climbed slowly and shyly.

श्लिष्यतः प्रियवधूरुपकण्ठं तारकास्ततकरस्य हिमांशोः ।
उद्वमन्नभिरराज समन्तादङ्गराग इव लोहितरागः ॥२७॥

Ślișyataḣ priyavadhurupakaṇṭhaṃ tārakastatakarasya himāṃśoḣ/
udvamannabhirarāja samantādaṅgarāga iva lohitarāgaḣ//27//

Translation:

Like the fragrant figure of a dear lady locked in the embrace of her lover and so pressed as to receive the rosy resins of her body, the chrysolite rays of the moon stretched tantalisingly in the firmament to hug the lights from the twinkling stars.

प्रेरितः शशधरेण करौघः संहतान्यपि नुनोद तमांसि ।
क्षीरसिन्धुरिव मन्दरभिन्नः काननान्यविरलोच्चतरूणि ॥२८॥

Preritaḣ śaśadhareṇa karaughaḣ saṃhatānyapi nunoda tamāṃsi/
ksîrasindhuriva mandarabhinnaḣ kānanānyaviraloccataruṇi//28//

Translation:

Assailed by the impact of the advancing arms of the moon, the outline of tall trees and the forests in this glimmsering night appeared like the choppy waves of the salt-ocean churned by the weird array of mount Mandara.

N.B. Mandara is the literary name of mount Sumeru used by the gods and demons as a churning rod when they churned the ocean for nectar. (Vide Canto V. Stanza 30)

शारतां अतितया शशिपादैश्छायया विटपिनां प्रतिपेदे ।
पुष्पशुक्लबलिचित्रतलाभिस्तुल्यता वसतिवेश्ममहीभिः ॥२९॥

Śāratāṃ atitayā śaśipadaiścchāyayā viṭapināṃ pratipede/
puṣpaśuklabalicitratalābhistulyatā vasativeśmamahîbhiḣ//29//

Translation:

The deep and long shadows of the tall trees deriving their strength from the moon-beam presented a strange chiaroscuro of light and shade on the surface of the earth like the paintings of sacrificial offerings (oblations) against the background of the diagram of white flowers at the basement (forecourt) of storied buildings.

N.B. Mallinātha's gloss of "gamitayā" (=going, moving or the marching of an assailant) does not give Bhāravi's idea of long and deep shadows meant by the word "atitayā" (=very much or exceedingly). In Raghuvaṃśam Kālidāsa has devoted several stanzas to describe the chequer-work of light and shade under moonbeam, when king Rāma describes to Sitā the different hues of the water of the Ganges and Jamunā at their confluence in what is Allahabad today. It is remarkable that the shadows under the light of the moon have exercised great fascination for Sanskritic poets and writers.

So also the gloss "nyasta" (=cast down or deposited) does not convey Bhāravi's idea of sacrificial altars painted with sacrifial offerings against the background of the diagram of white flowers before tall buildings by way of comparison. (Vide The Judicial Customs of Nepal Part I Chapter V). The line "puṣpaśuklavalicitratalābhistulyatā vasativeśmamahîbhiḣ" appears to be a window on the principles and practices of worship in Nepal from Kapilavastu to Kathmandu, which is true even to our own day

श्रातपे धृतिमता सह वध्वा यामिनीविरहिणा विहगेन ।
सेहिरे न किरणा हिमरश्मेर्दुःखिते मनसि सर्वमसह्यम् ॥३०॥

Ātape dhritimatā saha vaddhvā yāminîvirahiṇā vihagena/
sehire na kiraṇā himaraśmerduḣkhite manasi sarvamasahyam//30//

Translation:

The pair of ruddy ducks, who lived so happily under the heat of day, could not bear the pangs of seperation with the soothing beams of the moon. All good things of life have no meaning for oppressed minds.

गन्धमुद्धतरजःकणवाही विक्षिपन्विकसतां कुमुदानाम् ।
श्रादुधाव परिलीनविहङ्गा यामिनीमरुदपां वनराजीः ॥३१॥

Gandhamuddhatarajaḣkaṇavāhî viksipanvikasatāṃ kumudānāṃ/
ādudhāva parilînavihaṇgā yāminîmarudapāṃ vanarājîḣ//31//

Translation:

The mild rustle of wind bearing with it the balmy breath of the pollen-dusts of water lilies flowering at night mixed with dews, broke the stillness of the night in the forest and awakened the sleeping birds.

N.B. V.S. Āpte defines "kumuda" as white water-lily said to open at moon-rise, whereas Śhreê Koṣanātha in his Nepali Nighaṇṭu describes it as a small variety of white and blue water-lilies known technically as Nymphaea alba and monochoria hastaefolia and known in Nepali as Indu-kamala to-day. It appears to me that the use of the word "vîhañgā" for birds seem to be borrowed from Māna-deva's inscription of Cāngu-Nārāyaṇa Face III line 16 (vide Appendix).

संविधातुमभिषेकमुदासे मन्मथस्य लसदंशुजलौघः ।
यामिनीवनितया ततचिह्नः सोत्पलो रजतकुम्भ इवेन्दुः ॥३२॥

Saṃvidhātumabhisekamudāse manmathasya lasadaṃśujalaughaḣ/
yāminîvanitayā tatacinhaḣ sotpalo rajatakumbha ivenduḣ//32//

Translation:

Like youthful bride the night prepared herself to celebrate the coronation of her all-conquering king of love by lifting the silver bowl of the moon in the sky to shower the water of benediction.

तेजसापि खलु नूनमनूनं सत्सहायमभियाति जयश्रीः ।
यद्विभुः शशिमयूखसखः सन्नाददे विजयि चापमनङ्गः ॥३३॥

Tejasāpi khalu nûnamanûnaṃ satsahāyamabhiyāti jayaśhrêêh/
yadvibhuḣ śaśimayûkhasakhaḣ sannādade vijayi cāpamanañgaḣ//33//

Translation:

Cosmic existence remains unfulfilled all by itself though it may be full of energy. Most assuredly, the goddess of victory follows the law of synthesis (which is the basis of everything). It is the indisputable law of God that Erotes assumes his victorious bow when it is helped by the moon-beam to help it.

N.B. Mallinātha's glosses of "ojasā" (=virility or generative faculty of bodily strength), "nasahayamupayati" jayaśhrêê" (=the goddess of victory) does not follow the helpless" do not express Bhāravi's idea "tejasāpi"(=though full of energy) "satsahaya abhiyat' jayashree" (the goddess of victory follows good company or the law of synthesis') in a broad sense of the function of the god of love as a factor in the synthesis of the anti-thesis of our mortal existence. Obsessed by the Brāhmannic fabrication of the myth of the incineration of the god of love by the fire from the Third Eye of Śiva, Mallināttha misses the big idea of the coronation of Cupid by the all-pervading Night in the stupendous drama of God's creation. This personification of Night as the bride of the God of love with the rising moon as a silver goblet to pour the water of benediction of his coronaton challenges some of the most fundamental Brāhmannic theories and assumptions about the universe. The poet is not talking here about the virility or generative faculty by the word "oja" but "teja" or the electric vitality of the infinitesimal particles with negative and positive charges that are scintillating and blowing through the night of space seeking their union by their mutual attraction (satsahāya). What is true of the protons or electrons is also true about the contact points of the stars in our vast stage of the universe through the two way working "Tāra" (vide Canto XV stanza 43) where "virāva" (=explosion) is law in the workship of the Almighty Śiva. The same is true about the mutual attraction of men and women.

In the following stanzas Bhāravi describes the action of the Five Ms namely "madirā" (wine), māmsa (meat), maithuna (copulation), mudrā (physical attitude) and "mantra" (spell) in Nepal's scheme of "Kāraṇapûjā"(worship of reason and the flow of soul). From these five fundamental bases, rather than from Pañca-sîla (Five Moralities) or from Pañca-gavyas (five ambrosias), that our psychic power could be developed so that we could be in tune with the mysterious sources of power known as Śiva and Śakti.

सद्मनां विरचनाहित शोभैरागतप्रियकथैरपि दूत्यम् ।
संनिकृष्टरतिभिः सुरदारैर्भूषितैरपि विभूषणमीषे ॥३४॥

Sadmanāṃ viracanāhitaśobhairāgatapriyakathairapi dûtyam/
saṃnikriṣṭaraṭîbhih suradārairbhûṣitairapi vibhûṣaṇamîṣe//34//

Translation:

Under the inspiration of the god of love, the divine ladies took pains to rearrange the arbour of sports, which was already decked befitting the occasion. While the messengers brought the good tidings of the arrival of their friends, the ladies hustled about and added beauty aids in anticipation of the night of love-play.

न स्रजो रुरुचिरे रमणीभ्यश्चन्दनानि विरहे मदिरा वा ।
साधनेषु हि रतेरुपधत्ते रम्यतां प्रियसमागम एव ॥३५॥

Na srajo rurucire ramaṇîbhyascandanāni virahe madirā vā/
sādhaneṣu hi raterupadhatte ramyatām priyasamāgama eva //35//

Translation:

Neither garlands (woven with lovely flowers) nor aromatic sandal-pastes nor wine nor beauty of feature and frame are so much appreciated by love-lorn ladies as the company of their friends for purposes of intimacies. For beauty aids are not end in themselves and they become factors as they help the consumation of passions.

प्रस्थिताभिरधिनाथनिवासं ध्वंसितप्रियसखीवचनाभिः ।
मानिनीभिरपहस्तितधैर्यः सादयन्नपि मदोऽवलम्बे ॥३६॥

Prasthitābhiradhināthanivāsaṃ dhvaṃsitapriyasakhîvacanābhiḣ/
māninîbhirapahastitadhairyaḣ sādayannapi mado(ऽ)valambe //36//

Translation:

Some vain ladies took advantage of the situation to proceed straight to the chamber of the supreme lord to the neglect of the polite entreaties of their lady-friends,. Defeated in their game, and losing patience, these women had recourse to drinking in their state of frustration.

कान्तवेश्म बहु संदिशतीभिर्यातमेव रतये रणणीभि :।
मन्मथेन परिलुप्तमतीनां प्रायशः स्खलितमप्युपकारि ॥३७॥

Kāntaveṣma bahu saṃdiśatîbhiryātameva rataye ramaṇîbhiḣ/
manmathena pariluptamatînāṃ prāyaśaḣ skhalitamapyupakāri//37//

Translation:

The sensuous beauties chattered about obscene matters at random on their way to the home (club) of their male-friends for love-mongering, Even eccentricities become helpful to minds obsessed by passions.

आशु कान्तमभिसारितवत्या योषितः पुलकरुद्धकपोलम् ।
निर्जिगाय मुखमिन्दुमखण्डं खण्डपत्रतिलकाकृति कान्त्या ॥३८॥

Āśu kāntamabhisāritavatyā yoṣitaḣ pulakaruddhakapolaṃ/
nirjigāya mukhamindumakhaṇḍaṃ khaṇḍapa ratilakākritikāntyā//38//

Translation:

The fair ladies encountered their male friends (in the club) with their hair bristling with excitement. Though divested of the beauty make up of vermillion marks, their unadorned feature and form surpassed the splendour of the moon in no time.

Dialogue between a sensous lady and her matron:

The poet appears to introduce the following dialogue between the ladies to show what the Himālayan sexual behaviour was like in the overall scheme of Prajñāpāramitā (perfection of wisdom at its summit). Judging by Bhāravi's coinage of words and expressions, I have reason to feel that they are influenced by such ancient works as "Bodhisattvabhûmi, Pali Dhamma, Prasannapadā, Madhyāntavibhāga and other ancient works of the Perfections, rather than Vātsyāyana's Kāmasûtra, which gives a summary of Indian Society's sexual customs, taboos, wisdom, myth and foolishness before sexual acts.

उच्यतां स वचनीयमशेषं नेश्वरे परुषतां सखि साध्वी ।
श्रानयैनमनुनीय कथं वा विप्रियाणि जनयन्ननुनेयः ॥३९॥

Ucyataṃ sa vacnîyamaśeṣaṃ neśvare paruṣatā sakhi sādhvî/
ānayainamanunîya kathaṃ vā vipriyāṇî janayannauneyaḣ//39//

Translation:

A courtesan: Will you speak out all your dreams and desires and surrender yourself to your friend without leaving back (in the recesses of your mind)?

A lady: O! no!! my dear friend, frankness is contraindicated in dealing with men who are full of guile.

Courtesan: Then why do not you bring him to reason by reading a lecture to your man (lord or husband) about the irreversible exposition (on the forsaking of discrimination contained in Bodhisattvabhûmi)?

A lady: How could you convince an obssesed man, who is deranged with base passion, by telling him about the big method of law (prescribed by the Perfection of wisdom at its summit)?

What this lady means to say is that Love is blind and a man in love has no sense of discrimination.

N.B. The poet appears to have coined the expression of "anunîya kathaṃ" from the the Prajṇā literature, where we have discussions about developing supramundane faculties by following a series of rules known as "anudharma" in order to conquer carnal desires. In such a context Mallinātha's etymological explanation does not seem to be helpful.

किं गतेन न हि युक्तमपैतुं कः प्रिये सुभगमानिनि मानः ।
योषितामिति कथासु समेतैः कामिभिर्बहुरसा धृतिरूहे ॥४०॥

Kim gatena na hi yuktamapaituṃ kaḣ priye subhagamāninî mānaḣ/
yoṣitāmiti kathāsu sametaiḣ kāmibhirvahurasā dhritirûhe//40//

Ttranslation:

A courtesan: Where, then, is the pleasure of going to him in a spirit of non-attachment ? Is it useless to go and join the party ?

A lady: O proud and beautiful woman ! where is the demarcation (of caste, color or creed) in matters of love, which (like war) is the greatest leveller ? On hearing this interesting dialogue with the backing of practical examples, passionate men with a variety of tastes regained their confidence.

योषितः पुलकरोधि दधत्या घर्मवारि नवसंगमजन्म ।
कान्तवक्षसि बभूव पतन्त्या भूषणं लुलितमंडनतैव ॥४१॥

Yoṣitaḣ pularodihi dadhatyā gharmavāri navasaṃgamajanma/
kāntavakṣasi vabhûva patantyā bhuṣaṇam lulitamaṇḍanataiva//41//

Translation:

Their hair bristling by the new aesthetic experience and drops of sweat dripping from their breasts added to the vanishing beauty aids from the physical frames of the ladies like the warm and fleeting rain of summer.

N.B. Mallinātha's gloss of "maṇḍanaṃ" (=decoration or adornment Vide Canto X. 59) seems to be a poor substitue for Bhāravi's original of "bhuṣaṇam" (=articles for the make-up of ladies as aids to their beauty). What is happening is that the beauty aids are vanishing with the dripping sweat which is compared to the brisk shower of summer. The poet is describing the new aesthetic experience of the ladies in the crucible of "Rati-lîlā, which survives in Nepalese language as "Rateli" even to our own day. The poet gives us the origin of the custom of Rateli in Nepal.

शीधुपानविधुरासु निगृह्वन्मानमाशु शिथिलीकृतलज्जः ।
संगतासु दयितैरुपलेभे कामिनीषु मदनो नु मदो नु ॥४२॥

Śîdhupānavidhurāsu nigrihṇanmānamāśu śithilîkritalajjaḥ/
saṇgatāsu dayitairupalebhe kāminîsu madano nu mado nu //42//

Translation:

O how this well--cultured and well-cured potion inebriates and humbles the pride of eminent ladies as much as to deprive them of their sense of guilt by its association. Is this the god of love or wine?

N.B. It is remarkable that Bhāravi explains the thesis of "Madya" (intoxicating drinks) as a factor in the new scheme of "Kāraṇapûjā" vis-a-vis Bharata's Eight principal feelings of human nature. Evidently, wine is necessary to develop that permanent frame of human will known as "vîraraudrobhāva" by eliminating the tragic frailities inherent in man.

द्वारि चक्षुरधिपाणि कपोलौ जीवितं त्वयि कुतः कलहोऽस्याः ।
कामिनामिति वचः पुनरुक्तं प्रीतये नवनवत्वमियाय ॥४३॥

Dvāri akṣuradhipāni kạpolau jîvitaṃ tvayi kutaḥ kalaho(ऽ)syāḥ/
kāimîmiti vacaḥ punaruktaṃ prîtaye navanavatvamiyāya//43//

Translation:

"O! What is there to dispute our joy, when with hands over our head we were looking on the door with longing in anticipation of your coming ! O my dear ! how could we survive without you ?" Oft repeated these words from the lips of love-lorn men had rejuvenating effect on their loving partners.

N.B. This sign of putting hands overhead in anxiety exposes the vapidity of Mallinātha's explanation of "sîrapāne" (hands overhead= पुर्पुरोमा द्दातलाउन्) in Canto IV stanza 38.

साचि लोचनयुगं नमयन्ती रुन्धती दयितवक्षसि पातम् ।
सुभ्रुवो जनयति स्म विभूषां संगतावुपरराम च लज्जा ॥४४॥

Sāci locanayugaṃ namayantî rundhatî dayitavakṣasi pātaṃ/
subhruvo janayati sma vibhûṣāṃ sangatāvupararāma ca lajjā//44//

Translation:

Staring with their eyes askant and holding themselves with effort against the horseplay of their stripping male-partners, the coy ladies ingenuously brought into bold relief their sense of shame by the graceful dance of their eye-lashes during the foreplay of coitus.

सव्यलीकमवधीरितखिन्नं प्रस्थितं सपदि कोपपदेन ।
योषितः सुहृदिव स्म रुणद्धि प्राणनाथम अधिवाष्यनिपातः ॥४५॥

Savyalîkamavadhîritakhinnaṃ prasthitaṃ sapadi kopapadena/
yoṣitaḣ suhridiva sma ruṇaddhi prāṇanātha adhivāspanipātaḣ//45//

Translation:

Pretending to be oppressed by the guilty feeling of sex-pollution (generated in them by sex taboos and inhibitions), and walking with angry steps, the ladies somehow managed to control the discharge of vapour, when their affectionate malepartners stood in their way and held them for copulation.

Mallinātha's gloss of "mabhivāspa" (=discharged their tears excessively) does not give scientific report of sexual behaviour to people who derived their inspiration from the sexual customs, taboos, wisdom and foolishness of Vātsyāyana's kāmasûtra. By restoring Bhāravi to his original of "madhivāṣpanipātaḣ" (=discharge the vapour or sperm in advance), we get the poet's intimate knowledge of sexual behaviour. It has been established by sexual scientists that the loss of vapour (sperm) before the attainment of female climax is a disease which made sex solely the province of their male partners. It appears to me that Bhāravi's idea of sex was far in advance of Vātsyāyana's hedonistic manual known as Kāmasûtra.

शंकिताय कृतवाष्पनिपातामीर्ष्यया विमुखितां दयिताय ।
मानिनीमभिमुखास्थिररुचित्तां शंसति सा धनरोगविभेदः ॥४६॥

Śañkitāya kritavāṣpanipātāmirṣyayā vimukhitāṃ dayitāya/
māninîmabhimukhāsthiracittāṃ śaṃsati sma ghanaromavibhedaḣ//46//

Translation:

Feeling teased, excited and suspicious with her eyes downcast and brimful of tears due to suppression of sex, the very look of a proud woman shows that something has gone wrong and her mind upset by the very nature of her bristling hair consequent upon the nervous tension.

N.B. Mallinātha's gloss of "mukhāhitacittaṃ" (= her face noted for good qualities or in other words free from anger) gives a wrong meaning to the entire stanza, where the poet wants to show the imbalance and unsteadiness on the face of some of the proud ladies by the expression "māninîmabhimukhasthiracittaṃ". By restoring the poet to his original, we are in a position to appreciate his studies of the psychology of sex. Now we can say how the orgasmic impairment mentioned in staza 45 of this canto could be studied in the nervous looks of the proud and fair ladies, which reflect their tension and mental imbalance.

लोलदृष्टि वदनं वनितायाश्चुम्वति प्रियतमे रभसेन ।
व्रीडया सह विनीवि नितम्वादंशुकं शिथिलतामभिपेदे ॥४७॥

Loladriṣti vadanaṃ vanitāyāścumvati priyatme rabhasena/
vrîdayā saha vinîvi nitamvādaṃśukaṃ śithilatāmabhipede//47//

Translation:

What a pity ! even the bejewelled buckles of the chastity-belt of the girls became loose and lacked lustre in sympathy and shame with the modesty of the wearers, when the boys used force (in a spirit of raping as it were) to cover with kisses the stripped bodies of virgins who looked on with helpless and changeful eyes.

Mallinātha's glosses of "dayitā" (=a wife or beloved woman) and "mupapede" (=became) with the object of explaining Vātsyāyana's dictum:

"Vāhyamābhyantaraṃ ceti dvividhaṃ ratamucyate/
tatrādyaṃ cumvaṇāśleṣanakhadantaksatādikam//
dvitîyaṃ surataṃ sākṣānnānākaraṇakalpitam//

overlook the use of force by the male partners on the girls (vanitāyā= women in general) by their overpowering action meant by "abhipede". Evidently, Vātsyāyana does not explain these sexual mores and behaviours observed in the works of Bhāravi .

ह्रीतया पलितनीवि निरस्यन्नन्तरीयमवलम्बितकाञ्चि ।
मण्डलीकृतपृथुस्तनभारं सस्वजे दयितया हृदयेशः ॥४८॥

Hrîtayā palitanîvi nirasyannantarîyamavalambitakāñci/
maṇdalîkritaprithustanabhāraṃ sasvaje dayitayā hridayeśaḥ//48//

Translation:

As the lord of her mind (husband) reached out for stripping her time-worn underwear served with tinkling bells (used by the experienced ladies of Kānci), the (faithful) wife offered her plump round breast to be pressed and she embraced her husband (like an experienced woman that she was).

N.B. Here Bhāravi describes experienced category of wives by the word "dayitā" (= experienced wife of Canto VI stanza 13). Thus we see that "vanitā" (= girls in general) of stanza 47 are different category of women from "dayitā." (wives).

आदृता नखपदैः परिरम्भाश्चुम्बितानि घनदन्तनिपातैः ।
सौकुमार्यगुणलम्भितकीर्तिर्वाम एव सुरतेष्वपि कामः ॥४९॥

Ādritā nakhapadaiḥ parirambhāścumvitāni ghanadantanipātaiḥ/
saukumāryaguṇalambhitakîrtirvāma yeva surataṣvapi kāmaḥ//49///

Translation:

Richly honoured by the scratches of nails and passionately kissed to the extent of leaving behind deep impressions of tooth-bites, cruelty and pain became the badge of Erotes during guileful foreplay for the defloration of virgins by taking away their maidenhead during the horseplay for coupulaton to the consequent loss of their reputation as maidens.

N.B. Mallinātha's "saukumāryaguṇasaṃbhritakîrtiḥ" (=famous for the concentrated qualities of tenderness namely embrace, kisses etc) does not give us the in-depth survey of sexual behaviour implied by the poet's sentence of "saukumārya guṇalambhitakîrtiḥ" with reference to the tradition of "suvarna-kumāra" (= the golden prince) to whom the vestal virgins known as "Gaurîs" are married at the age of eight years. This is known as "Gaurî dharma or Gorîdhrama" in very ancient inscriptions in order to avoid the blight widowhood for women ever afterwards. Here the poet is talking about the defloration of maidens in this game of love when they have attained puberty. Mass marriages of Gaurîs to the *Belfruit* representing the Golden Prince are celebrated before important temples even to our own day. Mallinātha should have quoted Vātsyāyana's eight forms of love-scratches and other complicated manouvres of love contained in Kāmasûtra here with much better effect than in stanza 48, where Bhāravi exposes the weaknesses of such manouvres by actually describing the scene of revelry and its effect on men and women concerned.

Unlike Vātsyāyana our poet describes the response of married women and virgins to the attitude of Himālayan people and how sensuality is reflected in their behaviour. Sexual intimacy, whenever or whereever it occurs, takes place in the context of human relationship that is serious rather than casual. And in that context it grows less furtive and more open when it is practised in a club. It is not that men and women do not feel guilty about sex, specially as the Divine ladies are beginning a new phase from the paradise of Indra. In this Samyak Society, the feeling of guilt, whether it is touching the limb of a virgin or petting or kissing with the intention of sex-intimacy or actual intercourse of the married men and women.,— does not seem to stand in the way of their passionate behaviour. In this strange Gausṭhi (Club) of early 6th century A.D. even the youths and virgins seem to be relieved of anxieties when they inflict pain and leave permanent scars of love on their partners, rather than disguise their feelings beneath their cool facade of indifference. In such a permissive society, the god of love would find fulfilment in these acts of apparent cruelties among heroic men and women.

पाणिपल्लवविधूननमन्तः सीत्कृतानि नयनार्धनिमेषाः ।
योषितां रहसि गद्‌गवाचामस्त्रतामुपययुर्मदनस्य ॥५०॥

Pāṇipallavavidhûṇanamantaḣ sîtkritāni nayanārdhanimeṣāḣ/
yoṣitāṃ rahasi gadgadavācāmastratāmupayayurmadanasya//50//

Translation:

It is only when her hands begin to shake and vibrate, when she half-closes her eye-lids in coitus and when she stutters and lisps her words in primacy that a coy and sensuous maiden is said to have attained her orgasm with the arsenal of Erotes.

N.B. This frank description of the physiological nature of orgasm of the sensuous women in copulation sweeps away the sex mongering from the Vedic and Buddhistic periods and helps men and women to judge major sex disabilities including premature ejaculation, frigidity and impotence.

पातुमाहितरतीन्यभिलेषुस्तर्षयन्त्य पुनरुक्तरसानि ।
सस्मितानिवदनानि वधूनां सोत्पलानि च मधूनि युवानः ॥५१॥

Pātumāhitaratînyabhileśustarṣayantyapunaruktarasāni/
sasmitāni vadanāni vadhûnāṃ sotpalāni ca madhûni yuvānaḣ//51//

Translation:

O wine ! the potion, which is the main source of aesthetic pleasure in the scheme of eroticism and more tasteful when it is tasted, the smiling maidens helped themselves to the honey-drinks and drank the cups to the dregs of molasses side by side with their male partners.

N.B. In this and the following stanzas the poet describes the delights of drinking in Pāṇagoṣṭhis (clubs for drinking).

कान्तसंमगपराजितमन्यौ वारूणीरसनशान्तविवादे ।
मानिनीजन उपाहितसंधौ संदधे धनुसि नेषुमनङ्गः ॥५२॥

Kāntasaṇgamaparājitamanyau vāruṇîrasanaśāntavivāde/
māninîjana upāhitasaṇdhau saṇdadhe dhanuṣi neṣumanangaḣ//52//

Translation:

Their angry and fighting mood gone in the company of fair ladies, the proud maidens acted as sobering agents to disarm Erotes of his bows, and all of them started a healthy dialogue under the exhileration of spirituous liquor.

कुप्यताशु भवतानतचित्ताः कोपितांश्च वरिवस्यत यूनः ।
इत्यनेक उपदेश इव स्म खाद्यते युवतिभिर्मधुवारः ।।५३।।

Kupyatāśu bhavatānatacittāḣ kopitāṃśca varivasyata yunaḣ/
ityaneka upadeśa iva sma khādyate yuvatibhirmadhuvāraḣ//53//

Translation:

Pretending (acting) as if their mind were in rage with the adoration, the merry maidens finally helped themselves to the drinking of sweet wine in moderation according to the advice contained in manuals (of Kāraṇapûjā).

N.B. Judging by the wordings I have reason to feel that there were manuals to control drinking by men and women.

भर्तृभिः प्रणयसंभ्रमदत्तां वारूणीगतिरसां रसयित्वा ।
ह्रीविमोह विरहादुपलेभ पाटवं नु हृदयं नु वधूभिः ।।५४।।

Bhartribhiḣ praṇayasaṃbhramadattāṃ vāruṇîmatirasāṃ rasayitvā/
hrîvimohavirahādupalebhe pāṭavaṃ nu hridayaṃ nu vadhûbhih//54//

Translation:

Did the ladies become wiser and cleverer or gain in quickening of mind to the rejection of their mental stupor, modesty and melancholy, when they tasted the very delicious wine known as "Vāruṇî (dedicated to Varuna) so politely offered by their male partners in their state of intoxication?

स्वादितः स्वयमथैधितमानं लम्भितः प्रियतमैः सह पीतः ।
आसवः प्रतिपदं प्रमदानां नैकरूपरसतात्मिव भेजे ।।५५।।

Svāditaḥ svayamathaidhitamānaṃ lambhitaḥ priyatamaiḥ saha pîtah/
āsavaḥ pratipadaṃ pramadānāṃ naikarûparasatāmivabheje//55//

Translation:

Drinking the delicious potion out of the same cup, and feeling encouraged and proud to bring the drink to the lips of their male-partners gracefully with their own hands again and again, the dancing liquor appeared as something apart from the glamorous and voluptuous ladies in form (colour) and taste.

भ्रूविलाससुभगाननुकर्तुं विभ्रमानिव वधूनयनानाम् ।
आददे मृदुविलोलपलाशैरुत्पलैश्चषकवीचिषु कम्पः ।।५६।।

Bhrûvilāsasubhagānanukartuṃ vibhramaniva vadhunayanānām/
ādade mriduvilolapalaśairutpalaiścasakavîciṣu kampaḥ//56//

Translation:

O ! how the reflection of the play of the eye-brows of the beautiful damsels over the brimming cup synchronised with the ripples on the calm water by the fall of a soft and rosy petal of palāsa (brutea-frondosa) in the way of a suggestion for the synthesis of the antithesis of our existence.

ओष्ठपल्लवविदंशरुचीनां हृदयता मुपययौ रमणानाम् ।
फुल्ललोचनविनोलसरोजै रङ्गनास्यचषकैर्मधुवारः ।।५७।।

Oṣṭapallavavidaṃśarucînāṃ hridayatāmupayayau ramaṇānām/
phullalocanavinîlasarojairaṅganāsyacaṣakairmadhuvāraḥ//57//

Translation:

With the skilful promotion of drinking party, the thirst for enjoyment in the face and glint of their blue-lotus-like eyes became reflected over the sparkling bowl of wine when they drank again and again meeting lips with lips.

प्राप्यते गुणवतापिगुणानां व्यक्तमाश्रयवशेन विशेषः ।
तत्तथा हि दयिताननदत्तं व्यानशे मधु रसातिशयेन ।।५८।।

Prāpyate guṇavatāpiguṇānāṃ vyaktamāśrayavaśena viśeṣaḥ/
tattathā hi dayitānanadattaṃ vyānaśe madhu rasātisayena//58//

Translation:

As it is said (in the scientific works of alchemy) that the properties, though they are in the very quality of the matter, become manifest specially when they come together and act and react, so also the gift-maker (man and receiver wife) were both attracted and held together by the reaction of the extremely delicious wine.

वीक्ष्य रत्नचषकेष्वतिरिक्तां कान्तदन्तपदमण्डनलक्ष्मीम् ।
जज्ञिरे बहुमताः प्रमदानामोष्ठयावकनुदो मधुवाराः ॥५९॥

Vîkṣya ratnacaṣakesvatiriktāṃ kāntadantapadamaṇḍanalakṣmîm/
jagñire vahumatāḥ pramadānāmmoṣṭayāvakanudo madhuvārāh//59//

Translation:

On seeing the reflection of the beauty of the teeth of female partners over the emptied brim of bejwelled cups, the marks of the variety of colour and fragrance of their lip-sticks gave suggestions of individual taste to the cocktails.

लोचनाधरकृताहृतरागा वासिताननविशेषितगन्धा ।
वारूणी परगुणात्मगुणानां व्यत्ययं विनिमयं नु वितेने ॥६०॥

Locanādharakritāhritarāgā vāsitānanaviśeṣitagandhā/
vāruṇî paraguṇātmaguṇānāṃ vyatyayaṃ vinimayaṃ nu vitene //60//

Translation:

Distinguished for its own special variety of smell and taste the alchoholic liquor known as "Vāruṇi" did not barter away its properties from other varieties of wine, and constricted the fragrance of the unguents of the lips and also conditioned the faculties of the eyes of the revellers by its own superfine quality.

N.B. It appears from this description of "Vāruṇi" that the Nepalese alchemists were familiar with the use of alcohol very much earlier than the Persian scientists Rhazes and Avicenna during the medieval period.

तुल्यरूपमसितोत्पलमक्ष्णोः कर्णगं निरूपकारि विदित्वा ।
योषितः सुहृदिव प्रविभेजे लम्भितेक्षणरूचिर्मदरागः ॥६१॥

Tulyarûpamasitotplalamakṣṇoh karṇagaṃ nirupakāri viditvā/
yoṣitaḣ shridiva pravibheje lambhitekṣaṇarucirmadarāgaḣ//61//

Translation:

With its power of dilating the white pupils of the eyes and of paralysing the sense organs of the ears equally for all the smell of "vāruṇî" (alcohol) obliterated all obstacles and befriended all the revellers by depriving them of the logical and practical faculties under its rose-coloured passion.

N.B. This minute description of the symptoms of "vāruṇî" on all the members of the club gives clear indications that the Kirātas and the Licchavis were familiar with the use of alcohol.

क्षीणयावकरसोऽप्यतिपानैः आर्द्रन्तपदलम्भितशोभः ।
आययावतिरामिव वध्वाः सान्द्रतामधरपल्लवरागः ॥६२॥

Kṣîṇayāvakaraso (ऽ) pyatipānaiḣ ārdradantapadalambhitaśobhaḣ/
āyayāvatitarāmviva vadhvāh sāndratāmadharapallavarāgaḣ//62//

Translation:

O ! where is the line of demarcation between aesthetic experience and violence when tipsied people add to the adornment of the lips of the ladies with their saliva and tooth-bite in a bout of heavy drinking to the corresponding loss of their beauty aids?

N.B. Mallinātha's glosses of "Kāntadantapadasambhritaśobhaḣ" (= whose beauty is enhanced by the scars of he husband's teeth) do not give us the true picture of the scene of overdrinking, where the bloody marks of tooth-bite and saliva are left to scar their faces to their dwindling beauty make-up in such a turbulent scene. By restoring Bhāravi to his original of "Ārdradantapadalambhitaśobhaḣ" (whose face is adorned by the scars of tooth-bite and saliva of the tipsied lover) we get the scene of over-drinking in contravention of Bharata's traditional term of "rasa" (रस), which designates the aesthetic state of consciousness. Bharata recognises 8 forms of Rasa (aesthetic pleasure) as follows: 1. Rati (sexual delight), 2 hāsa (laughter), 3 soka (sorrow), 4 krodha (anger), 5. utsāha (exhileration), 6. bhaya (fear), 7. jugupsā (disgust) and 8. vismaya (wonder, surprise or astonishment) as the principal feelings of human nature. But as "Rasa" means not only tasting but also what is tasted, these 8 feelings of human nature become the factors of aesthetic experience and find expression among human beings in the following behaviour patterns, namely ṣrñgāra (erotic), hāsya (comic), karuṇa (pathetic), raudra (furious), vîra (heroic), bhayānaka (terrible), vibhatsa (odius) and adbhuta (marvellous).

Each of these mental states is accompanied by three elements namely Kāraṇa (causes), kārya (resulting effects in the form of work) and sahacara (concomitant elements). The causes are the facts of life, the effects are the physical reactions caused by it and the concomitant elements are the behaviour pattern accompanying it.

But because Bharata did not take note of the permanent human feeling of the Eight samyak paths (correct way) and the resulting mental attitude of "śānta" (calm-pacified) along the traditional line of thought propagated by Śākyamuni Buddha, Bhāravi does not accept this arbitrary and didactic division of "vibhāva" (factor), anubhāva (effect) and "vyabhicāri-bhāva (tragic frailties). The poet, therefore, introduces here the extreme state of drinking, where the infliction of pain, scorn and bleeding by tooth-bite, scratches of nails and saliva assume the form of pleasure for the drunkards. This mental imbalance goes beyond the boundary of the three kinds of delights mentioned by Bharata in his "Nātyaśāstra" namely Kāma-srñgāra (make-up for sexual pleasure), Artha-ṣrñgāra (make-up for the achievement of material prosperity) directed to the fulfilment of the economic or political end and Dharma-srñgāra (make-up for moral and religious duties). Oblivious of the transitions from Dharma-cakra to Bhairavi-cakra in Nepal and Himālayan countries, Bharata seems to be influenced by the pan-Indian concept of human life as being motivated by four purposes namely Kāma (pleasure or love), Artha (material prosperity), Dharma (religious duty) and Mokṣa (redemption or liberation of soul from the bonds of mortal existence). This was considered to be the supreme realisation known technically as "Paramārtha-siddhi."

In order to fulfil the above purposes, it was found necessary to cultivate "Sthāyi bhāva" (permanent state of consciousness) by going through the experience of "Rati" (sexual delight), "Krodha" (anger), "utsāha" (energy) and "Śama" (serenity), so that human beings may conquer the "vyabhicāribhāva" (tragic frailties or transitory mental states) which were 33 in number as follows:

1. nirveda (discouragement), 2. glāni (languor or weakness), 3. Śaṇkā (apprehension), 4. śrama (weariness), 5. dhriti (contentment), 6. jaḍatā (stupor), 7. harṣa (joy) 8. dainya (depression), 9. ugratā (cruelty), 10. cintā (anxiety), 11. trāsa (fright) 12. asûyā (envy), 13. amarṣa (indignation), 14. garva (arrogance,) 15. smriti (recollection), 16. maraṇa (death), 17. mada (intoxication), 18. supta (dreaming), 19. nidrā (slumber), 20. vivodha (awakening), 21. vriḍā (shame), 22. apasmāra (epilepsy), 23. moha (distraction), 24. mati (assurance), 25. ālasya (indolence), 26. āvega (agitation), 27. tarka (deliberation), 28. avahittā (dissimulation), 29. vyādhi (sickness), 30. unmāda (insanity), 31. viṣāda (despair), 32. autsukya (impatience) and 33. cāpala (inconstancy).

Among the anubhāva (consequents) were included the eight involuntary states namely 1. stambha (paralysis), 2. pralay (fainting or total loss of consciousness) 3. romāñca (horrent hair or bristling of hair), 4. sveda (sweating), 5. vaivarṇya (change of colour), 6. vepathu (trembling,) 7. aśru (tears or weeping), and 8. vaisvarya (change of voice).

Bharata felt that pleasure was the aim and end of "rati" (sexual intimacies), which would lead to the achievement of profit and right action, and further that anger and energy were associated with "artha" (material prosperity) and dharma (religious duties).

Against this background of pan-Indian thoughts Bhāravi introduces the actual scene of Pāṇagoṣṭhis (community drinking) to expose the limitations of Bharata's Nātyaśāstra, where we do not find the word "māna" (pride or self-respect). On the other hand, Bhāravi steadily introduces his idea of developing the adamantine mental state of "Vîraraudrobhāva" (the heroic mental frame of staring death in the face on this side of the grave) so that men may conquer the vyabhicāribhāva (tragic frailties) inherent in human nature.

रागकान्तनयनेषु नितान्तं विद्रुमारुणकपोलतलेषु ।
सर्वगापि ददृशे वनितानां दर्पणेष्विव मुखेषु मदश्रीः ॥६३॥

Rāgakāntanayaneṣu nitāṇtaṃ vidrumāruṇakapolataleṣu/
sarvagāpi dadriśe vanitānāṃ darpaṇeṣviva mukheṣu madaśhrêḣ//63//

Translation:

Though their entire body was overcome with intoxication, the charm of the alcoholic liquor could be seen on their coral red cheeks under tousy hair with glint of eyes reflecting their passion like in a mirror.

वद्धकोपविकृतीरपि रामाश्चारुताभिमततामुपनिन्ये ।
वश्यतां मधुमदो दयितानामात्मवर्गहितमिच्छति सर्वः ॥६४॥

Vaddhakopavikritîrapi rāmāścārutābhimatatāmupaninye/
vaśyatāṃ madhumado dayitānāmātmavargahitamicchati sarvaḣ//64//

Translation:

Although the looks of the lovely ladies were distorted by rage, they appeared all the more charming under the flavour of sweet wine (honey-wine) as the synthetic factor despite the antithetic factor in human nature that everybody works for his own delight out of self-interest.

वाससां शिथिलतामुपनाभि ह्रीनिरासमपदे कुपितानि ।
योषितां विदधती गुणपक्षे निर्ममार्ज मदिरा वचनीयम् ॥६५॥

Vāsasāṃ śithilatāmupanābhi hrînirāsamapade kupitāni/
yoṣitāṃ vidadhatîguṇapakṣe nirmamārja madirā vacanîyam//65//

Translation:

Their skirts loosening and going down to the point of revealing their navel at the expense of modesty in their present state of intoxication, O wine ! is it thy quality to respect the laws of scripture in its abeyance ?

N.B. The scriptures prescribed that a woman should not reveal her navel to anybody except her husband under any circumstance.

भर्तृषूपसखि निक्षिपतीनामात्मनो स्फुटमदोद्यमितानाम् ।
व्रीडया विफलया वनितानां न स्थितं न विगतं हृदयेभ्यः ॥६६॥

Bhartrişûpasakhi nikşipatînāmātmano sphutamadodyamitānāṃ/
vrîḍayā viphalayā vanitānāṃ na sthitaṃ na vigataṃ hridayebhyah//66//

Translation:

As the male-partner brought down his wife within the eye-shot of her friends, and as both their bodies went up and down under the explosive urge of the spirituous liquor, it was difficult to judge whether there was sense of shame or it had become a casualty, when shame itself had suffered a defeat in the heart of the ladies.

N.B. Mallinātha's gloss of "madhumado" (= honey wine or sweet wine) does not convey the idea of the explosive power of the alcoholic liquor known as "vāruṇî". On the other hand, Bhāravi introduces the word "sphuṭamado" deliberately to overrule the objection of the Buddhist logicians and Brahmannic Mimāṃsakas, who believed that the concept of "sphoṭa", according to their grammarians, was a vocality, eternal and without parts, distinct from the letters and manifested by "vyaṇj" (evocation). We have already pointed out elsewhere how Bhāravi was the earliest poet to notice explosions in the sky and associate the word "sphoṭa" with splitting. It appears to me that Bhāravi introduces a peculiar situation to explain the explosive nature of the alcohol, where the pair are united together in hot embrace within the sight and ear-shot of their friends and where they are behaving in a manner to outshame Shame itself. In such a situation the minds of the spectators become the prey of conflicting mental movements like "vrîḍa" (shame), "jugupsā" (disgust), "sprihā" (envy). Are the spectators in a state of indifference (tāṭasthya) in such a case of direct perception (pratyakṣa pramāṇa) ? The feelings of delight, sorrow, anger, disgust and envy, which pervade human beings in ordinary life, appear in a different setting in such a drinking party. How could we say that the sense of shame was there in the heart of women or it had left the hearts also of the spectators, when Shame itself was a casualty. It is only against the background of Vātsyāyaña's "Kāmasûtra", Bharata's "Nāṭya-śāstra," Buddhistic logicians and Brahmannic Mimāmsakas that we could assess the practical aspects of Bhāravi's bold descriptions of a drinking party.

रुन्धती नयनवाक्यविकासं सादितोभयकरा परिरम्भे ।
व्रीडितस्य ललितं युवतीनां क्षीबता बहुगुणैरनुजह्रे ॥६७॥

Rundhatî nayanavākyavikāsaṃ sāditobhayakarā parirambhe/
vrîḍitasya latlitaṃ yuvatînāṃ kṣîbatā bahuguṇairanujahre//67//

Translation:

Her voice choked by tears in her eyes and her hands locked in hot embrace, Shame itself took its lesson from the behaviour pattern of the intoxicated ladies in their present state of orgasm.

योषिदुद्धतमनोभवरागा मानवत्यपि ययौ दयितांकम् ।
कारयत्यनिभृता गुणदोषे वारुणी खलु रहस्यविभेदम् ॥६८॥

Yoṣiduddhatamanobhavarāgā mānavatyapi yayau dayitāñkam/
kārayatyanibhritā guṇadoṣe vāruṇî khalu rahasyavibhedam//68//

Translation:

The subconscious passions of her mind excited by drinking, even the supercilous beauty (queen) fell into the embrace of her lover. Indeed, the alcoholic liquor known as "vāruṇî", despite its contradictory constituents (properties) is an opener of the secrets of dormant feelings.

आहिते नु मधुना मधुरत्वे चेष्टितस्य गमिते नु विकासम् ।
आबभौ नव इवोद्धतरागः कामिनीष्ववसरः कुसुमेषोः ॥६९॥

Āhite nu madhunā madhuratve ceṣṭitāsya gamite nu vikāsam/
ābhabhau nava ivoddhatarāgaḥ kāminîṣvavasaraḥ kusumeṣoḥ//69//

Translation:

If modesty is the badge of womanly virtues, where was it in the rough sexual behaviour of the drunken women ? Nevertheless, this temporary state of passion under intoxication became a new experience for love-lorn beauties in the realisation of the subconsious feelings of their erotic self.

मा गमन्मदविमूढधियो नः प्रोज्झ्य रन्तुमिति शंकितनाथाः ।
योषितो न मदिरां भृशमीषुः प्रेम पश्यति भयान्यपदेऽपि ।।७०।।

Mā gamanmaḍavimûdhadhiyo naḥ projjhya rantumiti śaṅkitanāthāḥ'/
yoṣito na madirāṃ bhriśamîṣuḥ prema paśyati bhayānyapadespi//70//

Translation:

Some careful women went slow over the booze for fear that their husbands may apprehend them in their present state of unreliable behaviour and desert them. For, love sees danger of a wrong step, and it exercises control through fear even under the influence of strong drinks (in a permissive society).

चित्तनिर्वृतिविधायि विविक्तं मन्मथो मधुमदः शशिभासः ।
संगमश्च दयितैः स्म नयन्ति प्रेम कामपि भुवं प्रमदानाम् ।।७१।।

Cittanirvritividhāyi viviktaṃ manmatho madhumadaḥ śaśibhāsaḥ/
saṃgamaśca dayitaih sma nayanti prema kāmapi bhuvaṃ
pramadānāṃ//71/

Translation:

O ! how far does passion for pleasure carry voluptuous woman in her career of amor in this world, when she meets her lover in a solitary place under the conjunction of delicious honey-wine and the light of moon as the transforming factor of her mind for the orgyastic exercises of coitus !

CANTO IX

In the concluding seven stanzas Bhāravi describes the stark state of copulation. Vātsyāyana may turn in his paradise and wonder how the poet ever found the nerve to describe the experience of men and women in the actual state of copulation under intoxication, and re-defined the manual of "Kāmasûtra". But it is only in the stark practices of Adhigama that men and women find their orgasm and identity.

धाष्टर्चलङ्घितयथोचितभूमौ निर्दयं विलुलितालकमाल्ये ।
मानिनीरतिविधौ कुसुमेषुर्मत्तमत्त इव विभ्रममाप ।।७२।।

Dhārṣṭyalañghitayathocitabhûmau nirdayaṃ vilulitālakamālye/
māninîrativídhau kusumeṣurmattamatta iva vibhramamāpa//72//

Translation:

In total transgression of the accepted rules and disciplines, and cruelly disturbing their hair-do and garlands in their present state of intoxicated excitement, the proud and sexual women gave vent to their feelings by dizzying and crazy actions as if madness was the measure in the scale of the god of love.

शीधुपानविधुरेषु वधूनां विध्नतामुपगतेषु वपुःषु ।
ईहितं रतिरसाहितभावं वीतलक्ष्यमपि कामिषु रेजे ।।७३।।

Šîdhupānavidhureṣu vadhûnāṃ vighnatāmupagateṣu vapuḣṣu/
êêhitaṃ ratirasāhitabhāvaṃ vîtalaksyamapi kāmiṣu reje//73//

Translation:

Totally overcome by the effects of drinking and their bodies bea-ring cruel scars in the arms of their lovers, the women at that purpose-less and particular moment of orgasm in copulation appeared, nevertheless, to achieve the state of dispassion (which is the aim and end of saints in their quest of Nirvāṇa).

N.B. This explains the erotic motifs on the struts of our temples. It was realised during the time of Bhāravi that sexual orgasm was the highest bliss in the scheme of "Kāraṇapûjā" (worship of the causes and reason)

अन्योन्य रक्तमनसामथ विभ्रतीनां
चेतोभुवो सुरसखाप्संरसां निदेशम्।
वैबोधिकध्वनिविभावितपश्चिमार्धा
सा संहृतेव परिवृत्तिमियाय रात्रिः ॥७४॥

Anyonyaraktamanasāmatha vibhratīnāṃ
cetobhuvo surasakhāpsarasāṃ nideśam/
vaibodhikadhvanivibhāvitapaścimārdhā
sā saṃhriteva parivrittimiyāya rātriḣ//74//

Translation:

While thus frantically enjoying and drinking life to its lees in the company of their mundane friends under the spell of the god of love, the music makers and heavenly houris were disturbed by the awakening sound of the west to the effect that the night was not young after all.

N.B. Mallinātha's gloss of "harisakha" (= Indra's secretaries namely the music makers) does not give us the mundane atmosphere of the "pānagauṣṭhis" (= drinking clubs). It is only by restoring the poet to his original of "surasakhāpsarasāṃ" that we get the idea that all the members of the club were getting attracted to each other. Grammatical terminologies and etymological explanation would not be able to explain Bhāravi's expression of "vaivodhikadhvani" (=the awakening sound)vis-a-vis Bharata's "rasadhvani"(=the sound of "rasa" which may be juice or flavour). At this stage the poet defines the relationship between "rasa" (=fiavour,juice or enjoyment) and "dhvani" (=sound) which agitated the minds of Bharata and and his commentators as far as Abhinavagupta. Professor R. Gnoli in "The aesthetic experience according to Abhinavagupta" (Is. M.E.O. Rome 1956) discusses this point extensively. Now we see that, according to Bhāravi, there could be no such thing as "rasa-dhvani" (flavour of sound) and that "dhvani" (sound) has an awakening effect.

निद्राविनो दितनि तान्तरतिल्कमाना–
मायामिमङ्गलनिनादविबोधितानाम् ।
रामासु भाविविरहा कलितासु यूनां
तत्पूर्वतामिव समादधिरे रतानि ॥७५॥

Nidrāvinoditanitāntaratiklamānā-
māyāmimañgalaninādavibodhitānām/
rāmāsu bhāvivirahākalitāsu yûnāṃ
tatpûrvātāmiva samādadhire ratāni//75//

Translation:

Already overcome by sleep on account of fatigue generated by the orgies of the acts of coitus, the auspicious music of dawn had the awakening effect on the erotically benighted beauties; and copulation became the bridge of understanding among the love-hungry youths once again.

कान्ताजनं सुरतखेदनिमीलिताक्षं
संवाहितुं समुपयानिव मन्दमन्दम् ।
हर्म्येषु माल्यमदिरापरिभोगगन्धा-
नाविश्चकार रजनीपरिवृत्तिवायुः ॥७६॥

Kāntājanaṃ suratakhedanimîlitākṣaṃ
saṃvāhituṃ samupayāniva mandamandam/
harmyeṣu mālyamadirāparibhogagandhā-
nāviścakāra rajanîparivrittivāyuḥ//76//

Translation:

The soft morning breeze was now spreading the fragrance of garlands, wine and other articles of enjoyment, as if to serve the beauties lying with closed eyes in a state of erotic duress amid their luxurious pleasure houses (Hermyes).

N.B. The use of the Greek word "HERMYES" (pleasure abodes) by Bhāravi reminds us that the poet was familiar with the Greek art of love. Judging by the sensual scene depicted in this canto I have reason to feel that Bhāravi had also read Ovid's Ars Amatoria, which invited the resentment of Roman Emperor Augustus, because its doctrine was a direct challenge to this policy of moral reform. Whereas Ovid (43 B.C.— A.D. 17), with all his Bohemian vivacity and his keen interest in and enjoyment of life could not rise above the two Roman virtues of fides (social honour) and candor (kindly sincerity), Bhāravi achieves the identity of men and women in his own scheme of "Kāraṇapûjā" through the exercise of carnal pleasures.

आमोदवासितचलाधरपल्लवेषु
निद्राकषायितविपाटललोचनेषु ।
व्यामृष्टपत्रतिलकेषु विलासिनीनां
शोभां बबन्ध वदनेषु मदस्य शेषः ॥७७॥

Āmodavāsitacalādharapallaveṣu
nidrākasāyitavipāṭalalocaneṣu
vyāmriṣṭapatratilakeṣu vilāsinînāṃ
śobhāṃ vavandha vadaneṣu madasya śeṣaḣ//77//

Translation:

Their lips trembling like petals over the brimming cup of pleasure, their eye-lids dropping their shades under the creeping effects of sleep and their beauty spots gone, the intoxication of wine alone remained to testify to the charm of the sensual women in the hot embrace of coupling (in the small hours of the morning).

N.B. This description of intimacies under the spell of drinking in the small hours of the morning as an independent activity appears to have its own charm and a joy in itself.

गतवति नखलेखा दृश्यताम् अङ्गरागे
समददयितपीताताम्रबिम्बाधरोष्ठ्याः ।
विरहविधुरमिष्टा सत्सखिअङ्गनायाः
हृदयमवललम्बे रात्रिसंभोगलक्ष्मीः ॥७८॥

Gatavati nakhalekhā driśyatām añgarāge
samadadayitapîtātāmravimvādharoṣṭhyāḣ/
virahavidhuramiṣṭā satsakhiañganāyaḣ
hridayamavalalamve rātrisaṃbhogalakṣmî//78//

Translation:

Moving about aimlessly with the open scars of nails on their make-up and still smarting with pain of round sores on their cherry-red lips as a result of violent drinking offered by their lovers, the forlorn and beautiful ladies, nevertheless, cherished in their hearts the memory of the happy night of copulation like the company of a true and reliable friend.

N.B. Mallinātha's glosses of "laksatāmañgarāge" (= the violent marks of the foreplay of love visible), "vimvādharāṇām" (= with the reflection of disc on their lips) and "vānganānāṃ" (= tortured by the feeling of separation) do not give us Bhāravi's description of drunken women in the morning after the horseplay of love from the eight forms of scratches to more complicated manouvres of love, which have left indelible marks on their feature meant by the expression "driśyatāṃ". And those marks are as red as cherry fruits on their lips meant by "vimvādharosṭhyā". All the lovely ladies (añganā) have thoroughly enjoyed themselves during the night of copulation (rātrisambhogalaksmi) and that enjoyment has left behind marks on the general feature and lips like the fruits of cherry-for all to see. This transcends all the separately perceptible parts. and it is in the form of forlorn memory that the flavour of drinking and coitus survives in the heart of the fair ladies (añganāyāḣ). The poet closes this canto with mālini metre.

The end of Canto IX.

KIRĀTĀRJUNIYE
CANTO X

CANTO X

Summary

This Canto consists of 63 stanzas.

After a glamorous night of Eros, drinking and debauchery, the heavenly houris and music-makers proceed to the hermitage of Arjuna according to the injunction of Indra. The hermitage presents a peaceful scene, where the deer and tiger live in amity to the seasonal and timely call of Himālayan birds. With new physical make-up the ladies appear very attractive and they tease Arjuna for his lean and hungry look and try to tempt him from his austere practices on the traditional line of the temptation of Śākyamuni by the daughters of Māra.

Seeing how Anuparamagupta Gomî mentions only the Three Vedas (Rgveda, Śāmaveda and Yajurveda in his Pilaster of Harigāon vide Appendix), the mention of the fourth Veda known as Atharava-veda by Bhāravi in stanza 10 of this canto opens up a unique vista of Brāhmannic chronological development vis-a-vis the authentic chronologies of the Kirātas and Śākyas. According to Mallinātha, Atharvaveda is attributed to the Brāhmannic saint Vaṣiṣṭha. It is most interesting that the names of saints Vaṣiṣṭha, Vedavyāsa (Dvaipāyana) and Vaiśampāyana do not occur in the Brāhmannic chronology known as Śukla Yajurveda vamśa (शुक्ल यजुर्वेद वंश). This proves the contention of The Judicial Customs of Nepal Part I that the sacrificial school and Āgama (esoteric worship) was much older than the impact of Buddhism and Brāhmanism on the traditional worship of Sākyavardhana (Paśupati) and Śirī-mā devī (the Great Mother Goddess) in Kapilavastu.

CANTO X

We have already seen in Canto III how saint Dvaipāyana initiates Arjuna in the principles and practices of Āgama (esoteric worship). Seeing how saint Vaiśampāyana occurs in an inscription of the period of king Vasanta-deva in the scheme of Kāraṇapûjā and also how this particular saint is responsible for inditing Yudhiṣṭhira's prayer to Jayā and Vijayā (the victorious lady) on the eve of his Gupta-vāsa (retirement incognito) in the kingdom of Virāta, it is impossible for us to trace any relationship in time and place of the authenticity of the Brāhmannic chronology, where Vājasaneyin Tura Kāvaseya, connected with the consecration of Janmejaya III of the epic of Mahābhārata, could hold discussion on the subject and arouse the wrath of saint Viaiśampāyana. This only means that this part of the epic of Mahābhārata was indited sometime at the beginning of the sixth century A.D. For one thing, however, saint Yājnavalkya, who is believed to be the priest of king Janaka of Mithilā, has been credited with the composition of Vājasaneyi saṃhitā or the Śukla Yajurveda; and the epic of Mahābhārata makes Vaiśampāyana and Tura Kāvaṣeya both pupils of Yājnavalkya Vājasaneya. It is equally remarkable that Dādhyaṇc Ātharvana and Atharvandaiva do occur in the Kāṇva and Mādhyāndina recensions of Bṛhadāraṇyaka upanisad. We have pointed out in The Judicial Customs of Nepal Part I how there was a quarrel between Gārgî-lopā and Yājñavalkya. Later the sons and descendents of Gārgî-lopā known as Gārgîputra play important roles side by side with Pārasarî-putras (sons and descendents of Parāsara and Satyavatî), Bhāradvājîputras, Māṭharîputras and Vātsî Māṇdavîputras with strong metronymics. According to J. Brough's "Gotra-pravara-mañjari," Vaiśvāmitras were Māṭharas or people born from incestuous union.

Going back to saint Vaśisṭha as the author of Atharvaveda, his name is mentioned as the person who taught Śākyamuni Buddha the Brāhmî scripts in the texts of Lalita-vistara, whereas the life of Buddha contained in very early Khandaka (Skandhaka) works mention Krimi-varmān as the real teacher of Śakyamuni in his young days. We have pointed out in The Judicial Customs of Nepal Part I how this work was translated into Chinese in the second century A. D. According to the epic of Rāmāyaṇa, Vasistha was the head-priest at the Ikṣvāku-court of king Dasaratha of Ayodhya. Our Licchavi inscriptions and Kirātārjunîye may now help research workers to work out a satisfactory chronology for the development of earliest Indian thought specially after second century B. C., when the tides of foreign invasion and non-Brāhmannic teachings were at their zenith.

Then, too, the mention of Vijayavatî in stanza 13 of this canto brings us directly to the inscription of Princess Vijayavatî (vide Introduction) in the overall context of Kāranapûjā, which is still extant. It is remarkable, however, that Mallinātha's explanation of "Vijayavatîm" seems to be in line with the traditional methods of the use of facts and fictions, such as are found in the Life of Śākyamuni Buddha and their recensions in the Vinayas and Lalita-vistara and also in the epics of Rāmāyana, Mahābhārata, Raghuvaṃśa and Yaksa's Niruktam. Though some of the etymologies seem to be loose, yet Bhāravi has used them in such a factual and appealing way as not to conflict with the historical accounts contained in the Chronologies of the Kirātas and the Śākyas vis-a-vis the Brāhmannic chronologies which totally influence the Inscription of king Jayadeva during the declining phase of the Licchavi regime in Nepal.

Finally, the Divine women and Gandharvas (music-makers) make skillful attempts to promote sexual passions and disturb Arjuna from his meditation, but all to no purpose. The description of the rainy season after autumn show how many months have glided by since Arjuna addressed himself to penances, and also how the fauna and flora of the Himālayas are true to nature even to our own day.

अथ परिमलजामवाप्य लक्ष्मीमवयवदीपितमण्डनश्रियस्ताः ।
वसतिमभिविहाय रम्यहावाः सुरपतिसूनुविलोभनाय जग्मुः ॥१॥

Atha parimalajāmavāpya lakṣmîmavayavadîpitamaṇdanaśriyastāḣ /
vasatimabhivihāya ramyahāvāḣ surapatisûnuvilobhanāya jagmuḣ //1//

Translation:

Thoroughly refreshed after a satisfying night of sexual enjoyment, the ladies, then, adorned themselves with fragrant make-up and ornaments in the following morning; and they left their pleasure abodes with a feeling of fresh vigour and proceeded boldly to their appointed task of seducing the son of the king of gods (Arjuna). The poet pens this canto with ·Puṣpitā metre.

द्रुतपदमभियातुमिच्छतीनां गमनपरिक्रमलाघवेन तासाम् ।
अवनिषु चरणैः पृथुस्तनीनामलघुनितम्बतया चिरं निषेदे ॥२॥

Drutapadamabhiyātumicchatînāṃ gamanaparikramalāghavena tāsām /
avanisu caraṇaiḣ prithustanînāmalaghunitamvatayā ciraṃ niṣede //2//

Transtaltion :

Although the divine ladies wanted to spring to their destination with speed, their heavy breasts and bottom attracted them to the atmosphere of the earth to fidget with caution.

निहितसरसयावकैर्बभासे चरणतलैः कृतपद्धतिर्वधूनाम् ।
अविरलविततेव शक्रगोपैररुणितनीलतृणोलपा धरित्री ॥३॥

Nihitasarasayāvakairbabhāse caraṇatalaiḣ kritapaddhatirvadhūnām /
aviralavitateva śakragopairaruṇitanîlatriṇolapā dharitrî //3//

Translation:

The soft and green turf marked by the red resins of the orderly and measured steps of the fair ladies looked like the glowing embers of Sakra's fire.

ध्वनिरगविवरेषु नूपुराणां पृथुरशनागुणशिञ्जितानुयातः ।
प्रतिरवविततो वनानि चक्रे मुखरसमुत्सुकहंससारसानि ॥४॥

Dhvaniragavivaresu nûpurāṇām prithuraśanāguṇaśiñjitānuyātaḣ /
pratiravavitato vanāni cakre mukharasamutsukahaṃsasārasāni //4//

Translation:

The jingle of the anklets echoing through the silent caverns of the forest roused the ducks and cranes, who made their response in a state of curiosity on account of the familiarity of the grating chime.

अवचयपरिभोगवन्ति हिंस्रैः सहचरितान्यमृगाणि काननानि ।
अभिदधुरभितो मुनिं वधूभ्यः समुदितसाध्वसविक्लवं च चेतः ॥५॥

Avacayaparibhogavanti hiṃsraiḣ sahacaritānyamrigāṇi kānanāni / abhidadhurabhito muniṃ vadhūbhyaḣ samuditasādhvasaviklavaṃ ca cetaḣ //5//

Translation:

(At the outset) the minds of the sexually motivated ladies were confounded with fear, as they were unable to gauge the nature of the meditation of the saint (Arjuna) in the peaceful atmosphere of the forest where the carnivorous animals coexisted with the deer.

नृपतिमुनिपरिग्रहेण सा भूः सुरसचिवाप्सरसां जहार तेजः ।
उपहितपरमप्रभावधाम्नां न हि जयिनां तपसामलङ्घ्यमस्ति ॥६॥

Nripatimuniparigraheṇa sā bhûḣ surasacivāpsarasāṃ jahāra tejaḣ / upahitaparamaprabhāvadhāmnāṃ na hi jayināṃ tapasāmalañghyamasti //6//

Translation:

The heavenly music-makers and the fairies found themselves lacking in lustre on entering the hermitage and on observing the behaviour pattern of the Royal saint. O! What is there, which is beyond the reach of all-victorious dedications (tapasa), when one concentrates to achieve the irresistible light of truth.

सचकितमिव विस्मयाकुलाभिः शुचिसिकतास्वतिमानुषाणि ताभिः ।
क्षितिषु ददृशिरे पदानि जिष्णोरुपहितकेतुरथाङ्गलाञ्छनानि ॥७॥

Sacakitamiva vismayakulābhiḣ śucisikatāsvatimānusāṇi tābhiḣ / Kṣitiṣu dadriśire padāni Jiṣṇorupahitaketurathāñgalānchhanāni //7//

Translation:

Then the divine ladies were most astonished and awestruck to witness the miracle of the luminous and incomprehensible step of Jiṣṇu kicking up from the white sandy bank (of Surasaritā) like the banner of a chariot flouting the steep-grey sky.

N.B. We have in this stanza clear reference to the basrelief of "Viṣṇum vikrāntamûrttiṃ" at the confluence of the rivulets Trigañgā and Vāgwatî to the south-east of the temple of Paśupatinātha (Vide. Levi, 20, R. Gnoli III and The Judicial Customs of Nepal Part I and Plate No. XI with a comparative study of the Aśokan Inscription of Luṃbini.) Another identical basrelief of this category with the Inscription of king Mānadeva, which was erected side by side with the Inscriptions of Kṣema-sundarî and Nara-varmma in Lājanpāt, has now been put on display in the Nepal Museum. A few other basreliefs of Viṣṇu in Three Vedic Steps in the temple of Cāñgu-Nārāyaṇa,Śikhin-Nārāyana and other villages have been printed by Stella Kramrish, Waldschmidt, Madantjeet Singh and other writers, and they have commented on them in their own particular way.

This reference to the basrelief by Bhāravi helps us to identify the site of Arjuna's penances, which has been carved in Māmallapuram, south of Madras in 7th century. It is remarkable that the reliefs depicting the climax of Kirātārjunîye made Professor H. Goetz hazard a guess in his "Art of the World" that Bhāravi was a court poet of king Mahendravarman (Pallava).

अतिशयितवनान्तरद्युतीनां फलकुसुमावचयेऽपि तद्विधानाम् ।
ऋतुरिव तरुवीरुधां समृध्दया युवतिजनैर्जगृहे मुनिप्रभावः ॥८॥

Atiśayitavanāntaradyutînāṃ phalakusumāvacaye (ऽ) pi tadvidhānam / rituriva taruvîrudhāṃ samriddhyā yuvatijanairjagrihe muniprabhāvaḥ //8//

Translation:

The minds of the divine ladies were greatly influenced by the extremely luxuriant growth of the fruits, flowers and creepers stemming as much from the contributory factor of the prolific seasonal atmosphere as by the powerful personality of the saint (Arjuna).

मृदितकिसलयः सुराङ्गनानां ससलिलवल्कलभारभुग्नशाखः ।
बहुमतमधिकां ययावशोकः परिजनतापि गुणाय सद्गुणानाम् ॥९॥

Mriditakisalayaḥ surāñganānāṃ sasalilavalkalabhārabhugnaśākhaḥ / vahumatamadhikāṃ yayāvaśokaḥ parijanatāpi guṇāya sadguṇānām //9//

Translation:

The trees of Aśoka (saraca indica) with their soft barks, branches and sprouts dripping with drops of rain became extremely popular with the bevy of ladies and their retinue. For, sound and polite qualities are attractions in themselves as if they had inherited these virtues under the influence of the saint.

N.B. According to V.S. Apte "Aśoka is a tree having red flowers; (said according to convention of poets to put forth flowers when struck by ladies with the foot decked with jingling anklets). According to L. Petech's Northern India according to the Shui-ching-chu (Section A. p. 35 b) "The marvellous tree, which the excellent queen (Māyā-devî— the mother of Śākyamuni) grasped when the Buddha came to life, is called 'hsu-ko (Aśoka). King Aśoka made out of lapiz-lazuli, a statue of the queen in the act of grasping (the tree) and giving birth to the prince (Buddha Śākyamuni). When the old tree had no more offshoots, all the Śramaṇas took the old trunk and planted it; and over and over again it continued itself till the present time. The branches of the trees are as of old, and they still shelter the old statue." It is remarkable that the tree mentioned in Shui-ching-chu, which is acknowledged to be older than the visit of Fa-scien, was Aśoka, and the basrelief of the nativity of Buddha Śākyamuni was attributed to king Aśoka. The present basrelief representing the nativity of Śākyamuni in Lumbini can be safely attributed to king Kaṇiṣhka I (vide Judicial Customs of Nepal Part I Plates I and IV with the running commentary). We have not discovered the basrelief of the nativity of Śākyamuni attributed by the Chinese text of Shui-ching-chu to Aśoka the Great in our excavations of Kapilavastu up to this writing. According to the epic of Rāmāyaṇa, Sitā was confined to the arbour of Aśoka trees in Lankā (Ceylon). Aśoka is a tree of the variety of Saraca Indica which are described extensively in the group of medicinal plants under the term "Aśokādi-varga in the treatises of Āyurveda. The mention by Bhāravi of the trees of Aśoka as the favourite of the ladies is in line with the Buddhistic traditions of Nepal: and both Nepal and China have preserved a large number of basreliefs depicting the nativity of Buddha Śākyamuni.

However, there are other traditions that the tree, to which Māyā clung in her pang of delivery, was Śālaḣ (shorea robusta) which abound in the region of Lumbini.

यमनियमकृशीकृतस्थिराङ्गः परिददृशे विधृतायुधः स ताभिः ।
अनुपमशमदीप्ततागरीयान्कृतपदपङ्क्तिरथर्वणेव वेदः ॥१०॥

Yamaniyamakriśîkritasthirāñgaḣ paridadrîśe vidhritāyudhaḣ sa tābhiḣ /
anupamaśamadîptatāgarîyānkritapadapañktiratharvaṇeva vedaḣ //10//

Translation:

Though looking lean and thin due to steady pursuit of rules and disciplines of ascetical practices for the purposes of peace, yet the divine ladies were astonished to find Arjuna burnishing in incomparable panoply with bow (and arrows) like the synthesis of all contraditions in Atharva-veda.

N.B. We have pointed out how Atharvaveda does not find mention in Anuparama's inscription of the Pilaster of Hārigāon. This is the fourth and apocryphal Veda of the Aryans in two recensions, a fifth of it reproduces spells from Rig Veda, all of which was not accepted as a canonical Veda till the end of the fifth century. "Outline of religious literature of India (London, 1920) by Farquhar." Refer to our summary for the genesis of Atharvaveda in the scheme of Brāhmannic Philosophy.

शशधर इव लोचनाभिरामैर्गगनविसारिभिरंशुभिः परीतः ।
शिखरनिचयेमेकसानुसद्मा सकुलमिवापि वसन्महीधरस्य ॥११॥

Śaśadhara iva locanābhirāmairgaganavisāribhiraṃśubhiḣ parîtaḣ /
sikharanicayemekasānusadmā sakalamivāpi vasanmahîdharasya //11//

Translation:

Like the moon the saint was sitting all by himself in a halo of light so that his beautifully undulating rays covered the side of mount (Indra-kîla) in the form of a garment.

N.B. Mallinātha's gloss of "dadhan" (=held or possessed) seems to be a poor substitute for the poet's original of "vasan" (= garment).

सुरसरिति परं तपोऽधिगच्छन्विधृतपिशङ्गबृहज्जटाकलापः ।
हविरिव विततः शिखासमूहैः समभिलषन्नुपबेदि जातवेदाः ॥१२॥

Surasariti paraṃ tapo (ऽ) dhîgacchanvidhritapiśañgavrihajjaṭākalāpaḣ/
haviriva vitataḣ śikhāsamuhaiḣ samabhilaṣannupabedi jātavedāḣ //12//

Translation:

While practising his supreme penances by the bank of Surasaritā with his chrysolite braid of long hair, he (Arjuna) appeared like the stuttering flame of fire Rig-vedic altar fed with clarified butter and sacrificial offerings.

N.B. Surasaritā is not definitely the Gāṇges. Judging by reference to Vijayavatî in stanza 13, Surasarita appears to be a disguised name for that stretch of river Vāgvati known today as the gorge of Sûryaghāṭa where the Sivalinga (Vijayaśvara) is found inscribed with the inscription of Bhāravi's mother Vijayavatî. The reference to the basrelief of Visṇu in Three Vedic steps in stanza 7 and to princess Vijayanatî in stanza 13 establish the exact location of the scene of Arjuna's penances.

सदृशमतनुमाकृतेः प्रयत्नं तदनुगुणामपरैः क्रियामलङ्घयाम् ।
दधदलघु तपः क्रियानुरूपं विजयवतीं त तपःसमां समृद्धिम् ॥१३॥

Sadriśamatanumākriteḣ prayatnaṃ tadanuguṇāmaparaiḣ kriyāmalañghayām /
dadhadalaghu tapaḣ kriyānurûpaṃ Vijayavatîṃ ca tapaḣsamāṃ samriddhim //13//

Translation:

With the frail frame of man he (Arjuna) addressed himself to tasks, which were beyond the capacity of human endurance. Then, too he performed major acts of penitential practices seeing how the observances (associated with the worship of Pañca-lingas in the scheme of Kāraṇapûjā) in the wake of Vijayavatî's religious austerity was most conducive to the attainment of the ultimate best in the direction of human affairs.

N.B. Most fortunately, the Liñga of Vijayaśvara inscribed with the inscription of princess Vijayavatî in the Licchavi scheme of Kāraṇapûjā survives in the gorge of Sûryaghāta even to our own day to find for ourselves what Bhāravi means in this stanza. The peculiar name of "Sûryaghāṭa" for this unlit gorge may trace its origin to the name of "Surasaritā" given by Bhāravi. Historical assessment of Bhāravi's work, rather than etymological explanation, would yield practical results. On and from stanza 7 to this stanza Bhāravi most skilfully gives us his assessment of the cult of the Rig-vedic Three Incomprehensible steps of Viṣṇu and its cult of fire in the synthetic crucible of Atharva-veda.

यमनियमकृशोऽपि शैलसारः शमनिरतोऽपि दुरासदः प्रकृत्या ।
ससचिव इव निर्जनेऽपि तिष्ठन्मुनिरपि तुल्यरुचिस्त्रिलोकभर्तुः ॥१४॥

Yamaniyamakriśo (ऽ) pi śailasāraḣ śamanirato (ऽ) pi durāsadaḣ prakrityā /
sasaciva iva nirjane (ऽ)pi tiṣṭhanmunirapi tulyarucistrilokbhartuḣ //14//

Translation:

Though lean due to the routine practice of self-control, yet his physical frame appeared as firm as the rock; although he pursued the path of self-containment and peace, yet he looked awe-insipiring and irresible by his own nature; though he lived in solitude far and away from the hunt (alarms) of men, yet he commanded respect as though he were surrounded by secretaries; and although he lived like a recluse, yet he appeared as radiant as the Lord of the Three Worlds (Indra).

N.B. Mallinātha's gloss of "ciraniyama" (=giving himself up to practice of personal self-denial and bodily mortification for a long period) does not give the poet's idea of "yamaniyama" (=living by the routine discipline of the rules of self-control). The poet seems to be influenced by king Māna deva's inscription of Cāñgu-Nārāyaṇa (G.N.I.I. Face II line 18 vide Appendix), where queen Rājyavatî— his mother lived according to the rules of "sîla" (Pañca-sîla or the five moralities preached by Śākyamuni), "tyāga" (renunciation), "dama" (fidelity), "upavāsa" (fastings) and "Ekānta" (solitude), which tended to give moral weakness to her character, as and when king Dharma deva passed away, so that she was ready to perform "Suttêê" (self-immolation) with her dead husband. It was king Māna deva I, who had to use all his ingenuity and effort to wean her away from the cruel practice way back in Saṃvat 386 (464 A.D.). Indeed, life is full of contradictions and the poet tries to show the effect of various physical attitudes and austere practices on the physical frame of Arjuna. It is remarkable that the early sculptors of Nepal have been very particular about various images in their special "mudrās" (physical attitudes e. g. "bodhigñāna-mudrā, bhûmi-sparsa-mudra, śāntajñāna-mudrā etc. which are extensively discussed in Prajñāparāmitās (literature concerned with the perfection of wisdom).

तनुमवजितलोकसारधाम्नीं त्रिभुवनगुप्तिसहां विलोकयन्त्यः ।
अवययुरमरस्त्रियोऽस्य यत्नं विजयफले विफलं तपोधिकारे ॥१५॥

Tanumavajitalokasāradhāmnîṃ tribhuvanaguptisahāṃ vilokayantyaḥ/
avayayuramarastriyo(ऽ)sya yatnaṃ vijayaphale viphalaṃ tapodhikāre //15//

Translation:

On seeing the esoteric attitude of his body, which was devoid of substantive pose for the achievement of the illumination (associated with sattva-guṇa), the immortal ladies thought within themselves that Arjuna's means of penitential practices with the lust of gaining control over the three worlds were inadequate to achieve the fruits (ends) of victory by the very limitations of their functions.

N.B. Evidently, the divine ladies were surprised by the very nature of the esoteric worship of the Five Śiva-liñgas associated with the worship of Vijayaśvara, which has been inscribed with the inscriptions of princess Vijayavatî. "Kāraṇapûja" (worship of the causes of reason) was a new experience for these divine ladies from Indra's paradise, who were accustomed to the rites of Vedic sacrifices.

When I was translating this stanza, I revisited the temple of Paśupati, then climbed to the table-land of Kailāsa and descended down the gorge of Suryaghāṭa (Surasaritā) in order to survey the scene and verify if my rendering was as it was visualised by Bhāravi. When I revisited the Liñga of Vijayaśvara in the preciptous bluff of Sûryaghatā, where two of the five phalluses have been carried away by landslide during the intervening time between me and Bhāravi, the cliffs and caves and the surrounding forests gave me the impression that the poet would not notice much change in the sight and scene of Kirātārjunîye, if he were to return to us to-day.

मुनिदनुतनयान्विलोभ्य सद्यः प्रतनुबलान्यधितिष्ठतस्तपांसि ।
अलघुनि बहु मेनिरे च ताः स्वं कुलिशभृता विहितं पदे नियोगम् ॥१६॥

Munidanutanayānvilobhya sadyaḣ pratanuvalānyadhitiṣṭhatastapāṃsi / alaghuni bahu menire ca tāḣ svaṃ kuliśabhritā vihitaṃ pade niyogaṃ //16//

Translation:

Though the ladies were loath to seduce the emaciated figure of Arjuna in his present state of penitential practices, yet they were duty-bound to carry out the command of the wielder of thunderbolt (Indra) at that particular moment, which was superior to their sentiment of sympathy on balance.

अथ कृतकविलोभनं विधित्सौ युवतिजने हरिसूनुदर्शनेन ।
प्रसभमवततार चित्तजन्मा हरति मनो मधुरा हि यौवनश्रीः ॥१७॥

Atha kritakavilobhanaṃ vidhitsau yuvatijane Harisûnudarsanena / prasabhamavatatāra cittajanaṃ harati mano madhurā hi yauvanaśrîḣ //17//

Translation:

Then the ladies were determined: and attracted by the sight of the physical attitude of the son of Hari (Arjuna) they made themselves up with beauty culture in response to the sudden upsurge of passion within their heart, so that they may seduce and win his heart by the display of tender wiles at the zenith of their youth.

सपदि हरिसखैर्वधूनिदेशाद्ध्वनितमनोरमवल्लकीमृदङ्गैः ।
युगपदृतुगणस्य संनिधानं वियति वने च यथायथं वितेने ॥१८॥

Sapadi Harisakhairvadhûnideśāddhvanitamanoramavallakîmridangaiḣ/ yugapadritugaṇasya saṇnidhānaṃ viyati vane ca yathāyathaṃ vitene //18//

Translation:

At the command of the ladies with their steps set for dancing, the music makers filled the forests and the sky with enchanting misic of lyre (vallakî= a stringed musical instrument like "vîṇā" usually seen in the hands of Nîlasarasvatî of our Licchavi period) and tambourines (Mridargas musical drums of percussion with small bells to keep tempi with energetic dancers) in tune with the season of the year.

N.B. According to the Sanskritic literature there are six Rāgas namely 1. Bhairavaḣ 2. Kauśika, 3. Hindola 4. Dîpaka, 5. Śrî-rāga and 6. Megha-rāga and their six consorts, and their combination give rise to several musical styles. They have got to be sung according to season of the year.

Judging by the figures of dancers during the Buddhistic and Licchavi periods and repertory of musical instruments in our temples and museums, there was charming ingenuity and joy of life in every season of the year, which Bhāravi describes in the following stanzas:—

सजलजलधरं नभो विरेजे विहृतिमियाय रुचिस्तडिल्लतानाम् ।
व्यवहितरतिविग्रहैर्वितेने जलगुरुभिः स्तनितैर्दिगन्तरेषु ॥१९॥

Sajalajaladharaṃ nabho vireje vihritimiyāya rucistaḍillatānām /
vyavahitarativigrahairvitene jalagubhiḣ stanitairdigantareṣu //19//

Translation:

The dark rain-bearing clouds decked the sky, and flashes of lightnings, like besetting creepers, forked themselves for liaison, where thunderclaps delivered the coup to bring heavy shower as far as the distant horizon as the factor of contact between the earth and the sky.

N.B. Mallinātha's gloss of "vivriti" (=gaping. yawning or seperating) does not give Bhāravi's idea of the attempt at liaision by one of the ten modes of indicating love used by women by the world "vihritam". The word "latā" (creepers) are as important for entwining the trees as the the thunders and lightnings for encompassoing the nuptial of the earth and sky by heavy rain-shower during the season of rain. The poet opens the description of rainy season.

परिसुरपतिसूनुधाम सद्यः समुपदधन्मुकुलानि मालतीनाम् ।
विरलमपजहार बद्धबिन्दुः सरजसतामवनेरपां निपातः ॥२०॥

Parisurapatisûnudhāma sadyaḣ samupadadhan mukulānimālatînām /
viralamapajahāra vaddhabinduḣ sarajasatāsatāpavanerapāṃ
nipātaḣ //20//

Translation:

Now, then, the wildly growing creepers of Mālatî (Jasmine= चमेली अथवा वर्षा पुष्पा) in full blossom beset the hermitage of the son of the king of gods (Arjuna) and isolated it from the damp and mud of the rain-soaked forest and kept it bright and balmy despite the dripping rain.

प्रतिदिशमनुगच्छताभिमृष्टः ककुभविकाससुगन्धिनानिलेन ।
नव इव विबभौ सचित्तजन्मा गतधृतिराकुलितश्च जीवलोकः ॥२१॥

Pratidiśamanugacchatābhimriṣṭaḣ kakubhavikāsasugandhinānilena /
nava iva vibahbau sacittajanmā gatadhritirākulitaśca jîvalokaḣ //21//

Translation:

The fragrantic smell of wildly-flowering Kakubha (terminalia Arjuna =काहुलो) wafted by the breeze from all directions imperceptibly roused his (Arjuna's) erotic feelings even as the new seasonal experience overcame the sentient world with the uncontrollable sexual passion for mating at the cost of reason and patience.

N.B. Mallinātha's gloss of "abhigacchatā" (= going in the direction of or towards") does not give Bhāravi's scientific significance of "anugacchatā (= the spontaneous method of nature behind the routine of sentient existence, It is interesting to note that "anudharma" is a technical term in Prajñā literature, such as Bodhisattva-bhûmi, Mahdyānta-vibhāga and Pāli Dhamma, for the method behind "dhamma" (norm of law) and the series of supra-mundane faculties which mark the growth of wisdom. By taking an example from nature the poet shows that the seasonal law of nature is more powerful in influencing the feelings of men and animals than the wonder-working characteristic of Arjuna as Jiṣṇu with his feet in the sky (vide stanza 7) or the discussions of anudharma" in the literature concerned with the "Perfection of wisdom at its summit."

V.S. Āpte in his Students' Sanskrit-English Dictionary does not take note of the use of the word "kakubha" by Bhāravi. He quotes from Kālidāsa's Meghadûta and Uttararāmcarita, which do not identify the botanical species of "kakubha" (terminalia Arjuna). Generally it is known as "kāhulo" but in eastern hills of Nepal it is also known as "vegar or vevar".

व्यथितमपि भृशं मनो हरन्ती परिणतजम्बुफलोपभोगहृष्टा ।
परभृतयुवतिः स्वनं विचक्रे नवनवयोजितकण्ठरागरम्यम् ॥२२॥

Vyathitamapi bhriśaṃ mano harantî pariṇatajamvuphalopabhogahriṣṭā /
parabhritayuvatiḣ svanaṃ vicakre navanavayojitakaṇṭharāgaramyam //22//

Translation:

Happy with the feast of ripe rose-apple fruit (Jamvu=Syzigium cumini=जामुन), the ladies, who were brought up according to the law of adoption (of the cuckoo by the crow) thrilled by the modulation of their melodius voices even people with obsessed minds and enthralled them by their method of singing new and ever new melodies.

N.B. Śrî Koṣanātha Devkoṭā in his Nepali Nighaṇṭu Section 157 defines Jamvu as Artemisis vulgaris known as Tite-pati (तीते पाति) and in Sections 524 as Syzygium cumini (जामुन which does good to the throat.

अभिभवति मनः कदम्बवायौ मदमधुरे च शिखण्डिनां निनादे ।
जन इव न धृतेश्चचाल जिष्णुर्नहि महतां सुकरः समाधिभङ्गः ॥२३॥

Abhibhavati maṇaḣ kadamvavāyau madamadhure ca śikhandināṃ nināde /
jana ıva na dhriteścacāla Jiṣṇurna hi mahatāṃ sukaraḣ samādhibhañgaḣ //23//

Translation:

Neither breeze bearing with it the soft smell of Kadamva (anthocephalous Cadamva= कदम) nor intoxicatingly mellow notes of the peacocks could assail the mind of Arjuna. Like a man sitting apart and living all by himself, there was nothing that could disturb Jisnu's adamantine attitude of meditation. Indeed, it is not easy to disturb the concentration of perfect ones.

N.B. Mr. Devkotā in his Nepali Nighaṇṭu Section 434 describes different varieties of Kadamva (Kadam) occuring in the hills and vales of Nepal, which flower at different seasons of the year. This is a very popular tree, which is celebrated in songs even to our own day.

धृतबिसवलयावलिर्वहन्ती कुमुदवनैकदुकूलमात्तबाणा ।
शरदमलतले सरोजपाणौ घनसमयेन वधूरिवाललम्बे ॥२४॥

Dhritavisavalayāvalirvahantî kumudavanaikadukūlamàttavàṇā /
śaradamalatale sarojapāṇau ghanasamayena vadhūrivāvalamve //24//

Translation:

The forest of white and blue water lilies (kumuda = Nymphaea alba) strung like arrows over their sturdy stems resembling brocades of finely woven silver garments appeared to extend their arms to embrace the ladies with their flowering arms during the intermediate phase between the dense season of rain and autumn under a clearing autumnal sky.

समदशिखिरुतानि हंसनादैः कुमुदवनानि कदम्बपुष्पवृष्टया ।
श्रियमतिशयिनीं समेत्य जग्मुर्गुणमहतां महते गुणाय योगः ॥२५॥

Samadaśikhirutānī haṃsanādaiḥ kumudavanāni kadamvapuṣpavṛṣṭyā /
śriyamatisayinîṃ sametya jagmurguṇamahatàṃ mahate guṇàya yogaḥ //25//

Translation:

Now, then, the shrill notes of the passionate peacocks could be heard side by side with the cackles of the ducks; and the shower of the flowers of kadamava trees (anthocephalus cadamba, adina cordifolia, mytragyna parvifolia = varieties of Kadam) overspread the forest of white and blue water-lilies. Indeed, the combination of the superfine qualities of the season of rain and autumn contributed to the beauty and happiness of the transitional phase of (the seasons).

सरजसमपहाय केतकीनां प्रसवमुपान्तिकनीयरेणुकीर्णम् ।
प्रियमधुरसनानि षट्पदाली मलिनयति स्म विनीलबन्धनानि ॥२६॥

Sarajasamapahāya ketakînāṃ prasavamupāntikaṇîyareṇukîrṇam/
priyamadhurasanāni ṣaṭpadālî malinayati sma vinîlavandhanāni//26//

Translation:

(During this transitional period) large six-footed black-bees with their capacity of bearing two variety of pollen dusts carried the honey juice from the flowers of Ketaki (agave Americana =सुनकेरडा)

and dimmed with its juice the flowers of "nîla" (flacourtia jangomas = सुनपाति) for the purposes of pollination.

N.B. I wonder why Bimala Sharmā translates Nīla as "sattisàla" (= garcinia merilla) In ordinary use the word "nîla" means "dark-blue while "nîlaḣ" means indigo. Whereas Mallinātha does not identify the botanical species śrî Koṣanātha gives us the uses of the word in relation to plant, animal, mineral and water. As the poet is talking about the pollination of plants by the bees, I feell the word "nîla" in the present context refers to सुनपाति-तालिस पत्र or बर (= ficus Bengalansis).

मुकुलितमतिशय्य बन्धुजीवं धृतजलबिन्दुषु शाद्वलस्थलीषु ।
अविरलवपुषः सुरेन्द्रगोपा विकचपलाशचयश्रियं समीयुः ॥२७॥

Mukulitamatiśayya vandhujîvaṃ dhritajalavinduṣu śàdvalasthalîṣu /,
aviralavapuṣah surendragopā vikacapalāśacayaśriyaṃ samîyuh //27//

Translation:

Many forms of insect life (such as grass-hoppers, dragon-flies and their like) appeared with the intense growth of parasitic plants over the rain-drenched meadows, which was green with young grass, while the insects left the budding plants to add to the beauty of (a variety of) Palāśa (Butea monosperma) in full blossom.

In the following stanza Bhāravi describes the onset of winter in the Himalayas:—

अविरलफलिनीवनप्रसूनः कुसुमितकुन्दसुगन्धिगन्धवाहः ।
गुणमसमयजं चिराय लेभे विरलतुषारकणस्तुषारकालः ॥२८॥

Aviralaphalinîvanaprasūnaḣ kusumitakundaṣugandhigandhavāhaḣ /
guṇamasamayajaṃ cirāya lebhe viralatuṣārakaṇastuṣārakālaḣ //28//

Translation:

The forest became dense with the continuous ripening of the fruits of Phalinî (priyangu = Aglaia Roxburghinia), and the fragrance of "Kunda" (N. dayālo दमालो = jasminum multiflorum) still embalmed the transitional season of autumn with its own good qualities, while drops of frost indicated that the winter was not far behind.

N.B. I do not see any contradiction in the description of the transitional phase between autumn and winter in this stanza. Obsessed by his idea of the four gloomy months of rains (caturmāṣa चतुर्मास Mallinātha seems to be confounded by the factual description of the transitional season by Bhāravi. The poet's description of fauna and flora is not conventional but true to nature.

निचयिनि लवलीलताविकासे विदधति लोध्रसमीरणे च हर्षम् ।
विकृतिमुपययौ न पाण्डुसूनुश्चलति नयान्न जिगीषतां हि चेतः ॥२८॥

Nicayini lavalîlatāvikāse vidadhati lodhrasamîraṇe ca harṣam / vikritimupayayau na Pāṇdusūnuścalati nayānna jigîṣatāṃ hi cetaḥ //29//

Translation:

The efflorescence of a large variety of creepers of "lavalî" (rose-berries or cicca acida = गुलाफ जामुन) mixed with the balmy air blowing from "lodhra" (= symplococus racemosa = लोध) presently contributed to the brightness of the season. But this did not produce any change in the form and feature of Jiṣṇu (Arjuna); for curiosities do not affect the behaviour pattern of men preoccupied with the thought of achieving victory.

N.B. Mallinātha's gloss of "janayati" (= giving birth to) does not convey Bhāravi's sense of "vidadhati (= contributed to) the bright and happy atmosphere of the transitional phase of the season. Autumn is a very happy season in the Himalayan countries, when rose-berries ripen and the balmy breeze blowing from Lodhra (Lodha= simplecocus racemosa)add to the pleasure of the people. Poet Kalidāsa in his Raghuvaṃśa 2.29 and Kumārasambhava 7.9. speaks about the bright qualities of "Lodhra" in relation to women. It is remarkable that Bhāravi describes the trees and creepers of the Himalayas in their exact flowering season with reference to their habitat in scientific sense.

कतिपयसहकारपुष्परम्यस्तनुतुहिनोऽल्पविनिद्रसिन्दुवारः ।
सुरभिमुखहिमागमान्तशंसी समुपययौ शिशिरः स्मरैकबन्धुः ॥३०॥

Katipayasahakāıapuṣparamyastanutuh:no (ऽ) lpavinidrasinduvārah / surabhimukhahimāgamāntaśaṃsî samupayayau śiśirah smaraikavandhuḣ //30//

Translation :

O ! how many beautiful parasitic forms flowered and faded during the frigid Himalayan winter and how many varieties of "sinduvāraḣ" (white variety : vitex negundo and black variety:- justicia gendarussa; N. सिमाली) rejuvenated themselves to herald the spring as memorials to the spell of winter !!

The poet now describes the spring :

कुसुमनगवनान्युपैतुकामा किसलयिनीमवलम्ब्य चूतयष्टिम् ।
क्वणदलिकुलनूपुरं निरासे नलिनवनेषु पदं वसन्तलक्ष्मीः ॥३१॥

Kusumanagavanānyupaitukāmā kisalayinîmavalambya cûtayastim / Kvaṇadalikulanûpuraṃ nirāse nalinavaneṣu padam vasantalakṣmiḣ //31//

Translation

With the object of reviving the mountains, forests and flowers (from the spell of frigid winter), the god of love assumed a staff wreathed by sprouts (of five vernal flowers) and stepped into the forest of lotuses with his feet jingling with the hum of bees to herald the spring.

विकसितकुसुमाधरं वहन्तीं कुरबकराजिवधूं विलोकयन्तम् ।
ददृशुरिव सुरांगना निषण्णं सशरमनङ्गमशोकपल्लवेषु ॥३२॥

Vikasitakusumādharaṃ vahantiṃ kuravakarājivadhûṃ vilokayantaṃ/ dadrisuriva surānganā nisaṅṅaṃ sasaramanṅgamaśokapallaveśu//32//

Translation :

On seeing the never-fading and many coloured "kuravaka" (=amaranth) glow like lips amid the blossom of flowers, the Divine ladies felt like seeing Eros sitting in the midst of the foliage of the tree of Aśoka (= saraca Indica) armed with his infallible arrows.

N.B. Mallinātha's gloss of "hasantiṃ" (= laughing) does not convey the poet's idea of "vahantim" (=carrying or bearing) in describing the characteristic of plants of the genus of Amarantus which typified immortality on account of its non-fading characteristic in all the seasons of the year. The plant genus Amarantus of the family of of Amarantacaea contains several well-known garden-plants, such as love-lies-bleeding with dark purplish flowers crowded in drooping spikes. It is a hardy vigorous annual, which never withers in all the seasons of the year. In ancient Greece the amaranth was sacred to Ephesian Artemis. It was supposed to have special healing properties, and as a symbol of immortality it was used to decorate the images of the gods and tombs.

मुहुरनुपतता विधूयमानं विरचितसंहति दक्षिणानिलेन ।
अलिकुलमलकाकृतिं प्रपेदे नलिनमुखान्तविसर्पि पङ्कजिन्याः ॥३३॥

Muhuranupatatā vidhûyamānaṃ viracitasaṃhati daksiṇānilena /
alikulamalakākritim prapede nalinamukhāntavisarpi pankajinyāḣ//33//

Translation :

The formation (format) of the busy bees was broken by the gust of south-wind, while they reformed themselves like the serpentine locks of lady's hair over the lotus-flowers of the variety of nymphaea rubra.

N.B. There is no indication of the breeze of Malaya as explained by Mallinātha. The poet is speaking about the gust of south-wind with the onset of spring.

श्वसनचलितपल्लवाधरौष्ठी नवनिहितेर्ष्यमिवावधूनयन्ती ।
मधुसुरभिणि षट्पदेन पुष्पे मुख इव शाललतावधूश्चुचुम्बे ॥३४॥

svasanacalitapallavādharauśthi navanihiterśyamivāvadhûnayantī /
madhusuıabhiūi śatpadena puśpe mukha iva Śālalatāvadhûscucumve //34//

Translation :

Like the young bride (in the basrelief of Māyādevî) hodding her rosy lips tight with baited breath and trembling with the pangs of new birth (of Śākyamuni), the ladies hugged the branches of "Śala" (shorea robusta), whose faces, then, resembled fully blossomed flowers after their fragrant resins have been sucked by the sixfooted bees.

N.B. Mallināthaʼs gloss of "pallavadharosṭhe" (= their twig-tender red lips) totally misses Bhāraviʼs reference to the basıelief of Māyādevî, who is depicted as holding the branch of the Śāla tree with her lips tight and breathing hard under pangs of delivery at the birth of Śākyamuni in Lumbini by the expression "pallavadharośṭhā" (=holding her rosy lips tight). We have illustrated in "The Judicial Customs of Nepal" how such basreliefs are modelled upon the legends of Aṭṭakathāvatthu and Aśokāvadāna respectively. We have also proved that the basrelief of Lumbini was put up by king Kaniśhka. This stanza proves that the tree was "Śāla" and not "Aśoka".

प्रवभति न तदा परो विजेतुं भवति जितेन्द्रियता यदात्मरक्षा ।
अवजितभुवनस्तथा हि लेभे सिततुरगे विजयं न पुष्पचापः ॥३५॥

Prabhavati na tadā paro vijetuṃ bhavati jitendriyatā yadātmaraksā /
avajitabhuvanastathā hi lebhe sitaturage vijayaṃ na puśpacāpaḣ //35//

Translation :

It is impossible to conquer our enemies as long as self-interest and self-defence remains the motive of victory over the five passions. (For the same reason) the holder of the bow of flowers (god of love)in the cosmic world could not achieve victory over the owner of white horses (Arjuna).

N.B. Mallinātha's gloss of "puśpabhāsaḣ" (= spring) shows his obsession for the Brāhmannic legend of the incineration of Cupid by the fire belching forth from the Third Eye of Śiva. Judging by the inscription of Jisnu-gupta at the base of an image of Chhatra-caṇdeśvara within the quadrangle of the temple of Paśupati as well as the image Hari-Hara (GNI. XX) these myths were invented later than Bhāravi. We have discussed the entire question in "The Judicial Customs of Nepal" Part I. On the other hand, thepoet of identifies the state "jitendriyatā" with the conquest of the five sense organs(Indriya) our body namely, I beauty (rāpa), flavour (rasa), smell (gandha), touch (sparsa) and sound (savda). According to Bhairavi conquest of the five sense-organs is an abstract consideration as long as there is that motive of self-interest to guide the actions of human beings. Though Arjuna does not pretend to be affected, the god of love has remained unconquered in the scheme of cosmic existence.

कथमिव तव संमतिर्भवित्री सममृतुभिर्मुनिनावधीरितस्य ।
इति विरचितमल्लिकाविकासः स्मयत इव स्म मधुं निदाघकालः ॥३६॥

Kathamiva tava saṃmatirbhavitrî samamritubhirmuninâvadhîritasya /
iti viracitamallikāvikāsah smayata iva sma madhuṃ nidāghakāla //36//

Translation :

"O season of Summer ! how could thou disturb the concentration of the saint when similar seasons failed in their efforts ?" With these words the flowers of Mallikā (Jasminum arborescens N. लहरे बेली) seemed to smile ironically at the unsuccess of the season of heat, honey and perspiration (to disturb Arjuna from his concentration).

बलवदपि बलं मिथोविरोधि प्रभवति नैव विपक्षनिर्जयाय ।
भुवनपरिभवी न यत्तदानीं तमृतुगणः क्षणमुन्मुनीचकार ॥३७॥

Valavadapi valaṃ mithovirodhi prabhavati naiva vipaksanirjayāya /
bhuvanaparibhavî na yattadanîṃ tamritugaṇaḣ kśaṇamunmunî-cakara //37//

Translation :

A divided army, though most powerful in strength and composition, cannot achieve victory over its adversary. Similarly, the most experienced and world-conquering army of the seasons could not move the mental concentration of the saint (Arjuna) even for the fraction of a moment.

श्रुतिसुखमुपवीणितं सहायैरविरललाञ्छनहारिणश्च कालाः ।
अविहितहरिसूनुविक्रियाणि त्रिदशवधूषु मनोभवं वितेनुः ॥३८॥

Śrutisukhamupavîṇitaṃ sahāyairaviralalāñcchanahārinaśca kālāḣ /
avihitaharisûnuvikriyāṇi tridaśavadhūśu manobhavaṃ vitenuḣ //38//

Translation :

The efforts of the the three hundred and thirty three million gods to distract the concentration of the son of Hari (Arjuna) with their dance and melody to the accompanyment of the music of lyre and dulcimer amid an atmosphere lavished prodigally by the luxuriant endowment (of the fruits and flowers) of the respective seasons acted as boomeranges on their own minds.

न दलति निचये तथोत्पलानां न च विषमच्छदकुन्दयूथिकासु ।
अभिरतिमुपलेभिरे यथासां हरितनयावयवेषु लोचनानि ॥३९॥

Na dalati nicaye tathotpalānāṃ na ca visamacchadakundayûthikāsu /
abhiratimupalebhire yathāsāṃ haritanayāvayaveśu locanāni //39//

Translation :

Indeed, the eyes of the ladies were so enamoured of the physical frame of the son of Hari (Arjuna) that they could not derive similar pleasure from the sight of the blossom of the hosts of blue lotuses nor from "visamacchada" (alstonia scholaris N छतिवन) nor from "kunda" (jasminum multiflorum N. वनहाँस) nor from "yûthikā" (jasminum auriculatum. जूही).

N.B. Mallinātha's gloss of "gucchayuthikasu" (=bunches of jasminum auriculatum N जूही) to describe a tree known in conventional Sanskrit literature as "saptaparṇa'' or saptacchada or saptapatra" according to the lexicon of Amarakośa overlooks the different variety of flowers mentioned by Bhāravi, which are dear to the eyes of the ladies at the period.

According to Encyclopaedia Brittanica Jasmine and Jessamine is a genus of ever green aromatic shrubs or climbers of the family of oleaceae, and comprising about 100 species occuring in all parts of the world.

मुनिमभिमुखतां निनीषवो याः समुपययुः कमनीयतागुणेन ।
मदनमुपदधे स एव तासु दुरधिगमा हि गतिः प्रयोजनानाम् ॥४०॥

Munimabhimukhatāṃ ninîśavo yāḥ samupayayuḥ kamanîyatāguṇena / madanamupadadhe sa eva tāsu duradhigamā hi gatiḥ prayojanānāṃ //40//

Translation :

Then the ladies approached the saint (Arjuna) with the object of beguiling him by their innate charm. On the contrary, the saint maddened them by generating feeling of sexual passion in them. Indeed, it is impossible to assess the extent of means to be employed without judging the end in view.

प्रकृतमभिससार नाभिनेयं प्रविकसदङ्गुलि पाणिपल्लवं वा ।
प्रथममुपहितं विलासि चक्षुः सिततुरगेन चचाल नर्तकीनाम् ॥४१॥

Prakritamabhisasāra nābhineyaṃpravikasadañguli pāṇipallavaṃ vā / prathamamupahitaṃ vilāsi cakśuḥ sitaturagena cacāla nartakînāṃ //41//

Translation :

Neither the initial play of lustful eyes nor the gesticulation of the fingers of their palms nor the accomplished and libidinous acting of the dancers moved Arjuna from his state of concentration.

N.B. Mallinātha's gloss of "anusasāra" (= to the accompanyment or following) does not convey the idea of lustful and libidinous display of professional women who met Arjuna in his hermitage meant by the poet's original of "abhisasāra".

A work known as Sāhityadarpana defines and classifies the theatrical action of dancers (nartakîrabhinaya) as follows:- 1. general: conveyed by bodily acting; 2. conveyed by their works; 3. extraneous: conveyed by their dress, ornaments, make-up etc; and 4. internal: which is conveyed by the manifestation of internal feelings such as perspiration, thrills and frills. The said work assumes that "Abhinaya" (acting) is an immitation of the natural conditions of life. We will see in the following stanza how Bhāravi defines "Abhinaya" (acting).

अभिनयमनसः सुराङ्गनाया निहितमलक्तकवर्तनातिताम्रम् ।
चरणमभिपपात षट्पदाली धुतनवलोहितपङ्कजाभिशङ्का ॥४२॥

Abhinayamanasaḣ surāñganāyāḣ nihitamalaktakavartanātitāmraṃ /
caraṇamabhipapāta ṣatpadālî dhutanavalohitapañkajābhiśankā (/42//

Translation :

In their anxiety to produce the most dramatic effect (to entice Arjuna) by their acting, the divine ladies had overdone their make-up by the excessive use of fragrant and lustrous resins of red lac, so that the bees swarmed at their feet, which deceived them (the bees) by their resemblance to the newly-blown lotuses.

अविरलमलसेषु नर्तकीनां द्रुतपरिषिक्तमलक्तकं पदेषु ।
सवपुषमिव चित्तरागमूहुर्नमितशिखानि कदम्बकेसराणि ॥४३॥

Aviralamalaseṣu nartakînāṃ drutapariṣiktamalaktakaṃ padeṣu /
savapuṣamiva cittarāgamûhurnamitasikhāni kadamvakesarāṇi //43//

Translation :

Tinged by the spray of the unguents of red-copper paints and stirred by the swift movement of the feet of the dancers, the tufts of "Kadaṃva" (anthocephalus Cadamba N. कदम) and "Kesara"

(Mahonia Napalaunsis N. केसरी रूख) as if they all combined to give physical expression to the mental outline of sexual passions.

नृपसुतमभितः समन्मथायाः परिजनगात्रतिरोहिताङ्गयष्टेः ।
स्फुटमभिलषितं बभूव वध्वा कथयति हि संवृतिरेव कामितानि: ॥४४॥

Nripasutamabhitaḣ samanmathāyāḣ parijanagātratirohitāñgayaśṭeh / sphuṭamabhilaṣitaṃ vabhūva vadhwā kathayati hi saṃvritireva kāmitāni //44//

Translation :

When the ladies approached the son of the king (Arjuna) invitingly making foreplay with creepers to the mutual gaze of their friends, their passion for the saint became more real than apparent. For it is said (in Vātsyāyana's Kāma-sûtra) that the concealment of the secret parts of their bodies (by women) is an invitation to coitus under the spell of the god of love.

N.B. Mallinātha's gloss of "vadati" (= speaks or makes discourse or opens up) does not give Bhāravi's reference to Vātsyāyana's "Kāma-sûtra" by the use of the expression "kathayati" (= it is narrated).

अभिमुनि सहसा हृते परस्या घनमरुता जघनांशुकैकदेशे ।
चकितमवसनोरु सत्रपायाः प्रतियुवतीरपि विस्मयं निनाय ॥४५॥

Abhimuni sahasā hrite parasyā ghanamarutā jaghanāmśukaikadeśe / cakitamavasanoru satrapāyāh pratiyuvatîrapi vismayaṃ nināya //45//

Translation :

Their bright garments and girdles flown over by the squall of wind in the presence of the saint (Arjuna) to their utter amazement, even the ladies with their companions felt ashamed at the exposure of their graceful thighs (let alone the saints) .

N.B. The excavations of Kapilavastu has revealed many figures of dancing Yakśîs or daughters of Māra with their girdles and treefoil dresses overflowing in the air as they dance. We have already referred to the inscription in our Introduction, which describes the dishevelment of the dress of Viṣṇu in the midst of storm. Unlike Kālidāsa, who describes the mantling of the earth by the ocean at the crack of doom in Raghuvaṃśa, Bhāravi takes his examples from the "Life of Śākyamuni" and the relative sculptures of Kapilavastu and Kāthmāndu to illustrate the scene of the seduction of Arjuna.

धृतबिसवलये विधाय पाणौ मुखमभिरूषितपाण्डुगण्डलेखम् ॥
नृपसुतमपरा स्मराभितापादमधुमदालसलोचनं निदध्यौ ॥४६॥

Dhritavisavalayevidhāya pāṇau mukhamabhirûṣitapāṇḍugaṇḍalekhaṃ / nripasutamaparā smarābhitāpādamadhumadālasalocanaṃ nidadhyau //46//

Translation :

Still under the spell of sexual passion but without the urge of the intoxication of sweet wine, some other ladies looked with longing and indolent eyes on the son of the king (Arjuna) in a state of dismay by placing their extremely angry faces totally deprived of its make-up over hands criss-crossed like stalks of lotus.

N.B. Mallinātha's glosses of "nidhāya" (= putting down or depositing) and "ādhi" (an indeclinable prefix to verbs to express the idea of (over or above or besides or in addition) totally miss the atmosphere of the scene of seduction of Śākyamuni by the daughters of Māra and their disappointment at their failures by the attitude described. The early period of our history seems to be characterised by Mudrās (physical attitudes) to express the mental state of the persons. The various attitudes of early images of the Buddhas and saints are so many cases in point.

सखि दयितमिहानयेति सा मां प्रहितवती कुसुमेषुणाभितप्ता ।
हृदयमहृदया न नाम पूर्वं भवदुपकण्ठमुपागतं विवेद ॥४७॥

Sakhi dayitamihānayeti sā māṃ prahitavatî kusumeṣuṇābhitaptā / hridayamahridayā na nāma pûrvaṃ bhavadupakaṇṭhamupāgataṃ viveda //47//

Translation :

"O saint ! my lady friend has confided in me to bring these words to your kind notice. When I presented myself to you (in this case of love at first sight), I have not anticipated the consequence regardless of whether it would be reciprocated by love or by cruelty.

N.B. By making the ladies speak their mind Bhāravi departs from the expression of erotic sentiments prescribed by Vātsyāyana's "Kāmasûtra" (e.g. chasing the sparrow and the attack of the wild boar). We well see later how the attack of the wild-boar on Arjuna leads to battle between the king of the Kirāta and the hero of the epic of Bhārata.

चिरमतिकलितान्यपारयन्त्या परिगदितुं परिशुष्यता मुखेन ।
गतघृण गमितानि सत्सखीनां नयनयुगैः सममार्द्रतां वचांसि ॥४८॥

Cirmtikalitānyapārayantyā parigaditum pariṣuśyatā mukhena / gataghriṇa gamitāni satsakhînāṃ nayanayugaiḣ samamārdratāṃ vacāṃsi //48//

Translation :

"O man of dispassion ! how could I express the sensual passion of a long-suffering love-lorn friend, who has sent her message to you in a hysterical state with dried lips due to extreme depression and who was muttering her subconscious feelings in a choking voice with eyes brimful of tears.

N.B. Mallinātha's glosses of "ciramapi" (= also long seized by fit of fainting) and "manaṃsi" (= mental pain inducing tears) to describe the hysterical state of the lady who sent the message. By restoring Bhāravi to his original of "ciraatikalitāni" (= long suffering hysterical friend) and "vacāṃsi" (= choking vioce), we have translated the stanza.

अचकमत सपल्लवां धरित्रीं मृदुसुरभिं विरहय्य पुष्पशय्याम् ।
भृशमरतिमवाप्य तत्र चास्यास्तव सुखशीतमुपैतुमङ्कमिच्छा ॥४९॥

Acakamata sapallavāṃ dharitrîṃ mridusurabhiṃ virahayya puṣpaśayyām /
bhriśamaratimavāpya tatra cāsyāstava sukhaśîtamupaitumañkamicchā //49//

Translation :

Where is the need for words when the lady love has left the aromatic bed of flowers to lie on bare ground covered over with prickly sprouts ! There is, no doubt, that she wants to ease the heat of her passion in the cool happiness of your embrace.

तदनघ तनुरस्तु सा सकामा व्रजति पुरा हि परासुतां त्वदर्थे ।
पुनरपि सुलभं तपोऽनुरागी युवतिजनः खलु नाप्यतेऽनुरूपः ॥५०॥

Tadanagha tanurastu sā sakāmā vrajati purā hi parāsutāṃ tvadarthe /
punarapi sulabhaṃ tapo (ऽ) nurāgî yuvatijanaḥ khalu napyate (ऽ) nurûpaḥ //50//

Translation :

O Sinless One ! Would not you be responsible if, for that matter, this daughter of another person "shuffles off her mortal coil" out of passion for you in her present state of hysteria ? You may have occasions to apply yourself to ascetical practices again and again, but you would not find another woman, who is so overwhelmed with love for you.

जहिहि कठिनतां प्रयच्छ वाचं ननु करुणामृदु मानसं मुनीनाम् ।
उपनतमवधीरयन्त्यभव्याः स निपुणमेत्य कयाचिदेवमूचे ॥५१॥

Jahihi kaṭhinatām prayaccha vācaṃ nanu karuṇāmridu mānasaṃ munînāṃ /
upanatamavadhîrayantyabhavyāh sa nipuṇametya kayācidevamuce //51//

Translation :

O Saint ! shun your ruthlessness and speak. For, nothing behoves the spiritual framework of saintly mind as compassion. And some of the clever ladies approached him with due obeisance and said,"Nothing is so cowardly of chivalrous men as to spurn the polite offer of ladies."

N.B. Mallinātha's gloss of "upagatam" (= approaching or going near) seems to be a poor substitute for Bhāravi's "upanatam" (= approaching with polite salutations or obeisances).

Mallinātha explains that the following five stanzas are calculated to explain the tragic frailties (vyabhicāribhāva) inherent in the nature of women. How far such an interpretation would apply to the composition of the apostles of the "Kāraṇapûjā" to whom "poetry is word and content without defects possessing qualities and also ornaments, though not necessarily at the cost of facts !" We will see how the facts of life are stranger than fiction.

सललितचलितत्रिकाभिरामाः शिरसिजसंयमनाकुलैकपाणिः ।
सुरपतितनयेऽपरा निरासे मनसिजजैत्रशरं विलोचनार्धम् ॥५२॥

Salalitacalitatrikābhirāmāḣ sirasijasaṃyamanākulaikapaṇiḣ /
surapatitanaye(ऽ)parā nirāse manasijajaitraśaraṃ vilocanārdhaṃ //52//

Translation :

Some of the wanton damsels assumed the lilting triangular pose (tribhañga) and gave indications of the passion of their mind by placing one of their hands on their forehead (like a huntress), and they discharged the infallible arrows (of love) with their askant eyes on the son of the king of gods.

सकुसुमवलम्ब्य चूतमुच्चैस्तनुरिभकुम्भपृथुस्तनानताङ्गी ।
तदभिमुखमनङ्गचापयष्टिर्विसृतगुणेव समुन्ननाम काचित् ॥५३॥

Sakusumavalambya cûtamuccaistanuribhakumbhaprithustanānatāñgî /
tadabhimukhamanañgacāpayasṭirvisritaguṅeva samunnanāṃ kācit //53//

Translation :

Their bodies bent under the weight of their heavy breasts, which resembled plump and round pots, some of the ladies embraced exotic trees with all their blossom (like Yakṣî vrikṣakās) and directed with their sprouts the arrows of Cupid with all its power of seduction on him (Arjuna).

N.B. Mallinātha's gloss of "kusumita" (= flowered or furnished with flowers) does not convey the poet's picture of "sakusumam"(= with blossoms on them) to describe the pose of the damsel or daughters of Māra or Yakṣi Vrikṣakās who are depicted to show the poses of dancing in the sculptures of Kapilavastu (Vide Waldschmidt's Nepal: Art Treasures of the Himalayas Plates 1-8 and 10; The Judicial Customs of Nepal Part I Plates 13 A. and 15 A. and also H. Goetz's Art of the World p.50 showing 'Tree goddess Yakṣî VrikṣhakāChula Kokā devatā' from the Bharut balustrade).

सरभसमवलम्ब्य नीलमन्या विगलितनीवी विलोलमन्तरीयम् ।
अभिपतितुमनाः ससाध्वसेव च्युतरशनागुणसंयतावतस्थे ।।५४।।

Sarabhasamavalamvya nîlamanyā vigalitanîvi vilolamantarîyam /
abhipatitumanāḣ sasādhvaseva cyutaraśanāguṇasaṃyatāvatasthe //54//

Translation :

When the hip-belts of their garments became loose (in their sport of love), some of the ladies hastily held together their indigo-blue underwear by their hands, in which unreal act they were thwarted by the mess of their dresses to buckle the knots of their girdle.

N.B. Mallinātha's gloss of "saṃditavātasthe" (= bound down) does not give Bhāravi's idea of being restrained, tied up or fettered by the mess of their dresses with the use of the word "saṃyatā". The ladies are acting to disturb Arjuna's concentration.

यदि मनसि शमः किमङ्गचाप शठ विषयास्तव वल्लभा न मुक्तिः ।
भवतुः दिशति नान्यकामिनीभ्यस्तव हृदये हृदयेश्वरावकाशम् ।।५५।।

Yadi manasi śamaḣ kimañgacāpa śaṭha viśayāstava vallabhā na muktih /
bhavatu diśati nānyakāminîbhyastava hridaye hridayeśvarāvakāśaṃ //55//

Translation :

Why do you brandish your bow if you have peaceful intentions ? O perfidious man ! you seem to be lured to your ascetical practices with the object of enjoying the good things of life rather than for self-emancipation. There is nothing in your behaviour to convince us that your abstention from enjoying our company (at the present moment) is due solely to your lurking passion for the goddess of your heart (in the future).

N.B. The use of the expression "sathah" for a Thug or a Pretender seems to be borrowed from the inscription of Māna-deva (Vide Appendix).

इति विषमितचक्षुषाभिधाय स्फुरदधरोष्ठमसूयया कयाचित् ।
अगणितगुरुमानलज्जया सः स्वयमुरसि श्रवणोत्पलेन जघ्ने ॥५६॥

Iti viṣamitacakṣuṣābhidhāya sphuradadharosthamasûyayā kayācit /
agaṅitagurumānalajjayās aḣ svayamurasi śravaṅotpalena jaghne//56//

Translation :

With lips turned up in jealousy and scorn and crooked eyes some of the ladies became even so bold and intolerant asa to approach Arjuna in defiance of their sense of modesty and respect, so much so that they clapped him with their thighs and twigs to titillate his passion (and disturb his trance).

सविनयमपराभिसृत्य साचि स्मितसुभगैकलसत्कपोललक्ष्मीः ।
श्रवणनियमितेन तं निदध्यौ सकलमिवासकलेन लोचनेन ॥५७॥

Savinayamaparābhisritya sāci smitasubhagaikalasatkapolalaksmiḣ /
śravaṇaniyamitena taṃ nidadhyau sakalamivāsakalena locanena //57//

Translation :

Others approached Arjuna dramatically with oblique and charming smile beaming over their faces; and all of them skilfully clapped and tapped to divert the concentration of the saint and finally fix him by their sidelong glances.

करुणमभिहितं त्रपा निरस्ता तदभिमुखं च विमुक्तमश्रु ताभिः ।
प्रकुपितमभिसारणेऽभिनेतुं प्रियमियती ह्यबलाजनस्य भूमिः ॥५८॥

Karuṅamabhihitaṃ trapā nirastā tadabhimukhaṃ ca vimuktamaśru tābhiḣ /
prakupitamabhisāraṅe(ऽ)bhinetuṃ priyamiyatî hyavalājanasya bhûmiḣ //58//

Translation :

What a pity ! the ladies shed tears (of sorrow at their failure) specially as they had presented themselves before the saint to the rejection of their shame and modesty. Finṇally, they tried to influence him by their acting of anger, which is the last resource of women in their dramatic introduction to love.

N.B. Mallinātha's gloss of "anunetum" (= propitiating or conciliating) does not convey Bhāravi's idea of "abhinetum" (= influence by their highly dramatic action). These ladies are "Abhisārikās who have gone to the hermitage of Arjuna in order to influence him by their dramatic action.

असकलनयनेक्षितानि लज्जा गतमलसं परिपाण्डुता विषादः ।
इति विविधमियाय तासु भूषां प्रभवति मण्डयितुं वधूरनङ्गः ॥५९॥

Asakalanayanekśitāni lajjā gatamalasaṃ paripāṅdutā viśādaḣ /
iti vividhamiyāya tāsu bhûṣāṃ prabhavati maṇḍayituṃ vadhûranañgaḣ //59//

Translation :

Sidelong glances, modesty, indolence, excessive paleness and pining are the gifts of the god of love, with which he decks the fair sex to excite the passion of men.

अलसपदमनोरमं प्रकृत्या जितकलहंसवधूगति प्रयातम् ।
स्थितमुरुजघनस्तनातिभारादुदितपरिश्रमजिह्मितेक्षणं वा ॥६०॥

Alasapadamanoramaṃ prakrityā jitakalahaṃsavadhûgati prayātaṃ /
sthitamurujaghanastanātibhārāduditapariśramajihmitekśaṇaṃ vā//60//

Translation :

(In such a situation) the fair ladies had no alternative but to proceed with beautifully lazy steps beating the grace of swan in its spontaneity. Or did they fall back and sit down with downcast eyes and pendulus breasts as a result of the overplay of their thighs (to win back Arjuna to the sensual world ?

N.B. Mallinātha's gloss of "sthalātibhāra" (= sitting together on the ground in a state of fatigue with the overplay of their thighs) does not convey Bhāravi's original of "stanātibhāra" (= bowed down with the weight of their pendulus breasts) calculated to show their pitiable plight at their defeat. The commentator's equation of "jihmite" (= morally crooked) with "ghûrṇite" (= vibrated in the sense of inner movement) seems to be inadmissible. For "jihma" (awry or morally corrupt or crooked; vide Canto I. stanza 8 tathapi jihmah etc.) in the present context can mean "downcast". According to Pāśupatācāryas (Professors of practical psychology) "ghûrṇi" can be explained by the word "spanda" which means vibration. This vibration is a ceaseless force from which springs all that exists. This idea is followed by the Śaiva school of Kashmir.

भृशकुसुमशरेषुपातमोहादनवसितार्थपदाकुलोऽभिलापः ।
अधिकविततलोचनं वधूनामयुगपदुन्नमितभ्रु वीक्षितं वा ॥६१॥

Bhriśakusumaṣareśupātamohādanavasitārthapadākulo(ऽ)bhilāpaḥ / adhikavitatalocanaṃ vadhûnāmayugapadunnamitabhru vîkśitaṃ va //61//

Translation :

Judging by the mode of their inarticulate speech and unsteady steps it was difficult to say whether the behaviour of the ladies was due to intense shower of flowers (passion) or for that matter, the dilatation of their eye-lids was due to intense concentration and overplay of their eye-brows (on Arjuna).

N.B. Mallinātha's gloss of "ca" (= an indclinable particle expressing copulation or used to join words, which, in English is equivalent to 'as well as, also or) and "vā" in the present context of Bhāravi could mean "optionally" (vide Canto III. 13) : so that I have seen it fit to render it into English with or for that matter, Like a psychiatrist the poet describes every mood of the proud ladies in their defeat and decimation.

रुचिकरमपि नार्थवद् बभूव स्तिमितसमाधिशुचौ पृथातनूजे ।
ज्वलयति महतां मनांस्यमर्षे न हि लभतेऽवसरं सुखाभिलाषः ॥६२॥

Rucikaramapi nārthavadvabhûva stimitasamādhiśucau Prithātanûje /
jvalayati mahatāṃ manāṃsyamarṣe na hi labhate(ऽ)vasaraṃ sukhābhilāśaḥ //62//

Translation :

Though pleasant yet the dramatic action of the ladies could not have its effect on the adamantine concentration of the son of Prithā (Kuntî- the elder wife of king Pāṇḍu). Passion for pleasure does not find a place in the minds of ambitious men who are blazing with rage (to feed fat the ancient grudge).

स्वयं संराध्येशं शतमखमखण्डेन तपसा
परोच्छित्त्या लभ्यामभिलषति लक्ष्मीं हरिसुते ।
मनोभिः सोद्वेगैः प्रणयविहतिध्वस्तरुचयः
सगन्धर्वा धाम त्रिदशवनिताः स्वं प्रतिययुः ॥६३॥

Svayaṃ saṃrādhyeśam satamakhamakhaṇḍena tapasā
parocchittyā labhyāmabhilaṣati lakṣmîṃ Harisute /
manobhiḥ sodvegaiḥ praṇayavihatidhvastarucayaḥ
sagandharvā dhāma tridaśavanitāḥ svaṃ pratiyayuḥ //63//

Translation :

"O God ! Who art worship all by theyself !!

The wives of the Three Hundred and Thirty Three Million gods accompanied by the music-makers returned to their abode totally defeated and lacking lustre, as they were unable to seduce the son of Hari from his uninterrupted mortification (associated with fire-worship) in favour of the performer of one hundred horse-sacrifices with his mind obsessed by the desire to destroy his enemies and regain his fortune as early as possible.

N.B. Mallinātha's gloss of "yavam" (= in this manner or thus) totally misses Bhāravi's concept of "îśam" (= the supreme God who is worship all by Himself). The poet is preparing us for Ajruna's meeting and dialogue with Indra, (in the following Canto) who advises his son to devote himself to the worship of Paśupati so that he may receive the missile of Pāśupatāstra to conquer his enemies.

The metre in this stanza is Śikharinî.

The end of Canto X.

KIRĀTĀRJUNIYE
CANTO XI

CANTO XI

Summary

This Canto consists of 81 stanzas.

In this interesting Canto the poet describes how Indra visited the hermitage of Arjuna in the disguise of an emaciated "Muni" (saint). We have observed at the conclusion of Canto X how Bhāravi prepares us for the sublimity of the concept of "îśa" (Śiva) by one stroke of his pen. Then the father and the son engage themselves in a learned discussion as to the means and end of "Tapas" (austere practices) and the relative merits and demerits of the Paurānic legends, whereupon Arjuna tells him that Krishna Dvaipāyaṇa had advised him to meditate upon Indra as the "sun of power" in the esoteric scheme of Kāranapûjā so that he may acquire the necessary energy to wreck vengeance upon the gang of the Kauravas, who had taken advantage of the truthfulness of his eldest brother by recourse to foul play and condemned them to exile in defiance of equity, justice and fair play. In such a context Mokṣa (deliverance) does not seem to have any tangible significance for Arjuna. The play upon the word "Māna" (self-respect, pride, honour and virtue) seems to be an example of synchronic etymology, whereby the poet justifies the heroic qualities, wars and adventures of his grandfather (Māna-deva) vis-a-vis the concept of "Nirvāṇa" (blowing out) and "Mokṣa" (deliverance) propagated by the Buddhists and the Brāhmins.

Another interesting feature of this Canto is the use of the name "Kriśna Dvaipāyana", where the word "Kriśna" meaning black, is an adjective to Dvaipāyana (an island-born), the form being derived from "Veṇṭha-dipo" or Veṣtra-dîpo", where the worship of the Vedic god Viṣṇu seems to be prevalent among the Kausikan Brāhmins during our Buddhistic period (Vide The Judicial Customs of Nepal Part I). It would be interesting to point out at this stage that it was a Brāhmin from Veṇṭhadîpo, who was responsible for the distribution of the ashes of Śākyamuni Buddha among the tribes, who had gone to receive them in Kusinārā after the Great Passing.

Judging by Anuparama's eulogium to Dvaipāyana (vide The Judicial Customs of Nepal Part I Chapter XIV and The Appendix for its translation) he was the follower of Bhāgavatadharma and worshipped the image of holy Vāsudeva, before whose temple Anuparama erected the famous Pilaster of Hārigāon (op cit) surmounted by the image of Vainateya with palms folded. According to the author, this Dvaipāyana was an opponent of the Saugatas (Buddhists of different schools) who did not believe in the teachings of the Three Vedas. It appears to me that Bhāravi has taken up the name of Kriśhṅa Dvaipāyana from the "Life of Śākyamuni Buddha" contained in Mûlasarvāstivāda Vinaya, where the word Krśna is used precisely in the same sense of "black" as it is done by the poet in this Canto.

But if Bhāravi mentions the compiler of the epic of Mahābhārata as the faithful of the vedic cult of Indra, the "Life of the Buddha" says that the black tint of Krishna Dvaipāyana vanished and he became "Suvarṇa- Dvaipāyana (Dvaipāyana with a golden colour) when Gautama testified to his purity and sinlessness. This testifies to the historical references contained in Mûlasarvāstivāda Vinaya to the visit of Ānanda to the valley of Nepal, where his Śākya kinsmen had migrated after the attack of Virûdhaka on Kapilavastu. In such a historical context, it is remarkable how Bhāravi makes use of the names of Vyāsa, Dvaipāyana and Krishṇa Dvaipāyana as one and the same person.

Another remarkable feature of this Canto is the mention of Indra as a subordinate deity, who advised Arjuna to devote himself to the worship of Paśupati by subjecting himself to the discipline of "Vyûha" (fortress) literature. In this interesting scheme the stump or phallus of Śiva is being represented by Lokapālas (guardian deities) on the four cardinal compass corner. We know how the Śākyas of Kapilavastu worshipped Paśupati as Bhava (the self-existent creator of the cosmos) or Śākyavardhana and his consort as "Śirimā-devî or Bhavānî. This dialogue between Indra and Arjuna is a window on the ancient world of the Kirātas, Śākyas, Kolîs, Yakṣas and Kinnaras, and seems to be in line with the early sculptures of the Himalayan Janapadas (People's Republics) and "Gaṇa-rājyas" (confederacy of tribal republlics).

Against the background of these historical facts, I would now request my readers to go along with my translation of Canto XI of Bhāravi's Kirātārjunîye :—

अथामर्षान्निसर्गाच्च जितेन्द्रियतया तया ।
आजगामाश्रमं जिष्णोः प्रतीतः पाकशासनः ॥१॥

Athāmarśānnisargācca jitendriyatayā tayā /
ājagāmāśramaṃ Jiśṇoḥ pratîtaḥ pākaśāsanaḥ //1//

Translation :

Then on hearing the report from the divine ladies and music-makers that Arjuna had worked hard in the field of conquering passions and had already achieved victory over such petty obstacles as jealousy and spirit of competition as well as impurities associated with sensual passions and pollution of birth, the killer of the demon known as Pāka (Indra) visited the hermitage of Arjuna in a happy mood.

The metre in this Canto is Anuṣṭupa.

मुनिरूपोऽनुरूपेण सूनुना ददृशे हरिः ।
द्राघीयसा वयोतीतः परिश्रान्त इवाध्वना ॥२॥

Munirûpo (ऽ) nurûpeṇa sûnunā dadriśe Hariḥ /
drāghîyasā vayotîta pariśrāntah ivādhvanā //2//

Translation :

Hari was seen by his son in the feigned disguise of a holy man, who was bowed down with extreme old age and decriptitude, and so debilitated and tired by his life's long journey as to be on the verge of passing away.

N.B. Mallinātha's glosses of "puraḣ" (= in front or before him) and "pariklānta" (extremely tired) appear to be very bad examples replacing the original expressions of the poet by substitues and synonyms, which give us the impression that the remedy is worse than the disease.

In the first case the poet is talking about the make-up of Hari (Indra) as a holy man, which completely deceived him. So "puraḣ" seems to be redundant.

Where is the sense of explaining the word "parisrāntaḣ" by the word "pariklāntaḣ" if both the words convey the same meaning ? Evidently, the remedy is worse than the disease. For a comparison read princess Vijayavatî's description of king Māna-deva in his old age contained in the Introduction.

जटानां कीर्णया केशैः संहत्या परितः सितैः ।
पृक्तयेन्दुकरैरह्नः पर्यन्त इव संध्यया: ॥३॥

Jaṭānāṃ kîrṇayā keśaiḣ saṃhatyā paritaḣ sitaiḣ /
priktayendukarairahnaḣ paryanta iva saṇdhyayā //3//

Translation :

His white locks (tufts or tresses) covered over with white hair from their very roots presented him (Indra in disguise) like the very end of day embraced by the white arms (rays) of the moon.

विशदभ्रूयुगच्छन्नवलितापाङ्गलोचनः ।
प्रालेयावततिम्लानपलाशाब्ज इव ह्रदः ॥४॥

Viśadabhrûyugacchannavalitāpāñgalocanaḣ /
prāleyāvatatimlānapalāśāvja iva hradaḣ //4//

Translation :

The pupils of his eyes peeping through the wrinkles of the couter-folds of skin covered over with bushy-white eye-brows presented as pitiable a sight as the water peeping through apertures of a frost-covered pond overspread with faded lotus-leaves.

CANTO XI

N.B. Seeing how Bhāravi has already made a reference to the basrelief depicting the miracle of Visṇu in Three Vedic Steps in Canto X stanza 7, I have reason to see in the use of the word "valitā" a reference, in this scene of deception, to the legend of king Vali and Vāmana-the midget who defeated the powerful king of demons by his trick.The Brāhmannic legend has it that the Man-lion Incarnation of Viśṇu (Narasimha) killed the golden-eyed demon of gold-country (Hiraṇya-Kaśyapa of Suvarṇabhûmi) and restored the throne to his son Prahlāda who gave birth to a son known by the name of Virocana who ruled the world according to the Vedic laws. He begot a son known by the name Vali, who became as powerful as his great-great grandfather Hiraṇya-Kaśyapa; and he oppressed the Vedic gods by not offering oblations and sacrifices to the 333 million gods of Indra's paradise. In their dismay, these gods prayed to Viṣṇu who incarnated himself as a dwarf from the womb of Aditî and her husband Kaśyapa. This dwarf assumed the dress of a mendicant and approached king Vali with the request to make him a gift of Three Steps of land. Noted for his generosity, the king made the gift, whereupon the midget showed himself in his true form and measured the entire earth by his First Step and covered the heaven with the Second Step. Unable to provide space for his Third Step king Vali offered his own head.

At this stage the Brāhmannic legend assumes that Viṣṇu was entirely successful with his subterfuge whereas the Buddhistic legend of Kāraṇḍavyūha makes Viṣṇu sink with king Vali to the subterranean world, where he had to live as the gatekeeper of king Vali ever afterwards. We have pointed out in "The Judicial Customs of Nepal'' Part I how the basrelief of Narasiṃha holds the figure of a Buddha (Hiraṇya-Kaśypa) and how Māna-deva's basrelief of Viṣṇu brings out the entire myth according to the Brāhmannic and Buddhistic legends (Vide Plates V and XI). It is remarkable how the poet presents this nexux between deceit and success from the higher aims and ends of Śaiva-dharma.

आसक्तभरनीकाशैरङ्गैः परिकृशैरपि ।
आद्यूनः सद्गृहिण्येव प्रायो यष्ट्यावलम्बितः ॥५॥

Āsakatabharanîkāśairañgaiḣ parikriśairapi /
ādyûnaḣ sadgrihiḣneva prāyo yaṣtyāvalamvitaḣ '//5//

Translation :

Though lean and corpulent and bowed down with age and decripitude, yet he seemed to cling to life with his voracious appetite on the alms of his faithful wife in his last days of his existence, who acted as his staff (and sole prop of his mortal life).

गूढोऽपि वपुषा राजन्धाम्ना लोकाभिभाविना ।
अंशुमानिव तन्वभ्रमण्डलच्छन्नमण्डलः ॥६॥

Gûdho(ऽ)pi vapuṣā rājandhāmnā lokābhibhāvinā /
aṃśumāniva tanvabhramaṇḍalacchannamaṇḍalaḣ //6//

Translation :

Though his body was under a disguise, yet his refulgence appeared to pervade the atmosphere like the rays of the sun through mazes of diagrams.

N.B. Mallinātha's gloss of "paṭalacchannavigrahaḣ" (= like the disc of the sun hidden under the film of clouds) does not convey Bhāravi's idea of the halo round the disc of the sun or the mystical diagram used in reflecting the rays of the sun e.g. "ādarśa maṇḍalanibhāni samullasanti" (Canto V stanza 41). "Maṇḍala" may be disc of the sun or the halo round the sun or a kind of mystical diagram used in invoking a divinity or a mirror to reflect light. In Rigveda Maṇḍala is a division of the entire collection, which is contained in 10 Maṇḍalas.

जरतीमपि बिभ्राणस्तनुमप्राकृताकृतिम् ।
चकाराक्रान्तलक्ष्मीकँ ससाध्वसमिवाश्रमम् ॥७॥

Jaratîmapi vibhrāṇastanu aprākritākritiṃ /
cakārākrāntalakśmîkam sasādhvasamivāśramam //7//

Translation :

Fearing lest that his simulation of old age under unnatural make-up may disturb the beauty and serenity of the scene by being apprehended, he approached the hermitage with a feeling of fear and circumspection.

अभितस्तं पृथासूनुः स्नेहेन परितस्तरे ।
अविज्ञातेऽपि बन्धौ हि बलात्प्रह्लादते मनः ॥८॥

Abhitastaṃ Prithāsûnuḥ snehena paritastare /
avigñāte (ऽ) pi vandhau hi valātprahlādate manaḥ //8//

Translation :

The son of Kunti (Arjuna) melted with affection to find him (Indra) right before his hermitage. Indeed, happiness overwhelms the mind by the very force of nature at the sight of a relative, though he may be unknown.

आतिथेयीमथासाद्य सुतादपचितिं हरिः ।
विश्रम्य विष्टरे नाम व्याजहारेति भारतीम् ॥९॥

Ātitheyîmathāsadya sutādapacitiṃ Hariḥ /
Viśramya viṣṭara nāme vyājahāreti Bhāratîm //9//

Translation :

On receiving due hospitality and worship from his son, Hariḥ (Indra) addressed the following skilful words to the man of Bhārata after being seated on a bed of wood strewn over with grass and straws.

N.B. The expression "Bharatîm (=descended from king Bharata or the inhabitant of Bhāratavarsa namely India) seems to have a direct connection with Anuparama's eulogium to Dvaipāyana (GNI XI line 24). The compilation of the epic of Bhārata, which gives innumerable episodes of king Sagara, Bharata and their descendants is attributed to Dvaipāyana by Anuparama in the Pilaster of Hārigāon. Judging by the narration of the myths of the epic by

Indra, the poet appears to consider its compilation by many hands. The appearance of these baseless legends was the reason why Bhāravi put up the authentic chronology of the Kirāta-gaṇas in order to challenge the basis of the legends of the epic that were cropping up in the midst of sober history. (vide Introduction.)

त्वया साधु समारम्भि नवे वयसि यत्तपः ।
ह्रियते विषयैः प्रायो वर्षीयानपि मादृशः ॥१०॥

Tvayā sādhu samārambhi nave vayasi yattapaḥ /
hriyate viṣayaiḥ prāyo varṣîyānapi mādrisāḥ //10//

Translation :

O ! how is it that you have so readily addressed yourself to such austere practices at the zenith of your youth, when the five organs of the sense (viṣayaiḥ namely, eye, tongue, nose, touch and ear) sway the feelings of a man so far gone in age like myself ?

श्रेयसीं तव संप्राप्ता गुणसंपदमाकृतिः ।
सुलभा रम्यता लोके दुर्लभं हि गुणार्जनम् ॥११॥

Śreyasîṃ tava saṃprāptā guṇasaṃpadamākritiḥ /
sulabhā ramyatā loke durlabhaṃ hi guṇārjanam //11//

Translation :

How well that your very look speaks that you have achieved the richness (perfection) of merits ! How difficult it is to cultivate virtues in a world full of the good and beautiful things of life, which can be had for the asking (which can be achieved without effort) !!

शरदम्बुधरच्छाया गत्वर्यो यौवनश्रियः ।
आपातरम्या विषयाः पर्यन्तपरितापिनः ॥१२॥

Śaradambudharacchāyā gatvaryo yauvanaśriyaḥ /
āpātaramyā viṣayāḥ paryantaparitāpiṇaḥ //12//

Translation :

The smile of fortune and abundance of youth are as variable as the shadows of the clouds of autumn.

The pleasures of the five organs of sense are enjoyable with immediate effect while their functions are limited by sorrowful conclusions.

अन्तकः पर्यवस्थाता जन्मिनः सन्ततापदः ।
इति त्याज्ये भवे भव्यो मुक्तावुत्तिष्ठते जनः ॥१३॥

Antakah paryavasthātā janminahsantatāpadaḥ /
iti tyājye bhave bhavyo muktāvuttiṣṭhate janaḥ //13//

Translation :

Death is the end of all sentient beings, whose lives are beset with perpetual difficulties. With this (the inevitability of the law of nature in view), men find it proper to shun the very source of mortal existence and surrender themselves to the practices of deliverance.

चित्तवानसि कल्याणी यत्ते मतिरुपस्थिता ।
विरुद्ध केवलं वेषः संदेहयति मे मनः ॥१४॥

Cittavānasi Kalyāṇî yatte matirupasthitā /
virudhda kevalaṃ veṣaḥ saṇdehayati me manaḥ //14//

Translation :

Your predisposition shows that your heart is striving to achieve Kalyāṇî (Ardhanārîśvara or Two-in-one in the scheme of Sthāṇu Śiva or a happy or fortunate woman or a cow). However, your exclusive apparel (dress) alone betrays the contradiction of your precept and profession, which is what puts my mind into doubt and confusion.

N.B. Mallinātha's gloss of the indeclinable "Yattvaṃ (=yetatsvāṃ = from whom, from what or from which place or quarter you) overlooks Bhāravi's use of Ātmanepada of "yatte" in the sense of striving after or longing for or exerting yourself.

युयुत्सुनेव कवचं किमामुक्तमिदं त्वया ।
तपस्विनो हि वसते केवलाजिनवल्कले ॥१५॥

Yuyutsuneva kavacaṃ kimāmuktamidaṃ tvayā /
tapasvino hi vasate kevalājinavalkale //15//

Translation :

Why do you wear armour as if you were bent upon war as the sole means of achieving your end ? For, the Arhats of Jains sect, whose essence is absolute purity, wear the birch-bark leaves to live the real life of anchorites.

N.B. Here we have a clear connection between Jaina religion and Nepal. While Candra Gupta Maurya was driving out the last of the Brāhmannic Nanda kings from Magadha in about the year 312 B.C., Sambhutavijaya and Bhadravāhu- the author of the life and work of the founder of Jaina sect Mahāvira-were jointly responsible for the direction of Jaina community. After the death of Sambhutavijaya in 312 B.C. there was a famine in North-Bihar, so that Bhadravāhu went south to the Karnatic where food was plentiful. After the famine was over Bhadravāhu returned and resigned his leadership of the Jain sect and retired to Nepal in order to spend the rest of his life in penitence. But the monks,who had returned from Karnatic reproached the Jains of Magadha for their laxity of morals and heresy. A council of Jains was called at Pāṭaliputra (Patna), but they realised that they could not proceed in the matter until somebody knew about the mystic doctrines of Mahāvira contained in the 14 Parvas (chapters). Bhadravāhu was the only person who had the complete knowledge, and that he was in Nepal at the period. So a disciple of Sambhutavijaya known by the name of Sthulabhadra visited Bhadravāhu in Nepal and obtained the 14 Parvas, out of which he communicated 10 Parvas to the Jain Council at Pāṭaliputra. It is most interesting to a student of psychology how the poet makes Indra refer to the event and the penitential practices of Bhadravāhu in its pristine purity against the background of the Vedic sanctions of wearing an armour in austere practices.

प्रपित्सोः किं च ते मुक्ति निःस्पृहस्य कलेवरे ।
महेषुधी धनुर्भीमं भूतानामनभिद्रुहः ॥१६॥

Prapitsoḣ kiṃ ca te muktiṃ niḣsprihasya kalevare /
maheṣudhî dhanurbhîmaṃ bhûtānāmanabhidruhaḣ //16//

Translation :

Do you aim at deliverance by making your body free from attachment on this side of the grave ?

O me ! your awe-inspiring bow and quiver (sheath for containing arrows) strike terror into the mind of sentient existences (which is a contradiction in itself).

भयंकरः प्राणभृतां मृत्योर्भुज इवापरः ।
असिस्तव तपस्थस्य न समर्थयते शमम् ॥१७॥

Bhayaṃkaraḣ prāṇabhritāṃ mrityorbhuja ivaāparaḣ /
asistava tapasthasya na samarthayate śamam //17//

Translation :

O ! how your punitive sword strikes terror into the heart of all sentient creatures like the second arm of death !! This does not support your profession of peace and fair-play as an anchorite.

जयमत्रभवान्नूनमरातिष्वभिलाषुकः ।
क्रोधलक्ष्म क्षमावन्तः क्वायुधं क्व तपोधनाः ॥१८॥

Jayamatrabhavānnunamarātisvabhilāśukaḣ /
krodhalakśma kśamāvantaḣ kwāyudhaṃ kwa tapodhanāḣ //18//

Translation :

O gentleman ! if your sole object is the lust for victory over your enemies, where is the line of demarcation between the characteristics of anger and benignity or for that matter, between those people who bear arms or those who are anchorites.

यः करोति वधोदर्का निःश्रेयसकरीः क्रियाः ।
ग्लानिदोषच्छिदः स्वच्छाः स मूढः पंकयत्यपः ॥१९॥

Yaḣ karoti vadhodarkā niḣśreyasakarîḣ kriyāḣ /
glānidoṣacchidaḣ svacchāḣ sa mûdhah pañkayatyapaḣ //19//

Translation :

The Pretender, who poses to profess self-abnegation with the intention of annihilating other people (in his heart), such a stupid self deceiver muddies the clear and thirst-quenching water of life.

मूलं दोषस्य हिंसादेरर्थकामौ स्म मा पुषः ।
तौ हि तत्त्वावबोधस्य दुरुच्छेदावुपप्लवौ ॥२०॥

Mûlaṃ doṣasya hiṃsāderarthakāmau sma mā puṣaḣ /
tau hi tattvāvavodhasya durucchedāvupaplavau //20//

Translation :

The lust for pelf and power and passion for women are the root-causes of crime and murder. Do not nourish them. For, indeed, they are the hindering elements to the cultivation of supreme knowledge of this material world (for the Third Eye of Inner Illumination).

अभिद्रोहेण भूतानामर्जयन्गत्वरीः श्रियः ।
उदन्वानिव सिन्धूनामापदामेति पात्रताम् ॥२१॥

Abhidroheṇa bhûtānāmarjayangatvarîḣ sriyaḣ /
udanvāniva sindhûnāmāpadāmeti pātratām //21//

Translation :

Changeful fortune won rapidly by injuring the interest of other incumbents invites) its own doom like a vessel caught in the eddies and whirlpools at the confluence of the river and the ocean.

या गम्याः सत्सहयानां यासु खेदो भयं यतः ।
तासां किं यन्न दुःखाय विपदामिव संपदाम् ॥२२॥

Yā gamyāḣ satsahyānāṃ yāsu khedo bhayaṃ yataḣ /
tāsāṃ kiṃ yanna duḣkhāya vipadāmiva sampadām //22//

Translation :

That (affluence), which can be won by easy and available means, and the possession of which is fraught with danger and fear, but the loss of which leads to depression and sorrow; O ! why should you acquire that possessive instinct, which is the root-cause of all troubles in our mortal existence ?

दुरासदानरीनुग्रान्धृतेर्विश्वासजन्मनः ।
भोगान्भोगानिवाहेयानध्यास्यापन्न दुर्लभा ॥२३॥

Durāsadānarînugrāndhritervisvasajanmanaḣ /
bhogānbhognaivāheyāāndhyāsyāpanna durlabhā //23//

Translation :

As the inborn, inveterate and long-standing enemy of fortitude, courage and confidence among sentient beings, it is impossible to annihilate carnal passions by the enjoyment of resulting pleasures and longings (for the good things of life).

नान्तरज्ञाः श्रियो जातु प्रियैरासां न भूयते ।
आसक्तास्तास्वमी मूढा वामशीला हि जन्तवः ॥२४॥

Nāntarajñāḣ śriyo jātu priyairāsāṃ na bhûyate /
āsaktāstāsvamî mûdhā vāmasîla hi jantavaḣ //24//

Translation :

When the desire for amassing fortune for its own sake becomes the dominating passion (bottomless perdition), such obsessed infatuated individuals may, indeed, be classed as being on the wrong side of discipline and morality by their own character.

कोऽपवादः स्तुतिपदे यदशीलेषु चञ्चलाः ।
साधुवृत्तानपि क्षुद्रा विक्षिपन्त्येव संपदः ॥२५॥

Ko (ʃ) pavādaḣ stutipade yadisîleśu cañcalāḣ /
sādhuvrittānapi kśudrā vikśipantyeva saṃpadaḣ //25//

Translation :

Where is the calumny (censure) if one spends vile and changeful fortune to good and purposeful ends ? It is a pity, however, that even well-disposed persons waste their wealth in a state of confusion like mad man without plan and programme.

कृतवानन्यदेहेषु कर्ता च विधुरं मनः ।
अप्रियैरिव संयोगो विप्रयोगः प्रियैः सह ॥२६॥

Kritavānanyadeheṣu kartā ca vidhuraṃ manaḥ /
apriyairiva saṃyogo viprayogaḥ priyaiḥ saha //26//

Translation :

Seeing how coming together (intimate union) with the desirable person and seperation (dissociation) from the beloved person would affect the bereaved mind, the actor should behave with other individuals by making himself an example (to guide others).

N.B. The construction of this stanza seems to be influenced by Face II lines 1–14 of the inscription of king Māna-deva on the Victory Pillar of Cāngu-Nārāyaṇa (vide Appendix for its translation).

शून्यमाकीर्णतामेती तुल्यं व्यसनमुत्सवैः ।
विप्रलम्भोऽपि लाभाय सति प्रियसमागमे ॥२७॥

Śûnyamākîrṇatāmeti tulyaṃ vyasanamutsavaiḥ /
vipralambho (ऽ)pi lābhāya sati priyasamāgame //27//

Translation :

The vacuum becomes filled up, when we come into contact with those whom we love and achieve what we desire. Even deceit can pass for celebration when the trick of lies (false statements) brings out its own profit (gain).

तदा रम्याण्यरम्याणि प्रियाः शल्यं तदासवः ।
तदैकाकी सबन्धुः सन्निष्टेन रहितो यदाः ॥२८॥

Tadā ramyāṇyaramyāṇi priyāḥ śalyam tadāsavaḥ /
tadaikākî savandhuḥ sanniśṭena rahito yadā //28//

Translation :

What is fair becomes foul and what is healthful in our physcial frame becomes painful when a foreign body (a spear, javelin or dart or any cause of poignant grief) enters it, which makes it a cause for fomentation and surgical operation. Lacking the favourite god (of Āgama) within our heart a man feels alone, though he may be surrounded by friends and relatives.

N.B. This advice by the god of Nigama (Indra) to Arjuna to see God through his own eyes in the scheme of esoteric worship seems to be a unique contribution of Bhāravi to the world of fanatics who claimed that their sectarian gods were absolute.

युक्तः प्रमाद्यसि हितादपेत परितप्यसे ।
यदि नेष्टात्मनः पोडा मा सञ्जि भवता जने ॥२९॥

Yuktaḣ pramādyasi hitādapetaḣ paritapyase /
yedi nestātmanaḣ pîdā mā sañji bhavatā jane //29//

Translation :

O ! saint, who has become one with the Supreme Spirit !! It is all too natural for you to get intoxicated with success when you get everything to your heart's desire, and to get worried and sorrowful when all that (gave you happiness) vanishes. With this in view it would be well for you to take example from what gives you pain before you inflict pain on other people.

जन्मिनोऽस्य स्थितिं विद्वांल्लक्ष्मीमिव चलाचलाम् ।
भवान्मा स्म वधीन्न्याय्ये न्यायाधीना हि साधवः ॥३०॥

Janmino (ऽ) sya sthitiṃ vidvaṇllaksmîmiva calācalām /
bhavānmā sma vadhînnyāyye nyāyādhînā hi sādhavaḣ //30//

Translation :

Knowing how the law of nature conditions the existence of all those who take their birth (in thier cosmic world), which is as fickle as fortune, O Wise one ! do not kill the universal rule of this nature's law; for, good men must respect and abide by inexorable system of this law.

N.B. Mallinātha's gloss of "Nyāyadhārā" (= fitness, proriety or decorum according to the rule prescribed in Manusmriti) does not convey Bhāravi's concept of the universal rule of nature's law meant by

Nyāyādhînāh (= under the universal rule of nature's law). Evidently, this law of nature rules out the concept of Bhagavadgîtā (Canto II. 27) .We have already referred to the sense of justice prevailing in the court of king Duryodhana. The Judicial Customs of Nepal (Part I) shows how the sense of justice developed from the night-fold paths of law, equity, justice, virtue, righteousness, honesty and Five Moralities to Samyak Society by conquering the original. sin of Virûpākśa-kāma-jaṭilatā (Oedipus Complex) inherent in the nature of man in and through the means of Kāranapûjā (worship of reason and the flow of soul) with our Licchavi period of the fifth century A.D. (Vide The Judicial Customs of Nepal).

विजहीहि रणोत्साहं मा पतः साधु नीनशः ।
उच्छेदं जन्मनः कर्तुमेधि शान्तस्तपोधन ॥३१॥

Vijahîhi raṇotśahaṃ mā tapaḣ sādhu nînaśaḣ /
ucchedaṃ janmanaḣ kartumedhi śāntastapodhana //31//

Translation :

Give up your ambition of winning victories in war; devote yourself to the warmth of ascetical practices in a spirit of total renunciation : do not kill its spirit and content.

O ascetic rich in penance ! the path of peace is the only way to eradicate the lurking sense of sin associated with our birth.

जीयन्तां दुर्जया देहे रिपवश्चक्षुरादयः ।
जितेषुननु लोकोऽयं तेषु कृत्स्नस्त्वया जितः ॥३२॥

Jîyātam durjayā dehe ripavaścakṣurādayaḣ /
jiteṣunanu loko(ऽ)yaṃ tesu kritsnastvayā jitaḣ //32//

Translation :

Conquer the unquerable enemies like, for example, your eyes (the visual factors) that form part of your body. Indeed, you will have achieved victory over the entire body of sin in the world if you conquer the (six) enemies within yourself.

परवानर्थसंसिध्यौ नीचैर्वृत्तिरपत्रय :।
अविधेयेन्द्रियः पुंसां गौरवैति विधेयताम् ॥३३॥

Paravānarthasaṃsiddhau nîcairvrittirapatrapaḣ /
avidheyendriyaḣ puṃsāṃ gauravaiti vidheyatām //33//

Translation :

Only such persons of low profession who, for their own self-interest and subsistence, are compelled to work like bulls under the yoke of other people, do not find themselves in a position to control their passions, and they behave like brutes.

N.B. Mallināṭha's gloss·" nîcavritti"(= low professions like drawing carts and bearing burdens) does not give us the poet's force of adjective in the use of the word "nîcais" (low, bowing down humbly or in a depressed spirit) to qualify "vritti" (= profession or means of subsistence e.g. "nîcairgacchasyuparica-ca dasa cakranemikrameṇa" Meghadûta 109. 2).

श्वस्त्वया सुखसंवित्तिः स्मरणीयाधुनातनी ।
इति स्वप्नोपमान्मत्वा कामान्मा गास्तदंगताम् ॥३४॥

Śvastvayā sukhasaṃvittiḣ smaraṇîyādhunātanî //
iti svapnopamānmatvā kāmānmā gāstadangatām //34//

Translation :

Remembering how personal happiness of today will vanish like dream tomorow, will you decide right now not to fall into the mess of passions (of opulent minority to the neglect of the needs of the needy majority of people) !

श्रद्धेया विप्रलब्धारः प्रिया विप्रियकारिणः ।
सुदुस्त्यजास्त्यजन्तोऽपि कामाः कष्टा हि शत्रवः ।३५॥

Śraddheyā vipralavdhāraḣ priyā vipriyakāriṇaḣ /
sudustyajyastyajanto(ऽ)pi kāmāḣ kaṣṭā hi śatravaḣ //35//

Translation :

What makes the worshipful and respectable persons appear deceitful; and what is wholesome and fair appear foul; and what sticks to our mortal existence though it deserves to be shunned, all these are our enemies namely, cupidity and lustful pain consequent upon the desire to achieve the means and end of Eros.

विविक्तेऽस्मिन्नगे भूयः प्लाविते जन्हुकन्यया ।
प्रत्यासीदति मुक्तिस्त्वां पुरा मा भूरुदायुधः ॥३६॥

Vivikte (?) sminnage bhûyaḥ plāvite Jahnukanyayā /
pratyāsîdati muktistvāṃ purā mā bhûrudāyudhaḥ //36//

Translation :

There is no reason why you should be armed to the teeth over this lonely and uninhabited mountain (of Indrakîla), which is made sacred for the second time by the daughter of king Jahnu (river) and where you are near deliverance (from all the ills of mortal existence).

व्याहृत्य मरुतां पत्याविति वाचमवस्थिते ।
वचः प्रश्रयगम्भीरमथोवाच कपिध्वजः ॥३७॥

Vyāhritya marutāṃ patyāviti vācamavasthite /
vacaḥ praśrayagambhîramathovāca Kapidhvajaḥ //37//

Translation :

As the king of Maruta (wind-god) remained silent after delivering the above-said speech, the flyer of monkey-imprinted banner (Arjuna) very politely spoke the following profound word.

प्रसादरम्यमोजस्वि गरीयो लाघवान्वितम् ।
साकाङ्क्षमनुपस्कारं विष्वग्गति निराकुलम् ॥३८॥

Prasādaramyamojasvi garîyo lāghavānvitam /
sākānkśamanupaskāraṃ visvaggati nirākulam //38//

Translation :

Beautifully propitious, deep without verbosity, faultlessly wholesome, free from abstract reasoning (of logic) and universally acceptable because they gave concrete form to the language of the heart,.......

न्यायनिर्णीतसारत्वान्निरपेक्षमिवागमे ।
अप्रकम्प्यतयान्येषामाम्नायवचनोपमम् ॥३९॥

Nyāyanirṇîtasāratvānnirpekṣamivāgame /
aprakampyatayānyeṣāmāmnāyavacanopamam //39//

Translation :

The facts of material substance established after a thorough examination of the four kinds of truth recognised by the Naiyāyikas (logicians) and proved as infallible and irrefutable as the principles and practices of Āgama (esoteric worship associated with Kāraṇapûjā or the worship of reason) and like the incomprehensible words of the Vedas distilled from a thorough analysis of the Brāhmaṇas and Upanisadas.

N.B. It is remarkable that Mr. V.S. Āpte in his Sanskrit-English dictionary has taken this stanza as an example to explain the science of logic founded by saint Gautama.

However, the critics do not seem to be aware of Bhāravi's pun on the name of "Nirapeksa" (GNI IX p. 12) whose Brāhmannic precepts were contrary to the principles and practices of the esoteric worship known as Āgama vis-a-vis Nigama. As a comparative study of Anuparama's unqualified eulogium of Dvaipāyana, this assessment of the religious and cultural situation of the 4th to the beginning of circa 6th century seems to be incomparable. (Vide Assessment of Anuparama's eulogium to Dvaipāyana contained in The Judicial Customs of Nepal Part I. Chapter XIV. Also see the Appendix).

अलङ्घ्यत्वाज्जनैरन्यैः क्षुभितोवदन्वदूर्जितम् ।
औदार्यादर्थसंपत्तेः शान्तं चित्तमृषेरिव ॥४०॥

Alañghyatvājjanairanyaiḣ kṣubhitodanvadûrjitam /
audāryādarthasampatteḣ śāntam cittamriṣeriva //40//

Translation :

Unfordable by other people like the agitated waves of the ocean, benevolent and magnanimous in economic affluence and peaceful and calm like the mind of a saint,

इदमीदृग्गुणोपेतं लब्धावसरसाधनम् ।
व्याकुर्यात्कः प्रियं वाक्यं यो वक्ता नेदृगाशयः ॥४१॥

Idamîdrigguṇopetaṃ lavdhāvasarasādhanam /
vyākuryatkaḣ priyaṃ vākyaṃ yo vaktā nedrigāsayah //41//

Translation :

After having achieved all the above-said merits with the best means available it would be useful to speak the truth when opportunity presents itself. Whoever sugarcoats his words and minces matters with all the above qualifications to suit the need of the hour could not be said to speak his mind freely and frankly.

न ज्ञातं तात यत्नस्य पौर्वापर्यममुष्य ते ।
शासितुं येन मां धर्मं मुनिभिस्तुल्यमिच्छसि ॥४२॥

Na jñataṃ tāta yatnasya paurvāparyamamuṣya te /
śāsituṃ yena māṃ dharmaṃ munibhistulyamicchasi //42//

Tneslation :

O brother ! you do not seem to know the tradition of "varṇāśrama-dharma" (the Brāhmannic law applied to the four castes namely Brāhmana, Kṣatria, Vaiśya and Śûdra) at the back of these efforts of mine. The norm of law that you advised me to follow would inevitably lead me to the path of Munis (saints like Śākyamuni or Mahāvîıa who prescribed the path of Nirvāṇa as the goal for mankind).

अविज्ञातप्रबन्धस्य बचो वाचस्पतेरपि ।
व्रजत्यफलतामेव नयद्रुह इवेहितम् ॥४३॥

Avijñātapravandhasya vaco vācaspaterapi /
vrajatyaphalatāmeva nayadruha ivehitaṃ //43//

Translation :

Without the knowledge of of religious and social background, even the words of the Master of Speech would find itself into conflict with the concomitant situation and become fruitless against the logic of events.

श्रेयसोऽस्यते तात वचसो नास्मि भाजनम् ।
नभसः स्फुटतारस्य रात्रेरिव विपर्ययः ॥४४॥

Śreyaso (ऽ) sya te tāta vacaso nāsmi bhājanaṃ /
nabhasaḥ sphuṭatārasya rātreriva viparyayaḥ //44//

Translation :

O Respected Brother ! However wholesome and useful may be your advice, this means is not expedient to the values I represent in the context of my present situation like, for instance, the twinkling of the stars in course of day.

N.B. Here clearly we have a reference to the expediency in means mentioned in Saddharma-puṇdarika-sûtra (the White Lotus sûtra of true law).

क्षत्रियस्तनयः पाण्डोरहं पार्थो धनञ्जयः ।
स्थितः प्रास्तस्य दायादैर्भ्रातुर्ज्येष्ठस्य शासने ॥४५॥

Kśattriyastanayaḥ Pāṇdorahaṃ Partho Dhananjayaḥ /
Sthitaḥ prāstasya dāyādairbhrāturjyeśṭhasya śāsane //45//

Translation :

I am the son of (king) Pāṇdu of the caste of Kṣatriya born to his eldest wife Kuntî. My name is Dhananjaya (winner of wealth by conquering the country of Uttarakurus). Banished by our own relatives into exile from our inheritence, I have been abiding under the rule of my eldest brother (Yudhiśṭhira).

N.B. It is interesting how Mallinātha gives preference to the wife of Brāhmana of Naimiśāraṇye known by the name of Prithā in generating Kṣatriyas to the neglect of the gallant Śivis (followers of the cult of Śiva) in Madra-deśa. Śākala (Pali Śāgala) was the capital of the Madras way back in the 6th century B.C. According to the ancient texts, the Madras appeared to have occupied the modern district of Sialkot between the rivers Chenab and Rāvî or, according to Cunnigham, between the rivers Jhelum and Rāvî. It was known to the Chinese as She-chich-lo and to Patañjali as Bālhikagrama. It was the birthplace of Sāvitrî and Satyavāna. Bhāravi refers to the Bālhikas repeatedly in Kirātārjunîye as gallant fighters Evidently the geographical knowledge of the poet was far in advance of his commentator Mallinātha.

कृष्णाद्वैपायनावेशाद्बिभर्मि व्रतमीदृशम् ।
भृशमाराधने यत्तः स्वाराध्यस्य मरुत्वतः ॥४६॥

Krișhṇa-Dvaipāyanāveśādvibharmi vratamîdriśam /
bhriśamarādhane yattaḥ svārādhyasya marutvataḥ //46//

Translation :

I have undertaken this religious vow (of contradictions) with my meditations fixed on the king of gods under the direct advice of Kriśhṇa-Dvaipāyana.

N.B. This name of Krishṇa Dvaipāyana seems to be borrowed by Bhāravi from Mûlasarvastivāda Vinaya, where it is said that his dark colour became golden when Gautama testified to his purity. M. Levi's Appendix to *Le Nepal* quotes from this Buddhistic document to show how Śākyamuni and Ānanda visited the valley of Nepal to pay respects to the haloed places and meet their kinsmen who had taken refuge under Kirānta king Jitādasti after the attack of Virûḍhaka on Kapilvastu. The validity of the accounts have been proved by concrete evidences of arson in our present exacavations of Kapilvastu.

However, according to the epic of Bhārata and Anuparama's inscription Dvaipāyana was the son of the fisherwoman Satyavatî and saint Parāsara. From all accounts Āgama and sacrificial schools were older than Vyāsa (Vide Summary of this Canto).

दुरक्षान्दीव्यता राज्ञा राज्यमात्मा वयं वधूः ।
नीतानि पणतां नूनमीदृशी भवितव्यता ॥४७॥

Durakṣāndivatā rajnā rājyamātmā vayaṃ vadhûh /
nitāni paṇatāṃ nūnamidriśî bhavitavyatā //47//

Translation :

While revelling himself in a game of dice, whose lidos were loaded with false dies, the king staked his kingdom, himself, ourselves and common wife and lost the wager like pana (which is equal to 80 cowries in Nepalese inscriptions). This is the inevitability of our tragic situation.

तेनानुजसहायेन द्रौपद्या च मया विना ।
भृशमायामियामासु यामिनीष्वभितप्यते ॥४८॥

Tenānujasahāyena Draupadyā ca mayā vinā /
Bhriśamāyāmiyāmāsu yaminîṣvabhitapyate //48//

Translation :

In my absence he (king Yudhisṭhira) with all his three brothers including Draupadî will feel intensely benighted during every moment of the long night like the oppressive pall of darkness itself.

हृतोत्तरीयां प्रसभं सभायामागतह्रियः ।
मर्मच्छिदा नो वचसा निरतक्षन्नरातयः ॥४९॥

Hritottarîyāṃ prasabhaṃ sabhāyāmāgatahriyaḣ /
marmacchidā no vacasā niratakśannarātayaḣ //49//

Translation :

Carried to the Assembly Hall by force in a state of utter helplessness and defeat, and stripping her (Draupadî) to the gloating gaze of our enemies, the most filthy language used to the jeering of the members of the Assembly went deep into heart (added insult to injury).

उपाधत्त सपत्नेषु कृष्णाया गुरुसंनिधौ ।
भावमानयने सत्याः सत्यंकारमिवान्तकः ॥५०॥

Upādhatta sapatneṣu Kriṣṇayā gurusannidhau/
bhāvamānayane satyāḣ satyaṃkāramivāntakaḣ //50//

Translation :

The sadistic cruelty of ideas behind these extremes of insults offered to Kriṣna and her husbands in the presence of old and venerable persons (like Bhiṣma and Droṇa) were the very negation of "plighted troth" and were in the nature of an invitation to Death itself.

तामैक्षन्त क्षणं सभ्या दुःशासन पुरोगमाम् ।
अभिसायार्कमावृत्तां छायामिव महातरोः ॥५१॥

Tāmaikṣanta kṣaṇaṃ sabhyā Duḣsāsana purogamāṃ /
abhisāyarkamāvrittaṃ chhāyāmiva mahātaroḣ //51//

Translation :

For a while some of the same and civilised senators showed their deference and sense of civility by placing themselves directly before Duḣsāsana like the great and gigantic trees casting their long shadows with the setting sun (so that they may shield Draupadî from the shameful and sinful act of Duḣsāsana in dragging and stripping before the Assembly).

N.B. Mallinātha's gloss of "puraḣzaram" (= by going ahead) seems to be a poor substitute for the poet's "purogamān" (= by placing themselves before the eyes to shield Draupadî from her shame and sorrow). The indeclinable "puras"+"gam" is appropriate and sanctioned by usage in the present context.

अयथार्थक्रियारम्भैः पतिभिः किं निरीक्षितैः ॥
अरुध्येतामितीवास्या नयने बाष्पवारिणा ॥५२॥

Ayathārthakriyārambhaiḣ patibhiḣ kiṃ nirīkṣitaiḣ /
arudhyetāmitīvāsyā nayane vāṣpavāriṇā //52//

Transaltion :

In such a unpredictable and disgraceful beginning of a sadistic action, where was the glory of bearing eye-sights for husbands in witnessing such a pitiable scene ? The ultimate relief was provided by tears which covered the eyes of Draupadî in her present state of helplessness.

N.B. Mallinātha's gloss of "tavekṣitaiḣ" (=seeing by or bearing witness) for the poet's "nirikśîtaih"(=to the gaze of their husbands or beholding) to show the helplessness of her husbands in the face of the insults offered. e.g. "nirîksya" saṃraṃbha etc. Canto III. 21.

सोढवान्नो दशामन्त्यां ज्यायानेव गुणप्रियः ।
सुलभो हि द्विषां भङ्गो दुर्लभा सत्स्ववाच्यता ॥५३॥

Soḍhavānno daśāmantyāṃ jyāyāneva guṇapriyaḣ /
sulabho hi dviśāṃ bhañgo durlabhā satśvavācyatā //53//

Translation :

My eldest brother (king Yudhiśṭhira), who prizes virtues and merits, suffers these indignities voluntarily; for, he believes that destruction of enemies is an easy matter whereas the breach of trust and promise made by oneself is irremediable under all circumstances.

स्थित्यतिक्रान्तभीरूणि स्वच्छान्याकुलितान्यपि ।
तोयानि तोयराशीनां मनांसि च मनस्विनाम् ॥५४॥

Sthityatikrāntabhîrûṇi svacchānyākulitānyapi /
toyāni toyarāśînāṃ manāṃsi ca manasvināṃ //54//

Translation :

Like the prancing waves of the ocean, whose water ebbs and flows within itself, the mind of the high-minded persons keeps within its own bounds (though it may be disturbed temporarily).

N.B. It is remarkable that Bhāravi conceived of mind as the essence of matter which is comparable to the waves of the ocean. He seems to follow the concept of Nyāya philosophy to the effect that "Manas" (mind) is a "drabya" (material) which is different from "ātman" (soul).

धार्तराष्ट्रैः सह प्रीतिर्वैरमस्मास्वसूयत ।
असन्मैत्री हि दोषाय तटच्छायेव सेविता ॥५५॥

Dhārtarāṣṭraiḣ saha prîtirvairamasmāsvasûyata /
asanmaittri hi doṣāya taṭacchāyeva sevitā //55//

Translation :

Our blood-relationship with the sons of (king)Dhritarāṣṭra has become the cause of animosity (enmity) between our two families. Indeed, we are sorry to have fallen victims to the evils of bad company like, for example, taking shelter behind the shifting shadows of the slopes on the brink of the ocean.

N.B. Mallinātha's gloss of "kulocchāya" (= shadows on the shores of the river) do not convey Bhāravi's idea "taṭacchāyayeva" (like the shifting shadows on the slopes of the shore at the conjuction of the river and the ocean).

अपवादादभीतस्य समस्य गुणदोषयोः ।
असद्वृत्तेरहोवृत्तं दुर्विभाव्यं विधेरिव ॥५६॥

Apavādādabhîtasya samasya guṇadoṣayoḣ /
asadvritterahovrittaṃ durvibhāvyaṃ vidheriva //56//

Translation :

Afraid of calumny and malicious defamations, and considering the merits and demerits on balance, it is difficult to judge the good and bad attitude of men from their appearance like the unpredictable workings of destiny; which cannot be anticipated.

N.B. Mallinātha's gloss of "durvıbhava"(bad attitude of the three main divisions of Bhāva, anubhāva and vybhicāri-bhāva op cit) does not give Bhāravi's sense "duıvibhāvyam" (= inscrutable or unfathomable or difficult to anticipate e.g. "nisarga durvodha Canto I.6.)

ध्वंसेत हृदयं सद्यः परिभूतस्य मे परैः ।
यद्यमर्षः प्रतीकारं भुजालम्बं न लम्भयेत् ॥५७॥

Dhvaṃseta hridayaṃ sadyah paribhûtasya me paraiḣ /
yadyamarṣaḣ pratîkāraṃ bhujālamvaṃ na lambhayet //57//

Translation :

Suffering, as I do, from the spurns of my enemies, it is natural for me to be inclined to destructive ends, though it is said (in scriptures) that one should not resort to arms in a spirit of intolerance and jealousy or purposes of revenge.

अवधूयारिभिर्नीता हरिणैस्तुल्यरूपताम् ।
अन्योन्यस्यापि जिह्रीमः किं पुनः सहवासिनाम् ॥५८॥

Avadhûyāribhirnîtā hariṇaistulyarûpatām /
anyonyasyāpi jihrîmaḣ kiṃ punaḣ sahavāsināṃ //58//

Translation :

Discarded and defeated by the trick of our enemies, we have been reduced to the sorry plight like the statue of a deer; so much so that we have become the object of ridicule of other people not to speak of those who depend upon us for their subsistence. N.B. Mallinātha's gloss of "hariṇaistulyavrittitām" (=we have been reduced to the subsistence or profession of a helpless deer) does not seem to take note of the part played by the deer in the legends of the Himalayas from the period of Śākyamuni down to the period of Bhāravi. The deer in Indian literature are said to be of five kinds bearing pale, whitish, reddish, yellowish and white colour and with beautiful eyes like those of ravishing women. On the whole they are regarded as persecuted animals. In Śāivite literature it is the Golden Deer that lures and works out the salvation of Virûpākśa. There may be reference here to the statue of the deer squatting before Virûpakśa and his mother, Hû-sa close to the temple of Paśupati (vide The Judicial Customs of Nepal Part I Plates VII and XVI with the running commentary). It is a common sight in early sculptures to see the Eight-spoked Wheel of Dharma-cakra flanked by statues of deer in the monasteries of Nepal, Tibet and China. In the legend of the epic of Rāmāyaṇa, it is the "golden deer" that plays its part in the elopement of Sitā. By restoing Bhāravi to his original of "hariṇaistulya-rûpatām" (=like the statues of deer) we get an overall picture of how the statue of deer was being represented in Śaivite, Buddhistic statues and literature.

शक्तिवैकल्यनम्रस्य निःसारत्वाल्लघीयसः ।
जन्मिनो मानहीनस्य तृणस्य च समा गतिः ॥५६॥

Śaktivaikalyanamrasya niḥsāratvāllaghîyasaḥ /
janmino mānahînasya triṇasya ca samā gatiḥ //59//

Translation :

Politeness due to lack of power and incompetence, obsequiousness due to weakness and want of self-respect among those who have taken birth in this world are as worthless as straws (grass).

N.B. The play on the word "māna" (= pride, self-respect and self-reliance) seems to be very significant and worthy of the grandson of king Māna-deva I.

अलङ्घ्यं तत्तदुद्वीक्ष यदेवोच्चैर्महीभृताम् ।
प्रियतां ज्यायसीं मा गान्महतां केन तुङ्गता ॥६०॥

Alanghyaṃ tattadudvîkṣya yadevoccairmahîbhritāṃ
priyatāṃ jyāyasîṃ mā gānmahatāṃ kena tuñgatā //60//

Translation :

Seeing how impassable and impregnable are the hoary peaks of the gigantic mountains, is it not useful to judge and respect the progressive deeds of the confederation of the Himalayan kings with the high title of Deva ?

N.B. Mallinātha's gloss "yadyeduccai" (=incapable of being scaled due to their heights) does not seem to take note of the fact that the hoary heights of the Himalayas were not only unscalable but they were also impregnable under the protection of the leader of the confederation of Himalayan kings with the title of "Deva" e.g. Vrsa-deva, Śañkra deva, Dharmma-deva ,and Māna-deva.

तावदाश्रीयते लक्ष्म्या तावदस्य स्थिरं यशः ।
पुरुषस्तावदेवासौ यावन्मानान्न हीयते ॥६१॥

Tāvadāśrîyate lakśmyā tāvadasya sthiraṃ yaśah /
puruṣastāvadevāsau yāvanmānānna hîyate //61//

Translation :

Fortune favours those persons as long as their glorious reputation lasts as a useful entity for men to follow. That man deserves the title of "Deva" as long as he does not lose self-respect (to deserve respectful consideration).

N.B. Thus we see that the restoration of Bhāravi in stanza 60 yields precise significance. There was no "divine right of kings in the restless aristocracy of Paśupati-bhaṭṭārakas. The most deserving leader was honoured with the title of "deva". The play on the word "māna" shows clearly that the reference is to the gallant spirit of king Māna deva I.

स पुमानर्थवज्जन्मा यस्य नाम्नि पुरःस्थिते ।
नान्यामङ्गुलिमभ्येति संख्यायामुद्यताङ्गुलिः ॥६२॥

Sa pumānarthavajjanmā yasya nāmni purahsthite /
nānyāmañgulimabhyeti saṃkhyāyāmudyatañgulih //62//

Translation :

He is, indeed, a He-man who justifies his existence by occupying a front position among men. It is a truism that the thumb leads the other fingers in matters of calculation.

दुरासदवनज्यायान्गम्यस्तुङ्गोऽपि भूधरः ।
न जहाति महौजस्कं मानप्रांशुमलङ्घ्यता ॥६३॥

Durāsadavanajyāyāngamyastuñgo(ऽ)pi bhûdharah /
na jahāti mahaujaskaṃ mānaprāmśumalañghyatā //63//

Translation :

The mountains in the maze of overgrown forests, though they appear unassailable from distance, are negotiable (from close quarters), not so the morning twilight of self-respecting persons, whose ambitious designs broaden (into day) to bafile men by their invincibility (like the treeless and stark Himalayan giants).

गुरून्कुर्वन्ति ते वंश्यानन्वर्था तैर्वसुंधरा ।
येषां यशांसि शुक्लानि ह्लेपयन्तीन्दुमण्डलम् ॥६४॥

Gurûnkurvanti te vaṃśyānanvarthā tairvasuṇdharā /
yeṣāṃ yaśāmsi śuklāni hrepayantîndumaṇḍalaṃ //64//

Translation :

Those people alone add weight to their heraldry by making the earth yield her substance in the form of wealth, whose spotlessly white reputation put the halo round the moon into shame.

N.B. Mallinātha's gloss of "subhrāṇi" (= white radiance) does not seem to be any improvement upon Bhāravi's "sûklāni" (= spotlessly white) to qualify the Ikṣvāku dynasty of Raghu and Dilîpa, when the poet's mother Vijayavatīspeaks in the same term about the Lichhavi dynasty of Nepal (Vide Introduction). On the other hand, the poet has put up the tradition of Kirātas vis-a-vis the unfounded chronology of Sagara, which appears for the first time in the Inscription of king Vasanta deva (op. cit).

उदाहरणमाशीःषु प्रथमे ते मनस्विनाम् ।
शुष्केऽशनिरिवामर्षो यैररातिषु पात्यते ॥६५॥

Udāharaṇamāśiḣṣu prathame te mansvinām /
śuṣke(ऽ)śanirivāmarṣo yairarātiṣu pātyate //65//

Translation :

He becomes an example of self-respecting person, who leads the van of warriors in the battle-field in a mood of anger and emulation by striking his enemies with the sharp end of his missiles like a flash of lightning.

न सुखं प्रार्थये नार्थमुदन्वद्वीचिचञ्चलम् ।
न चानित्याशनेस्त्रस्यन्विविक्तं ब्रह्मणः पदम् ॥६६॥

Na sukhaṃ prārthaye nārthamudanvadvîcicañcalaṃ /
na cānityāśanestrasyanvivikataṃ Brahmaṇaḣ padaṃ //66//

Translation :

I am not praying for the good things and happiness of life nor for wealth, which is as transitory and changeful as the waves of the sea in a beach. Neither am I afraid of the unsubstantiality of our mortal existence to seek to achieve the rank and position of Brāhmaṇaḣ devoted to the quest of the Supreme Spirit.

N.B. Mallinātha's gloss of "nānityātāsane" (= destructible) for the poet's original of "na cānityā" (=nor for the unsubstantial).

प्रमार्ष्टुमयशः पंकमिच्छामि छद्‌मना गतम् ।
वैधव्यतापितारातिवनितालोचनाम्बुभिः ॥६७॥

Pramārṣṭumayaśaḣ pañkamicchāmi chhadmanā gataṃ /
vaidhavyatāpitārātivanitālocanāmvubhiḣ //67//

Translaiton :

Victim of fraud, it is my will and purpose to wash away the mud of bad reputation by the remorseful tears flowing out of the eyes of the widowed wives of my enemies.

N.B. Mallinātha's glosses of "miccheyam" (=it is my wish) and "chhadmanākritam" (= done by fraud) do not express the will and purpose of Arjuna implied by the poet's original of "icchāmi" and "cchadmanāgatam" as it is being translated by us.

अवहस्येऽथवा सद्‌भिः प्रमादो वास्तु मे धियः ।
अस्थानविहितायासः कामं जिह्रेतु मा भवान् ॥६८॥

Avahasye(ऽ)thavā sadbhiḣ pramādo vāstu me dhiyaḣ /
asthānavihitāyāsaḣ kāmaṃ jihretu mā bhavān //68//

Translation :

Though it may excite derisive smile from Pundits, yet it has become the obsession of my mind. O Respected Man ! do not be offended because your effort has been misplaced (in pursuading me to do the wrong thing at this critical juncture of my life).

N.B. Mallinātha's gloss of ''apahasya'' (=uproarious laughter) seems to be borrowed from the six kinds of laughter namely "smitaṃ" (gentle smile), "hasita" (a smile showing the teeth to some extent), "vihasita" (laughing with a soft sound), "upahasita" (laughter by shaking the head), "apahasita" (uproarious laughter accompanied by tears) and "atihasita" (convulsive laughter accompanied by the shaking of the entire body). The first two variety is attributed to people of high station, the second two variety to the men of middle station of life whereas the last two are attributed to people of the lowest station of life. Bhāravi introduces a new variety of derisive laughter (avahasita). Lollaṭa introduces an infinite variety of laughter. According to an Egyptian proverb "every backbone takes on laughter and every tooth is exposed."

वंशलक्ष्मीमनुद्धृत्य समुच्छेदेनविद्विषाम् ।
निर्वाणमपि मन्येऽहमन्तरायं जयश्रियः ॥६९॥

Vaṃśalakṣmîmanuddhritya samucchedenavidviṣām /
nirvāṇamapi manye(ऽ)hamantarāyaṃ jayaśriyaḣ //69//

Translation :

So long as I am not in a position to restore the prestige and prosperity of our dynasty by the utter annihilation of our enemies, I would be inclined to feel that even the achievement of "Nirvāṇa" (liberation or blowing out) is an impediment to the achievement of a victorious career.

N.B. It is remarkable that V.S. Āpte quotes this very stanza from Bhāravi to explain "Nirvāṇa" as the final liberation or emancipation from matter and reunion with the Supreme Spirit.

अजन्मा पुरुषस्तावद्गतासुस्तृणमेव वा ।
यावन्नेषुभिरादत्ते विलुप्तमरिभिर्यशः ॥७०॥

Ajanmā puruṣastāvadgatāsustriṇameva vā /
yāvanneṣubhirādatte viluptamaribhiryaśaḣ //70//

Translation :

The person is still-born or as good as a dead blade of grass till such time as he justifies his existence and fulfills himself by putting an end to his enemies by resort to arms.

अनिर्जयेन द्विषतां यस्यामर्षः प्रशाम्यति ।
पुरुषोक्तिः कथं तस्मिन्ब्रूहि त्वं तु तपोधन ॥७१॥

Anirjayena dviṣatāṃ yasyāmarṣaḥ praśāmyait /
puruṣoktiḥ kathaṃ tasminvrahi tvaṃ tu tapodhana //71//

Translation :

Will you enlighten me, O ascetic rich in the performance of penitential practices ! how, on the contrary, you could class such a (cowardly) person in the category of man, whose anger (spirit of emulation) sobers down without achieving victory over his inveterete enemies ?

N.B. The poet's use of the indeclinable "tu" (= on the contrary) as an adversative particle appears more appropriate than Mallinātha's "hi" (= for or because expressing a logical reason).

कृतं पुरुषशब्देन जातिमात्रावलम्बिना ।
योऽङ्गीकृतगुणैः श्लाघ्यः सविस्मयमुदाहृतः ॥७२॥

Kritaṃ puruṣaśavdena jātimātrāvalamvinā /
yo(ऽ)ñgîkritaguṇaiḥ ślāghyaḥ savismayamudāhritaḥ //72//

Translation :

Does the word superman embrace a caste or class of persons already known for their (peaceful or warlike) callings (like, for examples, the Brāhmaṇas and Kṣatriyas) ? That person alone deserves citations, who distinguishes himself by his qualities (of head and heart) and heroic actions (for all to follow) to the amazement of all people.

ग्रसमानमिवौजांसि सदसा गौरवेरितम् ।
नाम यस्याभिनन्दन्ति द्विषोऽपि समतः पुमान् ॥७३॥

Grasamānamivaujāṃsi sadasā gauraveritaṃ /
nāma yasyābhinandanti dviso(ऽ) pi samataḣ pumān //73//

Translation :

That individual is by unanimous verdict a superman, whose will to power and bravery finds most honorable mention in a spell-bound assembly and whose name is respected even by his adversaries.

N.B. Mallinātha's gloss of "pumānpumān" (= man among the caste of Kṣatriyas) overlooks Bhāravi's democratic expression of "samataḣ pumān" (= great man by the unanimous verdict of the Assembly).

यथाप्रतिज्ञं द्विषतां युधि प्रतिचिकीर्षया ।
मामेवाध्येति नृपतिस्तृष्यन्निव जलाञ्जलिम् ॥७४॥

Yathāpratijñaṃ dviśatāṃ yudhi praticikîrśayā /
māmevādhyeti nripatistriśyanniva jalānjaliṃ //74//

Translation :

I am duty-bound to slake off the thirst of revenge by the palmful of water even as the oath was administered by the king (Yudhiśṭhira) with my vow to do unto the enemies in the battle-field (as they have done to us in gambling).

N.B. The poet's vocative use of the expression "māme vādhyeti" etc. (=binds me with the sacred vow administered with a palmful of water") appears more appropriate than Mallinātha's glosses "māmaivādhyeti" etc.

स वंशस्यावदातस्य शशाङ्कस्येव लाञ्छनम् ।
कृच्छ्रेषु व्यर्थया यत्र भूयते भर्तुराज्ञया ॥७५॥

Sa vaṃśasyāvadātasya śaśāñkasyeva lāncchanaṃ /
kricchreṣu vyarthayā yatra bhûyate bharturājnayā //75//

Translation :

That person, who does not carry out his superior's command in times of danger and difficulty is a stain in the serene dynasty of kings like the dark spots on the moon.

कथं वादियतामर्व्याङ्मुनिता धर्मरोधिनी ।
श्राश्रमानुक्रमः पूर्वैः स्मर्यते न व्यतिक्रमः ॥७६॥

Kathaṃ vādîyatāmarvyāñmunitā dharmarodhinî /
āśramānukramaḣ pûrvaiḣ smaryate na vyatikramaḣ //76//

Translation :

How is it possible for me to reconcile the principles and practices, which are contrary to the precepts of Dharma (varṇāśrama-dharma pertaining to the four stages of life according to their caste and colour) prescribed by the saint (Manu) ? Do I have to think of the law (of caste) in advance or wait for its application in the wake of actions by respecting the law in its breach ?

N.B. Mallinātha seems to be confounded by this stanza, which evidently refers to the four Āśramas (stages of life) prescribed by the Brāhmannic saint Manu to their faithfuls namely, 1. celibacy, 2. marriage, 3. pursuit of the happiness of married life, and 4. renunciation. According to Brāhmannic Dharma-śāstras saint Manu was a Vedic counterpart of Noah, who was saved from the Great Flood by the first incarnation of Viṣṇu as a Fish related in the fable of Matṣya-purāṇa. There are already 14 Manus and the person referred to by Mallinātha is the 7th one known as Vaivasvat Manu who gave the law.

We have pointed out in The Judicial Customs of Nepal Part I how the metrical recension of Manusmriti show that it was compiled about 100 A.D. This is confirmed by Anuparama's inscription (op cit), which mentions Manu as a Brāhmannic prophet who compiled the Dharma-śastras in tune with the Three Vedas vis-a-vis the atheistical teachings of the Saugatas (Buddhists). It is remarkable that Bhāravi's assessment of the concepts of Brāhmaṇa, Nirvāṇa, Vinayas (Buddhistic rules of life) and this law pertaining to the four castes gives us the chronological development of Indian philosophy during the 5th and the first part of the 6th century A.D.

आसक्ता धूरियं रूढा जननी दूरगा च मे ।
तिरस्करोति स्वातन्त्र्यं ज्यायांश्चाचारवान्नृपः ॥७७॥

Āsaktā dhûriyaṃ rûḍhā janani duragā ca me /
tiraskaroti svātantryaṃ jyāyāṃścācāravānnripaḣ //77//

Translation :

The injunctions of my king and elder (brother), who conducts himself according to the disciplines of the four Āśramas (stages of life) as well as my mother, who lives so far away, limit my freedom of action and make me duty-bound to practise this(out of the way penance in contravention of the laws of Manu).

स्वधर्ममनुरुन्धन्ते नातिक्रममरातिभिः ।
पलायन्ते कृतध्वंसा नाहवान्मानशालिनः ॥७८॥

Svadharmamanurundhante nātikramamarātibhiḣ /
palāyante kritadhvaṃsā nāhavānmanaśālinaḣ //78//

Translation :

It is the self-respecting and war-like individuals, who respect the law (of Manu) and justify their existence by staring death in the face and by not showing their back in the battlefield under the heavy batterment of the enemies.

N.B. Evidently there is reference to Māna-deva's victory pillar Inscription (GNI I Face III)where the king takes the vow of a warrior by touching his vow in preference to the cultivation of Five Moralities, and where S. Levi quotes Manu exactly as Mallinātha has done here.

विच्छिन्नाभ्रविलायं वा विलीये नगमूर्धनि ।
आराध्य वा सहस्राक्षमयशःशल्यमुद्धरे ॥७९॥

Vicchinābhravilāyaṃ vā vilîye nagamûrdhani /
ārādhya vā sahsrākṣamayaśaḣśalyamuddhare //79//

Translation :

I am determined to get rid of the foreign growth of ill-fame in my body whether I can do it by meditative practices to the king of gods with thousand eyes (or sores op cit) or by recourse to surgical operations, even if I may drift away like clouds or disintegrate and lose myself on the summit of this mountain (Indra-kîla).

N.B. V.S. Āpte explains the expression "śalya-muddhare" as that part of surgery, which related to extraction of extraneous matter from the body by resort to surgical operation.

इत्युक्तवन्तं परिरभ्य दोर्भ्यां तनूजमाविष्कृतदिव्यमूर्तिः ।
अघोपघातं मघवा विभूत्यै तस्मै भवाराधनमादिदेश ॥८०॥

Ityuktavantaṃ parirabhya dorbhyāṃ tanûjamāviskritadivyamûrtiḣ /
aghopaghātaṃ maghavā vibhûtyai tasmai Bhavārādhanamādideśa//80//

Translation :

While he was being addressed in such a manner, Maghavā (Indra) discarded his make-up to show his true form and held his son in the folds of both his hands and very sincerely advised him (his son Arjuna) to apply himself to the worship of Bhava (source of all existences) for deliverance from his sufferings.

N.B. Mallinātha's gloss of "bhavodbhava" (= the self-existent cause of the universe) overlooks the fact that the word "Bhava" seems to be called by the poet from Śākyamuni's vocabulary. The Śākyas of Kapilavastu worshipped Śākyavardhana and Śiri-mā or Bhava or Bhavānî, which were the Śākyan names of Paśupati and Pārvatî (the daughter of the mountains).

By restoring Bhāravi to his original of "tasmai" we get the adverbial force of the expression to guide Arjuna to the real path.

प्रीते पिनाकिनी मया सह लोकपालै-
र्लोकत्रयेऽपि विहिताप्रतिवार्यवीर्यः ।
लक्ष्मीं समुत्सुकयितासि भृशं परेषा-
मुच्चार्य वाचमिति तेन तिरोबभूवे ॥८१॥

Prîte Pinākini mayā saha lokapālai-
rlokatraye(ऽ)pi vihitāprativāryavîryaḣ /
lakśmîṃ samutsukayitāsi bhriśaṃ pareṣā-
muccārya vācamiti tena tirovabhûve //81//

Translation :

"By offering your loving adoration to the holder of the bow Pinãka (Śiva-Tripurãntaka as the destroyer of the Three Fortresses op cit) along with the Guardian deities of the four cardinal compass corners including myself (in the overall scheme of Sthāṇu or vyûha) and acquiring thereby the irresistible spiritual energy and power to transcend the bounds, of the Three Worlds, you will tempt the fortune of your adversaries by dint of your supreme will." With these words, he (Indra) vanished from the scene.

N.B. It is remarkable that this claim of the Vedic god Indra to have formed part of the scheme of Sthāṇu-Śiva gives a clue to the origin of the cult of Matsyendra in Nepal. So far he was known as "Atikāruṇika or Mahākāruṇika" or in other words the most compassionate Lord who was later identified with Avalokiteśvara or the compassionate god with the glancing look. In Canto XVIII. 22. Arjuna opens with a prayer to Atikāruṇika. During the early Buddhistic period of our history the four Guardian deities of the four cardinal compass points were Virûpākṣa (West), Kuvera (north), Dhattaratha (East) and Virulhaka (south). This syncretism of the Buddhistic and Brāhmannic gods in the Śaivite scheme of Vyûha (fortress) marks a great quckening of human ideas during the age of Bhāravi.

For a classical basrelief of Śiva–Tripurañtaka and its myth, please see Plate XV in The Judicial Customs of Nepal. The Kailāsa rock temple of Elura gives its own version of the God in the middle of the 8th century A.D. We have already pointed out in our Introduction how the legend of Kirātārjunîye was getting popular in South India.

The end of Canto XI

KIRĀTĀRJUNIYE

CANTO XII

CANTO XII

Summary

This Canto consists of 54 stanzas in Udgatā metre.

After the exit of Indra from the scene, Arjuna applies himself to the meditation of Śiva-Tripurāntaka in the scheme of Vyûha as advised by his father Indra. Arjuna felt extremely encouraged and practised the "Tapas" for the development of his will-power. The singularity of Arjuna's meditative practices far surpassed the "Yogic exercises" of the Siddhas (the Perfect ones). Disturbed by the event the forest-guards and the Siddhas proceeded to Kailāsa, where they have difficulty in having a sight of "Bhava and Bhavānî". But when they close their eyes and meditate, they finally have a vision of Śiva in a halo of light in the company of his consort, which is represented in the traditional inscriptions, basreliefs and sculputres of Nepal, some of which are traced with Licchavi scripts. Then the saints and forest-guards give Bhava and Bhavānî the impression that Arjuna may be the incarnation of the Vedic God Viṣṇu. Then Śiva assuages the Perfect Ones and points out the special qualities of his austere practices, while telling them with his knowledge of the past, present and future how an apocalyptic demon known by the name Mûka was trying to kill Arjuna under the disguise of a hog and how this incarnation of Viṣṇu was helpless against the attack of the Brute. Under the circumstances Bhava feels inclined to save Arjuna by the use of his Pāśupatāstra (animal-in-man-killing missile) in the disguise of a Kirāta. The Master of the Battle, then, orders the Siddhas and the forest-guards to return to their posts and watch how Arjuna would misinterpret his best of intentions and dispute his good turn by offering Him a battle.

On the other side of the drama Arjuna sees the gigantic wild-boar making towards him in full murderous career while the Kirātas are in pursuit to shoot him from the right place and at the right moment. But before Arjuna shoots, the king of the Kirāta has already delivered the fatal shot, so that the Beast struggles to his death with eyes of vengeance on Arjuna right before his hermitage. Then, Gaṇeśa (the Lord of the Gaṇas) approaches the hermitage of Arjuna accompanied by his followers known as the Gaṇas (Himalayan peoples composed of mixed tribes in the confederacy of Kirāta-gaṇa-rājyas).

When the dramatic situation gets most intriguing, the poet gives us glimpses of the flora and fauna of the Himalayas and also of the myths of Śiva-Tripurāntaka, which enables us to identify the basrelief of this god on the terraces to the north of the temple of Paśupati (vide The Judicial Customs of Nepal Part I Plate XV) and also to see how the myths of the ancient world were getting consolidated into solid facts of history.

Moreover, Bhāravi's description of Bhava and Bhavānî not only links up this canto to the traditional concept of the historical Buddhas but it also gives a tremendous perspective to the inscription of king Gaṇa-deva and his prime-minister Bhauma-gupta dated Śaṃvat 489 (= 570 A.D. GNI P.28), where the dialouge between Bhavānî and Śrî criticize the homosexual image of Hari-Hara (Śaṅkara-Nārāyaṇa) as the ultimate cause of creation. At a time, when the Ābhîras were trying to invent the myth of the incineration of the god of love by creating the image of Chhatra-caṇḍeśvara (the image of Śiva with a parasol), the poet's assessment of the situation with such expressions as "dhāturudaya-nidhane-jagatāṃ (coming into existence of the cosmic universal principle and its destruction in stanza 33) seems to give it a link directly to the record of Piprahavā Buddhist vase epitaph (Vide the Judicial Customs of Nepal Part I p. 12.). No doubt the quest for "anādinidhana" (state of timelessness or permanent beatitude) was sparkled by the expression of "salilanidhana" (corporal remains) occuring in the said epitaph of Śākyamuni.

Under these historical circumstances, I have interpreted such terms as "nayanavinimesa" (winkless eyes), kakuda-vṛṣasya (the hump of the bull), "bhuvanaikapuruṣa" (the only body of essences) against the background of Bhāvanî as His creative counterpart. It is a pity that Mallinātha has glossed over all the important words to give his etymological rather than historical interpretation. As for example we may have to trace the origin of such expression as "amalavapuṣa" (bodily essence free from three impurities) to the Buddhistic rather than Brāhmannic sources.

Finally, I have taken pains to identify the Himalayan fauna and flora described by the poet to show how keen was his observation of nature. I would presently request my readers to go along with my translations of the stanzas of Canto XII of Kirātārjunîye:

अथ वासवस्य वचनेन रुचिरवदनस्त्रिलोचनम् ।
क्लान्तिरहितमभिराधयितुं विधिवत्तपांसि विदधे धनंजयः ॥१॥

Atha Vāsavasya vacanena ruciravadanastrilocanaṃ /
klāntirahitamabhirādhayituṃ vidhivattapāṃsi vidadhe Dhanañjayaḣ //1//

Translation :

Then (after the exit of Indra from the scene) Dhanañjaya felt himself rejuvenated and encouraged; and he applied himself indefatigably to the worship of Śiva with the Third Eye according to the rules prescribed (for His meditation).

अभिरश्मिमालि विमलस्य धृतजयधृतेरनाशुषः ।
तस्य भुवि बहुतिथास्तिथयः प्रतिजग्मुरेकचरणं निषीदतः ॥२॥

Abhiraśmimāli vimalasya dhritajayadhriteranāśuśaḣ /
tasya bhuvi vahutithāstithayaḣ pratijagmurekacaraṇaṃ niśîdataḣ //2//

Translation :

Turning towards the sun with his mind disabused of all impurities and standing with one leg on earth, he spent many days (praying to Śiva) with the object of achieving final victory over his enemies.

वपुरिन्द्रियोपतपनेषु सततमसुखेषु पाण्डवः ।
प्रापनगपतिरिव स्थिरतां महतां हि धैर्य अविचिन्त्य वैभवम् ॥३॥

Vapurindriyopatapaneşu satatamasukheşu Pāndavah /
prāpanagapatiriva sthiratām mahatām hi dhairya avicintya vaibhavam //3//

Translation :

By constantly subjecting himself with great fortitude to severe penances at the cost of physical comforts and to the rejection of the demands of the five organs of sense, Pāṇḍava (Arjuna) achieved the sublime stability of mountains with the object of winning will and power (to subjugate his enemies).

N.B. Mallinātha's gloss of "vyāpa" (= obtained or achieved) to explain the poet's original of "prāpa" does not appear to be happy and his gloss of "avibhāvya" (= incapable of being anticipated) seems to be a poor substitute for Bhāravi's original of "avicintya" (=unthinkable).

न पपात संनिहितपक्तिसुरभिषु फलेषु मानसम् ।
तस्य शुचिनि शिशिरे च पस्यभृतायते हि सुतपः सुकर्मणाम् ॥४॥

Nā papāta sannihitapaktisurabhișu phaleșu mānasam /
tasya śucini śiśire ca pasyamritāyate hi sutapaḣ sukarmaṇām //4//

Translation :

His (Arjuna's) mind was not attracted by the sweet-smelling and ripe fruits of the season nor did he slake his thirst by the cool and clear water from the lakes. With a feeling that penances undertaken with good intents and purposes, like nectar, are rewards in themselves, he carried on.

न विसिस्मिये न विषसाद मुहुरलसतां न चाददे ।
सत्वमुरुधृति रजस्तमसी न हतः स्म तस्य हतशक्तिपेशले ॥५॥

Na visismiye na viṣasāda muhuralasatāṃ na cādade /
satvamurudhriti rajastamasî na hataḣ sma tasya hatasaktipeśale //5//

Translation :

He (Arjuna) did not get overwhelmed nor very much agitated nor did he get crest-fallen with the slow progress of his austere efforts. Concentrating on the luminous quality constituted within himself (satva-guṇa), he was not disturbed by the dynamic and powerful quality (rajaḥ) nor obstructed by the inert and stupid quality (tamah). In sum all the three qualities balanced themselves in the form of a mixture as when different drugs are pounded by the pestle on a grounding stone.

N.B. Mallinātha's gloss of "pelave" (= frail-transitory-delicate-fine-soft, lean-thin or tender) seems to be out of context. Seeing how the word "pesala" (= the pestle and the grounding stone to pound and pulverise materials) is used in the inscription of Bhāravi's mother Vijayavatî (vide Introduction), the poet uses the same word to show that the fruits of Arjuna's austerities, by virtue of contact between "sattva", "rajaḥ" and "tamaḥ" balanced themselves like substances pulverised with a pestle in a mortar. Thus we see that Bhāravi feels that the three states are animated by "druti" (fluidity), "vistāra" (dilatation) and "vikāśa" (expansion) and acquire the emergent state of "sattva" like the different ingredients of matter when they are pounded to yield effective result as a medicinal mixture.

तपसा कृशं वपुरुवाह स विजितजगत्त्रयोदयम् ।
त्रासजननमपि तत्त्वविदां न तदस्ति यन्न सुकरं महात्मभिः ॥६॥

Tapasā kriśaṃ vapuruvāha sa vijitajagattrayodayam /
trāsajananamapi tatvavidāṃ na tadasti yanna sukaraṃ mahātma-bhiḥ //6//

Translation :

Though lean yet his body spoke for itself that his physical frame was tending to assume the adamantine posture to conquer the Three Worlds. Though it may be awe-inspiring, yet there is nothing impracticable (unfeasible) for those who know the realities of material existence (vis-a-vis the skilfully conjured up magical performance which gives the semblance of reality).

N.B. Mallinātha's glosses of "kimidāsti" (=how is it ?) to express doubt and "manasvibhiḥ" (= men of mental stature) for the poet's original of "na tadāsti" (= there is nothing insuperable) for "mahātamabhiḥ" (= the high-souled) do not carry the positive sense intended. I do not see any ground for questioning nor any reference to the adventure of the human mind.

According to Nyāya philosophy mind is something like "dravya" (material) which is distinct from soul. According to Bhāravi reality is not an illusion nor a super-imposition nor an imitation but the cultivation of will and power by conditioning the three constituent elements of "sattva", "rajaḥ" and "tamaḥ", which are part and parcel of our life. At this point the state of emergence of "sattvaguṇa" is to be seen increasingly in the body of the high-souled person who goes on practising austerities.

ज्वलतोऽनलादनुनिशीथमधिकरुचिरम्भसां निधेः ।
धैर्यगुणमवजयन्विजयी ददृशे समुन्नततरः स शैलतः ॥७॥

Jvalato(ऽ)nalādanunisîthamadhikarucirambhasāṃ nidheḥ /
dhairyaguṇamavajayanvijayî dadriśe samunnatatarah sa śāilataḥ //7//

Translation :

Emerging from the deep water (of the obstructive and painful quality) of "tamaḥ" (pall of darkness that shrouds our life), he appeared as luminous as the flaming embers of fire during midnight. As he went on cultivating the qualities of patience to conquer the unconquerable (within himself) he appeared taller than the mountain.

जपतः सदा जपमुपांशु वदनमभितो विसारिभीः ।
तस्य दशनकिरणैः शुशुभे परिवेषभीषणमिवार्कमण्डलम् ॥८॥

Japataḥ sadā japamupāṃśu vadanamabhito visāribhiḥ /
tasya daśanakiraṇaiḥ śuśubhe pariveśabhîṣaṇamivārkamaṇḍalaṃ //8//

Translation :

When Arjuna uttered the spell (of esoteric worship) with a flourish of his broad face, the refulgence of his clean white teeth showed itself like the tense halo surrounding the sun.

कवचं स बिभ्रदुपवीतपदनिहितसज्यकार्मुकः ।
शैलपतिरिव महेन्द्रधनु परिवीतभीमगहनो विदिद्युते ॥९॥

Kavacaṃ sa vibhradupavîtapadanihitasajyakārmukaḣ /
śailapatiriva mahendradhanu parivîtabhîmagahano vididyute //9//

Translation :

Wearing a dazzling mail-coat (armour) and quiver full of arrows exactly at the spot where he wore the sacred thread (given by the Vedic priests to Brāhmins and Kṣatriya as marks of their baptism), he dangled an awe-inspiring bow, which gave the impression of the forest-clad king of mountains studded with a rainbow.

प्रविवेश गामिव कृशस्य नियमसवनाय गच्छतः ।
तस्य पदविनमितो हिमवान्गुरुतां नयन्ति हि गुणा न संहतिः ॥१०॥

Praviveśa gāmiva kriśasya niyamasavanāya gacchataḣ /
tasya padavinamito himavāngurutāṃ nayanti hi guṇā na saṃhatiḣ //10//

Translation :

When he walked down the forested slopes to the river-bed for his morning ablutions according to rules (prescribed for his ascetical practices), his lean frame added to the weight of the Himalayan landscape; for, it is quality that adds to the merit of matters rather than bulk (quantity).

परिकीर्णमुद्यतभुजस्य भुवनविवरे दुरासदम् ।
ज्योतिरुपरि शिरसो विततं जगृहे निजान्मुनिदिवौकसां पथः ॥११॥

Parikîrṇamudyatabhujasya bhuvanavivare durāsadaṃ /
jyotirupari śiraso vitataṃ jagrihe nijānmunidivaukasāṃ pathaḣ //11//

Translation :

When the saint stretched out his Titanic arms over his refulgent head in the attitude of encompassing the union (marriage) of the earth and sky, his adamantine pose appeared to obstruct the paths of the planets.

N.B. The Vedic concept of "dvavyaprithivi" (= the nuptial of the earth and sky) seems to be a favourite theme with Bhāravi.

रजनीषु राजतनयस्य बहुलसमयेऽपि धामभिः ।
भिन्नतिमिरनिकरं न जहे शशिरश्मिसंगमयुजा नभः श्रिया ॥१२॥

Rajanîśu rājatanayasya vahulasamaye(ऽ)pi dhāmabhiḥ /
bhinnatimiranikaraṃ na jahe śaśiraśmisaṃgamayujā nabhaḥ śriyā //12//

Translation :

Even during the dark-half of the ebbing moon the refulgence of the king (Arjuna) brightened the atmosphere.

महता मयूखनिचयेन शमितरुचि जिष्णुजन्मना ।
ह्रीतमिव नभसि वीतमले न विराजतिस्म व पुरंशुमालिनः ॥१३॥

Mahatā mayukhanicayena śamitaruci Jiśṇujanmanā /
hrîtamiva nabhasi vîtamale na virājatisma va puraṃśumālinaḥ //13//

Translation :

The conjunction of various forms of light and energy generated by Jiśṇu (as the incarnation of Vedic god Viṣṇu) put into shade the luminosity of the disc of sun in the specless sky, as though the sun was not the source of all existence.

N.B. Taking the word "virāja" from Manusmriti 1.32 in the sense of 1. beauty, splendour, 2. a man of Kṣatriya caste and 3. first proeny from the four-headed androgenous Brahmā, the poet makes a veiled attack on the cult of Viṣṇu as the Puruṣa (the first person born) and the source of life, sustenance and destruction rather than the sun.

तमुदीरितारुणजटांशुमधिगुणशरासनं जनाः ।
रुद्रमनुदितललाटदृशं ददृशुर्मिमन्थिषुमिवासुरीः पुरः ॥१४॥

Tamudîritāruṇajaṭāṃśumadhiguṇaśarāsanaṃ janāḥ /
Rudramanuditalalāṭadriśaṃ dadriśurmimanthiṣumivāsurîḥ puraḥ //14//

Translation :

On seeing him (Arjuna) on a cage (bed) of arrows with the red glow of his overflowing lock of hair in adamantine attitude of battle, the people (Siddhas and forest-guards) had the feeling of seeing Rudra himself with his forehead high and intent on reducing the (three) impregnable fortresses of the demons (made for their preservation by their architect Maya).

N.B. Mallinātha's gloss of "puri" (= city or town) does not underscore the historical significance of "puraḣ" (fortified town) surrounded by moat and canals from the Moheñjodāro and Harappā to Kapilavastu. The excavation of Kapilavastu has revealed this unique feature already noticed by archaelogists in the urban civilisation of the Indus valley associated with rice-culture vis-a vis nomadic civilisation of barley culture represented by the Indo-Aryans at the outset of their career of conquests. It is remarkable to note that the cities of Nepal are known as "puraḣ" and not "puri" e.g. Lalitpuraḣ, Kāntipuraḣ and Bhaktapuraḣ, which, no doubt, trace their origin to their traditional form.

It is equally remarkable that the Master of the Battle (Paśupati) was also recognised as their storm-god Rudra by the Brāhmins.

मरुतां पतिः स्विदहिमांशु अथ पृथुशिखः शिखी तपः ।
तप्तुमसुकरमुपक्रमते न जनोऽयमित्यवयये स तापसैः ॥१५॥

Marutāṃ patiḣ svidahimāṃśu atha prithuśikhaḣ śikhî tapaḣ / taptumasukaramupakramate na jano(ऽ)yamityavayaye sa tāpasaiḣ //15//

Translation :

Hallo ! could he be the god of the storm or the sun himself ? To judge this marvellous person by his insuperable ascetical practices here and now he may be (Buddha) Śikhî himself in a state of trance with his blazing and gigantic top-knot over-flowing like a flame of fire.

N.B. Mallinātha's glosses of "svidahimāṃśuruta" (= could he be sun ?) does not seem to take adequate note of the indeclinable particle of interrogation "svid", often implying doubt and translatable by "Hallo, Hey etc", V.S. Āpte quotes this particular stanza to show how the poet uses the word disjunctly in the sense of "either" with "tu", "uta" and "tā". Here the poet is using the indeclinable particle "atha" as a sign of auspiciousness which could be translated in the present context "here and now" e.g. "Omnkāraścāthasavdaśca dvāvetau brahmaṇapurāḣ/kaṇṭhaṃbhitvā viniryātau tena māñgalikā-vubhau // Under the circumstances we have here a clear reference to the ascetical practices of Buddha Śikhî— the second historical Buddha who followed the Lotus theory of the first historical Buddha Vipaśsi represented symbolically by the first vowel "Omṇ". The stupa of Buddha Śikhî still exists in a place known historically as Dhyānocca by the temple of Śikhî-Nārāyaṇa on the road of Dakṣiṇakālî.

न ददाह भूधरवनानि हरितनयधाम दूरगम् ।
न स्म नयति परिशोषमपः सुसहं बभूव न च सिद्धतापसैः ॥१६॥

Na dadāha bhûdharavanāni Haritanayadhāma dûragam /
na sma nayati pariśoṣamapaḣ susahaṃ vabhûva na ca siddhatāpasaiḣ //16///

Translation :

The far-spreading heat proceeding from the body of the son of Hari did not start a forest-fire over the mountains nor did it drain the water dry. This strange factor (of the Third Eye of Inner Illumination) struck the Siddhas (Perfect ones) by the singularity of the practices, which excited their wonder and jealousy.

N.B. Mallinātha's gloss of "bhûruha" (trees) do not carry the idea of the geographical situation of forest-clad mountains "bhûdharavanāni" seeing how the forests are always full of trees.

विनयं गुणा इव विवेकमपनयभिदं नया इवः ।
न्यायमवधय इवाशरणाः शरणं ययुः शिवमथो महर्षयः ॥१७॥

Vinayaṃ guṇā iva vivekamapanayabhidaṃ nayā iva /
nyāyamavadhaya ivāśaraṇāh śaraṇaṃ yayuḣ Śivamatho mahar-
ṣayaḣ //17//

Translation :

Baffled by the unwonted practices (of Arjuna to achieve Śivadrṣṭi the Third Eye of Inner Illumination) the eminent saints had no alternative but to betake themselves to the protection of the ever auspicious Śiva, who embodied in Himself the quintessence of all the discipline (of Buddhistic Vinaya), who had the power of discrimination to see the reality of things beyond the veil of (materialistic) illusions with the power of healing and who represented the spirit of Timelessness with correct balance (between creation, existence and destruction).

परिवीतमंशुभिरुदस्तदिनकरमयूखमण्डलैः ।
शंभुमुपहतदृशः सहसा न च ते निरीक्षितुमभिप्रसेहिरे ॥१८॥

Parivîtamamṃśubhirudastadinakaramayûkhamaṇḍalaiḣ /
Śaṃbhumupahatadriśaḣ sahasā na ca te nirîkṣitumabhiprasehire //18//

Translation :

Blinded by the unaccustomed brilliance of light enshrouding Śambhu, which surpassed the light of the sun, they (the Siddhas-Perfect ones) could not bear the sight of Śaṃbhu at the outset.

अथ भूतभव्यभवदीशमभिमुखयितुं कृतस्तवाः ।
तत्र महसि ददृशुः पुरुषं कमनीयविग्रहमयुग्मलोचनम् ॥१९॥

Atha bhûtabhavyabhavadîśamabhimukhayituṃ kritastavāḣ /
tatra mahasi dadriśuḣ puruṣaṃ kamanîyavigrahamayugma-
locanaṃ //19//

Translation :

It was only when the anchorites offered their prayer with devotion (as the highest form of human emotion) that they could have a desirable sight of the Supreme Being with the Third Eye, who could divine into the past, present and future.

ककुदे वृषस्य कृतबाहुमकृशपरिणाहशालिनि ।
स्पर्शसुखमनुभवन्तमुमाकुचयुग्ममण्डल इवार्द्रचन्दने ॥२०॥

Kakude vriṣasya kritavāhumakriśapariṇāhaśālini /
Sparśasukhamanubhavantamumākucayugmamaṇḍala ivārdra-candane //20//

Translation :

Then they saw the vision of Śiva sitting upon the hump of his bull (Nandi) with his plump and long arms holding the sandal-besmea red breasts of Umā in his loving embrace and experiencing the pleasures of life through perception.

N.B. It is remarkable that this vision of Umā-Maheśvara form the subject of most of the Licchavi scultpures. In the Brāhmannic legends "Kakudasthaḥ" is an epithet of Puranjaya, who was the son of the solar dynasty of Ikṣvākus. Defeated by the demons, Indra and and 333 million gods sought the aid of Puranjaya, who consented to help them provided Indra carried him on his shoulder. Accordingly, Indra assumed the form of a bull and carried him on his hump.So, Puranjaya got the title of Kākutstha and his solar dynasty inherited the title. According to Pāṇini V. 4. 146-147 Kakud is the form to be substituted for Kakuda in adjective or *vahuvrihi* composition.

What is more interesting than this cheap myth of 'Kākudasthaḥ' is Bhāravi's discussion of the cognition of Śiva through devotional prayer, which is the highest form of human emotion. The emerging vision of Umā-Maheśvara is their apprehension of the world of physical things in relation to their own ideas of this cosmic world, which can be described as external object. This is normal adult perception of our daily life.

स्थितमुन्नते तुहिनशैलशिरसि भुवनातिवर्तिना ।
साद्रिजलधिजलवाहपथं सदिगश्नुवानमिव विश्वमोजसा ॥२१॥

Sthitamunnate tuhinaśailaśirasi bhuvanātivartinā /
Sādrijaladhijalavāhapathaṃ sadigaśnuvānamiva viśvamojasā //21//

Translation :

Though manifesting from one corner of the plumed summits of the Himalayas right across the paths and accesses of the (monsoon) clouds from the sea, yet he appeared to dominate the enitre universe by his sheer energy (in the form of Sthāṇu Śiva).

अनुजानुमध्यमवसक्तवितवपुषा महाहिना ।
लोकमखिलमिव भूमिभृता रवितेजसामवधिनाऽभिवेष्टितम् ॥२२॥

Anujānumadhyamavasaktavitavapuṣā mahāhinā /
lokamakhilamiva bhûmibhritā ravitejasāmavadhinā(ऽ)bhives-ṭitam //22//

Translation :

Like a Collosus He bestrode the world from the base of high mountains of mists and snow, and his majestic form appeared to stretch in the direction of the universe beyond the pale of the solar system lit up by the rays of the sun.

N.B. Mallinātha's gloss of the indeclinable "adhi" (= over or above) does not convery the meaning of "in the direction of or towards) implied by the poet's use of the indeclinable prefix "abhi". This concept of Śiva as a Collosus striding the universe beyond the solar system appears to be a reply to the Miracle of Viṣṇu in three Vedic Steps.

परिणाहिना तुहिनाराशिविशदमुपवीतसूत्रताम् ।
नीतमुरगमनुरञ्जयता शितिना गलेन विलसन्मरीचिना ॥२३॥

Pariṇāhinā tuhinarāśiviśadamupavîtasūtrartām /
nîtamuragamanurañjayatā śitinā galena vilasanmarîcinā //23//

Translation :

The endless snake adorning his dark neck like a sacred thread over his expansive snow-white body presented its own contrast of light and shade.

प्लुतमालतीसितकपालकुमुदमुपरुद्धमूर्धजम् ।
शेषमिव सुरसरित्पयसां शिरसाविकाशि शशिधाम बिभ्रतम् ॥२४॥

Plutamālatîsitakapālakumudamuparuddhamûrdhajam /
śeṣamiva surasaritpayasāṃ śirasāvikāśi śaśidhāma vibhratam //24//

Translation :

Then the saints saw the emerging vision of Śiva with the pate of his head covered over with fragrant white jasmine and bright with the soaring rays of the moon like a Śiva-liñga by the bank of Surasaritā.

N.B. The reference here is to the Śîvaliñgas erected by the prominent ladies of the period to the memory of their husbands by the bank of river Vāgwatî and not definitely to the Ganges.

Some people have inserted the following stanza between stanzas 24 and 25 reading :

बहुभिश्च बाहुभिरहीनभुजगवलयैर्विराजितम् ।
चन्दनतरुभिरतनुभिः श्रमलायतैर्मलयमेदिनीभृतम् ॥

Vahubhiśca vāhubhirahînabhujagavalayairvirājitaṃ /
candanatarubhiratanubhih amalāyatairmelayamedinibhritam // //

Translation :

Though formless and without formulas and empirical action they saw the myriad hands of the Lord wreathed with Endless snake (= ināh or Anantanāga) and worshipped with sandal wood like the king of Malaya.

N.B. It is a pity that the commentators have made the confusion worst confounded by their glosses. The commentators should keep themselves aloof from their own judgment. For, all human epochs are "immediate to God" seeing how the actors from the Indus valley to the valleys of the Himalayas were partakers of the hopes, fears and faith of their own time, country and kind.

मुनयस्ततोऽभिमुखमेत्य नयनविनिमेषनोदिताः ।
पाण्डुतनयतपसा जनितं जगतामशर्म भृशमाचचक्षिरे ॥२५॥

Munayastato(s)bhimukhametya nayanavinimeṣanoditāḥ /
Pāṇḍutanayatapasā janitaṃ jagatamaśarma bhriśamācacakśire //25//

Then (after they had obtained the vision of Śiva) and interrogated with the twinkle of His eyes, the Siddhas apprised the Lord about the effect of the austere practices of the son of Pandu, which was unberable to them.

तरसैव कोऽपि भुवनैकपुरुष पुरुषस्तपस्यति ।
ज्योतिरमलवपुषोऽपि रवेरभिभूय वृत्र इव भीमविग्रहः ॥२६॥

Tarasaiva ko(ऽ)pi bhuvanaikapuruṣa puruṣastapasyati /
jyotiramalavapuṣo(ऽ)pi raverabhibhûya vrita iva bhîmavigrahaḥ//26//

Translation :

O Sole and Supreme Being of the Universe ! an unknown person with his body as awe-inspiring as Britrāsura (the demon of darkness and night) is addressing himself to powerful and austere practices transcending the sun in his resplendance.

स धनुर्महेषुधि बिभर्ति कवचमसिमुत्तमं जटाः ।
वल्कमजिन मतिचित्रमिदं मुनितावरोधि न च नास्य राजते ॥२७॥

Sa dhanurmaheṣudhi vibharti kavacamasimuttamaṃ jaṭāh /
valkamajina aticitramidaṃ munitāvirodhi na ca nāsya rājate //27//

Translation :

He equips himself with a gruesome bow and wears his armour with a sharp and fine bladed sword encased in a skin sheath, (which is un-like the birch-bark habiliment of saints). Despite this overdrawn and overlaid picture, it is a matter of wonder that these contradictions do not show any adverse effect on his profession of saintliness.

N.B. Mallinātha's gloss of the indeclinable/particle "iti" ("Thus" to mark the conclusion) does not convey Bhāravi's idea of "excessively overdrawn picture by the use of the indeclinable prefix "ati" (excceding-ly or excessively) with adjectives and adverbs (aticitramidaṃ=this exceedingly overdrawn picture). Judging by the miniature paintings and the description of paintings occuring in Licchavi inscriptions, the age of Bhāravi seems to be famous for superb paintings.

चलनेऽवनिश्चलति तस्य करणनियमे सदिङ्मुखम् ।
स्तम्भमनुभवति शान्तमरुद्ग्रहतारकागणयुतं नभस्तलम् ॥२८॥

Calane(ऽ)vaniscalati tasya karaṇaniyame sadiñmukhaṃ /
Stambhamanubhavati śāntamarudgrahatārakagaṇayutaṃ nabhasta-laṃ //28//

Transaltion :

The entire world moves with the movement of his mind; and the principles and practices with which he conducts himself before the stump (of Sthāṇu Śiva in the scheme of Kāraṇapûjā) with four. cardinal compass corner-images during the eleven periods of day and night makes him one and at peace with the wind, planets and the firmament studded with stars.

N.B. Mallinātha does not seem to realise that the poet is here discussing the nature of "reality" in Yogācāra Buddhism in its association with the scheme of Kāraṇapûjā. The school of Yogācara Buddhism teaches that the entire world, which surrounds us, is a creation of our own mind. In other words, nothing exists outside mind or our consciousness. This is the zist of such works as "Laṃkāvatāra sûtra, Aṣṭāsāhasrikā-prajñāpāramitā, Vajracchedikā, Mahāyanasutralaṃkāra, Slokavartika-nirālamvanavāda, Tattva-saṃgraha. Sloka-vārttika śunyavāda and allied works.

स तदोजसा विजितसारममरदितिजोपसंहितम् ।
विश्वमिदमपिदधाति पुरा किमिवास्ति यन्न बत तेन दुष्करम् ॥२९॥

Sa tadojasā vijitasāramamaraditijopasaṃhitam /
viśvamidamapidadhāti purā kimivāsti yanna vata tena duṣkmaram //29//

Translation :

What, Alas ! is beyond his cognition, when, by dint of the spiritual essences thus attained, he may achieve victory over the entire world inhabited by gods and demons ?

N.B. Mallināths'a gloss of "yenna tapasāmaduṣkaraṃ" (= what is beyond his power of asceticism ?) does not convey Bhāravi's idea of the cognition and spiritual essences meant by "yenna vata tena duṣkaram "What, Alas, ? is beyond his cognition ?). The use of the indeclinable particle "vata", which is the equivalent of Alas in English seems to be calculated to express the amazement and regret of the anchorites. (Vide the Judicial Customs of Nepal Part I.)

विजिगीषते यदि जगन्ति युगपदथ संजिहीर्षति ।
प्राप्तुमभवमभिवाञ्छति वा वयमस्य नो विषाहेतुं क्षमा रुचः ॥३०॥

Vijigîṣate yadi jaganti yugapadatha saṃjihîrsati /
prāptumabhavamabhivāncchati vā vayamasya no viṣahituṃ kśamā rucaḥ //30//

"O Lord ! We are not in a position to assess whether he is eager to conquer the world or to achieve simultaneously the adamantine state of permanent absolute or whether he wants to transcend the consciousness after achieving the innumerable essences. (Whatever his ulterior motive) we have not been able to bear the nature of his lustre of (conceptual thinking at the back of his austere practices)."

N.B. Mallinātha's etymological explanation does not underscore the historical significance of this interesting stanza, where the poet gives his assessment of "Yogācāra doctrine as it developed through such Buddhistic logicians as Asañga, Vasuvandhu and Diṅnāga long after the death of Śakyamuni Buddha, who taught that consciousness was the only reality and that the diversity of the world is a creation of our conceptual thinking. The moment a man rises above the level of discursive knowledge, the phenomenal world with all its variety comes to an end. For, according to Dhammapada (V. 154.) Śakyamuni says the following with the dawn of his illumination; "O ! Ego born of ignorance, creator of the World-House !! I have cognised thee well. Now thou wilt not be able to construct this house again. Because all the tools necessary for the construction of this house have been broken, the walls of the house have fallen. Because the mind (consciousness) i. e. cittaṃ (चित्तम्) has become pure by the cessation of desires and removal of impressions."

We find a beautiful description of this state of mind in Kevatta-sûtra :

"There is not that earth, water, fire and wind and long and short and fine and coarse; pure and impure no footing find.

Both name and form die out leaving no place behind, when the intellect ceases, they all cease."

किमुपेक्षसे कथय नाथ तव न विदितं न किंचन ।
त्रातुमलमभयदार्हसि नस्त्वयि मा स्म शासति भवत्पराभवः ॥३१॥

Kimupekşase kathaya Nātha tava na viditaṃ na kiṃcana /
trātumalamabhayadārhasi nastvayi mā sma śāsati bhavatparābhavaḥ //31//

Translation :

Why are you silent O Self-Immanent God ! for, there is nothing that is not known to you ? O Saviour ! it is up to you to assuage our fears; for, there is no defeat under your rule and law.

इति गां विधाय विरतेषु मुनिषु वचनं समाददे ।
भिन्नजलधिजलनादगुरु ध्वनयन्दिशां विवरमन्धकान्तकः ॥३२॥

Iti gāṃ vidhāya virateşu munişu vacanaṃ samādade /
bhinnajaladhijalanādaguru dhvanayandiśāṃ vivaramandhakān-takaḥ//32//

Translation :

When the saints remained silent after speaking these words, the Dispeller of darkness (Śiva) uttered the following words through the air in a vioce as deep as the depth of water (when it is sounded).

बदरीतपोवननिवासनिरतमवगात मान्यथा ।
धातुरुदयनिधने जगतां नरमंशमादि पुरुषस्य गां गतम् ॥३३॥

Vadarîtapovananivāsaniratamavagāta mānyathā/
dhāturudayanidhane jagatāṃ naramaṃsamādi puruṣasya gāṃ gataṃ//33//

Translation :

A permanent resident anchorite of the penance grove in the midst of the jujube forest known by the name of Badarî, he comes here as the human incarnation of the Supreme Person, who is responsible for bringing into existence the cosmic universal principle and its ultimate dissolution.

N.B. It is remarkable that the penance grove of Badarî was as famous in the days of Bhāravi as it is today for Hindu pilgrims. This place is regarded as one of the many sources of the river Ganges, which was famous for the hermitage of Nara and Nārāyaṇa. On the other hand, Bhāravi appears to have borrowed the expression of "dhāturudayanidhane" (coming into existence of the cosmic universal principle and its disssolution) directly from the Piprahavā Buddhist vase epitaph enshrining the mortal remains of Buddha Śākyamuni and of his kiths and kins vis-a-vis Anuparama's expression of "nāśotnādana-yoga" contained in line 61 of Anuparama's inscription of the pilaster of Hārigāon to define the nature of Vāsudeva (Viśṇu) as being exempt from all polarity of destructṇion and production, as He represented the lysis of all dialysis because he is eternal and everlasting, he stands apart from the attributes of matter (dharmmairayogāt). We have shown in our translation of Anuparama's eulogium to Dvaipāyana how he attacks the Buddhists and how he is unable to prove God's compact solitude and also how it does not isolate him from the consciousness of the past, present and future except by calling upon the Brāhmannic saint to do so.

By making Śiva quote the expression from the Piprahavā-Buddhist vase epitaph, Bhāravi resolves the contradictions of Yogācāra-doctrine and Vedic Revelations in the sheme of Pāśupata-dharma. Due to his insatiable hunger for sources Bhāravi, unlike Anuparama, does not lose his way in the tangled jungles of Yogācāra doctrines and Bhāgavata-dharma. The poet has breathed such a spirit of the transition known as Bhairavi-cakra-pravartana that the expression of "anādinidhana" (state of permanent beatitude)) had formed part of our confession fidei in liew of "salilanidhana" (corporal remains) to our own day.

If the expression led to the difference between the two early school of Theravāda and Hemavata factions in the first two Buddhist Councils of Rājagriha and Vaisāli, the new confessio fides appears to have become a subject of heated debate between the protagonists of Pāśupata-dharma and Bhāgavata-dharma in the Inscription of king Gaṇa deva and Bhauma-gupta (vide GNI XX p 28). In such a context, Bhāravi deserves credit for welding the contradictions of Buddhistic and Brāhmannic dharma into one harmonious whole through the śoice ṃiva.

द्विषतः परासिसिषुरेषु सकलभुवनाभितापिनः ।
क्रान्तकुलिशकरवीर्यबलान्मदुपासनं विहितवान्महत्तपः ॥३४॥

Dviśataḣ parāsisiṣureṣu sakalabhuvanābhitāpinaḣ /
krāntakuliṣakaravîryavalānmadupāsanaṃ vihitavānmahattapaḣ //34//

Translation :

This person, who is responsible for such a heat and consternation among you in the world, and that with the might to subdue the king of gods, is now concentrating on me so that he might achieve victory over his enemies.

अयमच्युतश्च वचनेन सरसिरुहजन्मनः प्रजाः ।
पातुमसुरनिधनेन विभू भुवमभ्युपेत्य मनुजेषु तिष्ठतः ॥३५॥

Ayamacyutaśca vacanena sarasiruhajanmanaḣ prajāḣ /
pātumasuranidhanena vibhû bhuvamabhyupetya manujeśu tiśṭhataḣ //35//

Translation :

This person (Nara) and the Imperishable One (Nāra-yaṇa) incarnate themselves to protect the peoples (of the world) by killing the demons at the behest of Brahmā, who is born from the lotus and by living among them.

सुरकार्यमेतदवगम्य निपुणमिति मूकदानवः ।
हन्तुमभिपतति पाण्डुसुतं त्वरया तदत्र सह गम्यतां मयाः ॥३६॥

Surakāryametadavagamya nipuṇamiti Mûkadānavaḥ /
hantumabhipatati Pāṇdusutaṃ tvarayā tadatra saha gamyatāṃ mayā//36//

Translation :

With the full knowledge fo the coming success of the Divine purpose, a monster known by the name of Mûka is trying to upset the progress of the new system by killing the son of Pāṇḍu. So, prepare yourselves with all speed to follow me where I go.

N.B. Mallinātha's gloss of "surakritya" (= execution of a divine task) overlooks the force of the passive participle of Bhāravi's original expression of "surakārya" (= Divine purpose or the norm of Divine law). Elsewhere the poet uses the expression in the sense of the esense of execution of a task e.g. "kriyāpavargesuanujîvisāt kritāḥ" or "kriyā suyuktai nripacārcakśuso"etc.

The poet seems to be influenced in the use of the expression by Face III line 8 of the Victory Inscription of king Māna-deva (GNI I) e.g. "rājyaṃ putraka kārayāham" etc. (vide Appendix) .

विवरेऽपि नैनमनिगूढमभिभवितुमेष पारयन् ।
पापनिरतिरविशङ्कितया विजयं व्यवस्यति वराहमायया ॥३७॥

Vivare(ऽ)pi nainamanigûḍhamabhibhavitumeṣa pārayan /
pāpaniratiraviśañkitayā vijayaṃ vyavasyati varāhamāyayā //37//

Translation :

Addicted to a career of crime, he feels secure in his hiding pothole under the disguise of a wild-boar, so that he may attack Arjuna all on a sudden and overcome him without a qualm of conscience.

निहते विडम्बितकिरातनृपतिवपुषा रिपौ मया ।
मुक्तनिशितविशिखः प्रसभं मृगयाविवादमयमाचरिष्यति ॥३८॥

Nihate vidamvitaKirātanripativapuśā ripau mayā /
muktaniśitaviśikhaḥ prasabhaṃ mrigayāvivādamayamā-
cariśyati //38//

Translation :

When I would have despatched the enemy in the assumed form of the king of the Kirātas, then Arjuna would dispute with me as to whose arrow first struck and dealt the fatal blow to kill the brute.

तपसा निपीडितकृशस्य विरहितसहायसंपदः ।
सत्वविहितमतुलं तुलयोर्बलमस्य पश्यत मृधेऽधिकुप्यतः ॥३९॥

Tapasā nipîḍitakriśasya virahitasahāyasaṃpadaḥ /
satvavihitamatulaṃ tulayorvalamasya paśyata mridhe(ऽ)dhikupya-
taḥ //139//

Translation :

Though reduced and thin of body on account of penitential practices and without the aid of an army and camp-followers to back him, yet you will notice how he will give a display of his unchallengable capacity to fight for what he believes to be right, specially when he is provoked, which cannot be weighed by weights of the scale.

N,B. Mallinātha's gloss of "bhujayorvalamasya" (= the weight of his arms) does not give Bhāravi's idea of Arjuna's will and power to stand up to the challenge when provoked, which cannot be weighed by the standard of weighing balance.

इति तानुदारमनुनीय विषमहरिचन्दनालिना ।
घर्मजनितपुलकेन लसद्गजमौक्तिकावलियुतेन वक्षसा ॥४०॥

Iti tānudāramanunîya viṣamaharicandanālinā /
gharmajanitapulakena lasadgajamauktikāvaliyutena vakṣasā //40//

Translation :

After saying these benevolent words (to the Siddhas and the forest guards) Śiva besmeared his body with the unguent of red-sandal wood (pterocarpus santalinus),and his hair bristling with the thrill and perspiration of the season of summer, He emerged under the disguise of the king of the Kirātas with the folds of his battle-scarred-breast decorated with pearly beads extracted from the temple of elephants.

N.B. Mallinātha's gloss of "mauktikāvaliguṇena" (= decorated by the strings or threads of pearls from the temple of elephants) does not give the picture of a warring Kirāta king with battle scars on the folds of his skin" meant by the poet's original of "mauktika-valiyutena". The poet is here describing the attributes of the Kirāta king as a warrior, whose hair stood erect with thrills of war and whose breast was battle-scarred and besmeared with the paste of red-sandal wood and decorated with beads extracted from the temples of elephants.

It is remarkable that Stella Kramrish in her "Art of Nepal," Asia House Gallery (1964) Statue No 1 and Waldschmidt's "Art Treasures of the Himalayas"(1967) Plate IX have discussed the portrait of a Kirāta king, which was discovered by Sri Yogi Narahari Natha in the forecourt of the temple of Vāsudeva with Anuparama's Pilaster of Hārigāon.

It is a matter of interest for the entire human community that the Kirātas are one of the most durable peoples in the history of mankind, who occcur in the eastern part of Nepal. In this sense Nepal is a laboratory of different ethnic groups.

वदनेन पुष्पितलतान्तनियमितविलम्बिमौलिना ।
विभ्रदरुणनयनेन रुचं शिखिपिच्छलाञ्छितकपोलभित्तिना ॥४१॥

Vadanena puṣpitalatāntaniyamitavilamvimaulinā /
vibhradaruṇanayanena rucaṃ śikhipicchalāncchitakapola-
bhittinā//41//

Translation :

His face lit up by a hair-style held in proper place by a coronet of creepers decked with wild flowers and its top knot flourishing feathers, his (Kirāta's) rosy eyes beamed bellicose spirit.

बृहदुद्वहज्जलदनादि धनुरुपहितैकमार्गणम् ।
मेघनिचय इव संववृते रुचिरः किरातपृतनापतिः शिवः ॥४२॥

Vrihadudvahajjaladanādidhanurupahitaikamārgaṇam /
meghanicaya iva saṃvavrite rucirah Kirātapritanāpati Śivah //42//

Translation :

Śiva in the disguise of a king of the Kirātas holding his gigantic bow (Pināka) strung with an arrow appeared like the refulgent heap of rain-bearing clouds.

अनुकूलमस्य च विचिन्त्य गणपतिभिरात्तविग्रहैः ।
शुलपरशुशरचापभृतैर्महती वनेचरचमूर्विनिर्ममे ॥४३॥

Anukûlamasya ca vicintya Gaṅapatibhirāttavigrahaih //
śûlaparaśuśaracāpabhritaiimahatî vanecaracamurvinirmame //43//

Translation :

Convinced within themselves that the appearance of Śiva as the Lord of the Gaṇas (Himalayan tribes) provided the most wholesome leadership for them, the soldiers comprised by the tribes of the forest-dwelling Kirātas armed themselves with tridents, battle-axes, arrows and bows in battle-array.

N.B. Gaṇapati is Śiva-Tripurāntaka and the acknowledged lord of the Himalayan tribes. So far the concept of the elephant-headed Hindu-god of auspices known as Gaṇapati and Gaṇesa does not appear in Nepal. (Vide The Judicial Customs of Nepal Part I Plate XV).

विरचय्य काननविभागमनुगिरमथेश्वराज्ञया ।
भीमनिनदपिहितोभुरुवः परितोऽपदिश्य मृगयां प्रतस्थिरे ॥४४॥

Viracayya Kānanavibhāgamanugiramathesvarāgyayā /
Bhīmaninadapihitorubhuvah parito(ऽ)padiśya mrigayāṃ pratas-thire //44//

Translation

Then, following the sacrament of Iśa's (God's) command they (the Kirāta officers and men) made disposition according to the terrain of the forest. Rending the earth with their fearful noise they (the hunters) skielfully proceeded to circumvent the brute (by putting off the scent).

क्षुभिताभिनिःसृतविभिन्नशकुनिमृगयूथनिःस्वनैः ।
पूर्णपृथुवनगुहाविवरः सहसा भयादिव ररास भूधरः ॥४५॥

Kśubhitābhiniḣsritavibhinnaśakunimrigayûthanihsvanaih /
pûrṇaprithuvanaguhāvivaraḣ sahasā bhayādiva rarāsa bhûdharaḣ//45//

Translation :

Terrified by the uncanny noise, the variety of birds of prey and herds of beasts left their nests, caves and holes of the dense forest while the mountains reverberated to the echo.

न विरोधिनी रुषमियाय पथि मृगविहङ्गसंहतिः ।
घ्नन्ति सहजमपि भूरिभियः सममागताः सपदि वैरमापदः ॥४६॥

Na virodhinî ruṣamiyāya pathi mrigavihañgasaṃhatiḣ /
ghnanti sahajamapi bhûribhiyaḣ samamāgatāḣ sapadi vairamā-papaḣ //46//

Translation :

All the birds and beasts, who have been enemies by their own nature, forgot their anger, and they did not obstruct the paths of their prey. On the other hand, they made common cause against the common enemy in their trepidition (from this new threat from hunters).

चमरीगणैर्शिववलस्य बलवति भयेऽप्युपस्थिते ।
वंशविततिषु विषक्तभृशप्रियवालवालभिराददे धृतिः ॥४७॥

Camarîgaṇairśivavalasya valavati bhaye(ऽ)pyupasthite /
vaṃśavitatiṣu viṣaktabhirśapriyavālavālabhirādade dhritih //47//

Translation :

Intensely engaged in grazing among the bamboo thickets of the mountains, herds of yaks who formed part of the transport of Śiva's army, did not (however) stampede amid the din and bustle of the beaters. They chewed (the bamboo shoots) patiently with leisurelly whisks of their thick and luxuriant yak-tails.

N.B. Mallināttha's gloss of "gaṇavalasya" (= forming part of the army of tribes) and explaining the same term by the poet's original of "Śivavalasya" does not appear to make any sense. Similarly, the commentator's gloss of "viṣaktaprithu" (= adhering thickly broad) does not describe the yak-tail as faithfully as the poet's original of "viṣaktabhriśa" (= wide and dense). Judging by Mallināttha's identification of the yaks with the species of deer, he does not appear to know that the yaks belong to the bovine species. Its habitat is above 10,000 feet in the Himalayan region. Judging by ancient sculptures the tails of yaks seem to be used extensively as fly-whisks.

The poet is giving us a panoramic view of the Himalayan highlands inhabited by yaks down to the valleys and the Tarai infested by elephants and tigers with a vivid account of the avi-fauna. The account seems to be as true during the period of Bhāravi as it is today.

हरसैनिकाः प्रतिभयेऽपि गजमदसुगन्धिकेसरैः ।
स्वस्थमभिददृशिरे सहसा प्रतिबोधजृम्भितमुखैर्मृगाधिपैः ॥४८॥

Harasainikāḥ pratibhaye(ऽ)pi gajamadasugandhikesaraiḥ /
svasthamabhidadriśire sahasā prativodhajrimbhitamukhairmrigādhipaiḥ//48//

Translation :

Roused from their sleep by the awe-inspiring din of the beaters, the kings of the beasts (lions and tigers) yawned lazily and looked on the army of Śiva with their ruffled manes scented by the ichor of elephant (who are believed to be their prey.)

N.B. It is remarkable that the African lions figure prominently in the tradition of the Śākyas due to their early contacts with the Pārsavas (Persians). The Heraldic Lion of the Śākyas has been accepted as the mount of Durgā. According to Mahāparinirvāṅa-sûtra and Buddhacarita, Śākyamuni is said to have entered "viṣkandaka samādhi" (=concentration which is like the Lion's Yawn).The Licchavis appear to have inherited the same tradition from the Śākyas of Kapilavastu. Under the circumstances I have reason to feel that Bhāravi seems to be influenced by Māna-deva's pillar Inscription of Cāngu-Nārāyaṇa Face III 16 reading : "nirbhîh siṃha ivākulotkaṭasaṭaḣ pāscādhbhuvañ jagmivān" (vide Appendix for its translation.) Accordingly, the Lion has been accepted as the Heraldic Beast by the subsequent dynasties of the kings of Nepal to our own day.

विभरांवभूवुरवितत जठरशफरीकुलाकुलाः ।
पंकविषटमितताः सरितः करिरुग्ण चन्दन रसारुणं पयः ॥४९॥

Vibharāṃvabhûvuravitata jaṭharaśapharîkulākulāḣ /
pañkaviṣamitataṭāḣ saritaḣ karirugṇacandan rasāruṇaṃ payaḣ //49//

Translation :

Forced out of their nests in river beds by the spreading confusion consequent upon the stampede of terrified elephants and blinded and their stomach upset by the bitter sandal pastes, the shoal of fishes found themselves stranded in the mud-plasterd banks.

महिषक्षतागुरुतमालनलदसुरभिः सदागतिः ।
व्यस्तशुकनिभशिलाकुसुमः प्रणुदन्ववौ वनसदां परिश्रमम् ॥५०॥

Mahiṣakṣatāgurutamālanaladasurabhiḣ sadāgatiḣ /
vyastaśukanibhaśilākusumaḣ praṇudanvavau vanasadāṃ
pariśramam //50//

Translation :

The cool breeze blowing from the tall Tamāla (cinnamomum tamala तेजपात or garcinia morilla =सतिशाल) and the fragrant roots of Nalada (vetiveria zizaniorides = उशीर from which scents are extracted) bruised by the buffaloes in their grazing as well as from the

Śilākusumaḥ (saxi–fraga) bearing the faded colour of a parrot, relieved the privations and fatigue of the Kirātas in beating the different zones of the forests (alotted to them for the task).

N.B. In this stanza we get a glimpse of the range of Bhāravi's minute observation of the fauna and floıa fom the frigid zones of the Himalayas inhabited by yaks down to the fragrant belt of Tamāla and Nalada, where the buffaloes graze. On my way to Lhasa I have personally observed "śilākusuma" (saxi fraga) which grows among the dark stones of the Himalayan region and disintegrate the rocks. By a few deft strokes of his pen the poet gives us glimpse of the stupendous scenery of the Himalayas, where the Kirātas lived and worked from the snow-covered tundras down to the steaming and lush valleys through the coniferous pine forests.

मथिताम्भसो रयविकीर्णमृदितकदलीगवेधुकाः ।
क्लान्तजलरुहलताः सरसीर्विदधे निदाघ इव सत्त्वसंप्लवः ॥५१॥

Mathitāmbhaso rayavikîrṇamriditakadalîgavedhukāḥ /
Klāntajalaruhalatāḥ sarasîrvidadhe nidāgha iva sattvasaṃ-
plavaḥ //51//

Translation :

As if for the relief and preservation of life during the dry season of summer, the canalisation of water from the swift-moving mountain rivers sprinkled the banana-groves and animal fodders amıd terraced farms full of hay-lofts, where the stems of water lilies in the pools conserved water appeared to be inviting the fatigued hunters (for of slaking their thirst or for having their bath).

इति चालयन्नचलसानुवनगहनजानुमापतिः ।
प्राप मुदितहरिणीदशनक्षतवीरुधं वसतिमैन्द्रसूनवीम् ॥५२॥

Iti cālayannacalasānuvanagahanajānumāpatiḥ /
prāpa muditahariṇîdaśanakṣatavîrudhaṃ vasatimaindrasû-
navîṃ//52//

Translation :

It was while the husband of Umā was beating the forest to rouse the denizens of the woods from their retreat along the slopes of the silent and immovable sylvan mountains, the flocks of deer approached the hermitage peacefully nibbling the creepers as usual, where the son of Indra practised his penitential practices.

स तमाससाद घननीलमभिमुखमुपस्थितं मुनेः ।
पोत्रनिकषणविभिन्नभुवं दनुजंदधान अतिसौकरं वपुः ॥५३॥

Sa tamāsasāda ghananîlamabhimukhamupasthitaṃ muneh̀ /
potranikaṣaṇavibhinnabhuvaṃ danujaṃdadhāna atisaukaraṃ vapuh̀//53//

Translation :

Finally He (the king of Kirāta) spotted the gigantic body of the demon in the form of a cloud-dark wild-boar burrowing through the various soils with his hard tusks, so that he may ambush the saint (Arjuna and kill him on the spot).

N.B. I do not see any reason why Mallinātha needed the indeclinable particle "atha" (= there or now) used at the beginning of words as a sign of auspiciousness to give continuity to the story, when the facts of beating the forests to spot the brute and his discovery are being related as they came in surprising sequence of things. According to Mr. V.S. Āpte "ati" is an indeclinable particle used with adjectives and adverbs meaning "very, too, exceedingly or excessively" and showing "utkarṣa" (high-spirt or self-conceit), which would be appropriate in the present context.

कच्छान्ते सुरसरितो निधाय सेनामन्वीतः स कतिपयैः किरातवर्यैः ।
प्रच्छन्नस्तरुगहनैः सगुल्मजालैर्लक्ष्मीवाननुपदमस्य संप्रतस्थे ॥५४॥

Kacchānte Surasarito nidhāya senāmanvîtah̀ sa katipayaih̀ Kiratāvar-yaih̀ /
pracchannastarugahanaih̀ sagulmajālairlakśmîvānanupadamasya saṃpratasthe //54//

Translation :

Leaving the bulk of the army on the bank of the rivulet known as Surasaritā for rear-guard action, the fine-looking and smart king cf the Kirātas hid himself amid the foliages of the dense jungle (like an expert hunter that he was) and followed the track of the wild-boar accompanied only by the pick of the Kirāta contingent.

N.B. The metre here is Praharśiṅî".

In total ignorance of historical and geographical knowledge Mallinātha identifies Surasaritā with the sources of the Ganges known as Mandākinî. We have pointed out how Surasaritā is a disguised name for river "Vāgwatî".

The End of Canto XII

REFERENCES

Bibliography

1. Amarakoṣa
2. Annals of China
3. Āpte V.S., Students' Sanskrit English Dictionary
4. Aṣṭāsārikā–prajŋāpāramitā
5. Aśvaghoṣa, Buddhacarita
6. Bhagvadgītā
7. Bharata, Naṭyasāstra
8. Bhavabhūti, Uttararamacarita
9. Bodhisattvabhûmi
10. Bṛhadāraṇyaka upaniṣad
11. Brough, J., Gotrapravara-mañjari
12. Davids, Prof. Rhys, Life of the Buddha
13. Devkotā, Koṣanātha, Nighanṭu (Nepali)
14. Encyclopaedia Brittanica
15. Gnoli, Prof. R., Nepalese Inscriptions in Gupta Characters
16. Goetz, Professor H., Art of the World
17. Hsūan-Tsāng, Travel Accounts
18. Kathāsaritsāgara
19. Kālidāsa, Kumārasaṃbhava
20. " " Meghadūta
21. " " Raghuvaṃśa
22. K.C., Kaisher Bahadur, The Judicial Customs of Nepal, Part I
23. K.C., Kaisher Bahadur, The Kirātārjunîye
24. Lalitavistara
25 Lañkāvatāra
26. Levi, M., Le Nepal
27. Madhyāntavibhāga
28. The Mahābhārata
29. Mahāparinirvāṇasûtra

30. Mahāyānasūtralaṃkāra
31. Manu, Manusmriti
32. Ovid, Ars Amatoria
33. Pali Dhamma
34. Petech, L., Northern India According to Shui-Ching-chu
35. The Rāmāyaṇa
36. Śharmā, Bimala, Nepali Translation of the Kirātārjunîye
37. Ślokavārtika-niralamvanavāda
37. Ślokavārtika-Śunnyavāda
39. Stella Kramrish, Art of Nepal
40. Tattva Saṃgraha
41. Tucci, G., Preliminary Report on Two Scientific Expeditions of Nepal
42. Vajrachhedikā
34. Vātsyāyana, Kāmasūtra
44. Viswanāth Kavirāj, Sāhityadarpaṇa
45. Waldschmidt, Art Treasurer of the Himalayas
46. Yakṣa, Nirukta
47. Yājnavalkya, Vājasaneyi saṃhita

List Of Inscriptions

1. Inscription of King Rāmadeva
2. Inscription of Mahendravarman
3. Lichhavi Inscriptions
4. Mānadeva's Inscription of Cāngu Nārāyaṇa
5. Anuparamagupta Gomi's Pilaster of Hārigāon
6. Inscription of King Vasantadeva
7. Inscription of Jayadeva
8. Aśokan Inscription of Lumbinī

Errata

Page	Line	Incorrect	Correct
2	9	Guptānmaṭh	guptānmatha
8	30	Saṃpida	Saṃpiḍa
13	19	Ākîrnā	Ākīrṇā
13	19	Vilāsinīmu	vilāsiniṇamu
13	29	Apatanti	Āpatanti
14	18	raining	reining
18	8	mādahde	mādadhe
22	1	Ārodhuh	Āroḍhuh
23	3	krîdanta	Krîḍanta
29	4	canto	camp
32	12	yaşti	yaşṭi
32	13	daştaustakarā	daşṭausthakarā
33	29	Madra	Madras
34	12	by prodigally	prodigally by
34	15	yield	yield the
34	20	factural	factudal
34	27	is great	is a great
36	25	temple	tempi
37	20	five	fire
37	29	jaghanean	jaghanena
39	22	hiṁsāra	niṁsāra
40	21	drankards	drunkards
40	29	mani	maṇi
40	29	navasni	navasai
41	8	Madias	Madras
41	28	sputa	sphuṭa
44	14	Kalaṃsa	Kalahaṃsa
46	3	parilodita	pariloḍita
46	18	māndanen	maṇḍanena
47	17	vilînaşṭpade	vilînasatpade
50	—	—	Canto VIII
50	13	danam	ḍanaṃ
52	7	kritanu	kritānu
54	24	nimianna	nimîlanna
56	14	priyopakantham	priyopakaṇṭhaṃ
56	20	in state	in a state

56	25	rūdh	rūḍha
58	18	twiligh	twilight
69	10	varida	vārida
73	5	see Bhāravi	seen how Bhāravi
74	17	illusive	ellusive
74	26	nirodhānirodhā	nirodhā
76	28	sputa	sphuṭa
78	22	śaśipadais	śaśipādais
84	3	ucyataṃ	ucytāṃ
85	1	Tti anslation	Translation
85	13	pularodihi	pulakarodhi
86	16	Kāimimiti	Kāmināmiti
87	8	प्राणनाथम	प्राणनाथ
87	29	सा	स्म
88	19	priyatme	priyatame
90	9	widowhood	of widowhood
91	2	गद्गवा	गद्गदवा
93	11	vibhramaniva	vibhramāniva
93	12	palaśai	palāsai
95	3	shridiva	suhridiva
95	13	आर्द्रन्त	आर्द्रदन्त
95	14	वतिरामिव	वतितरामिव
99	10	sphuta	sphuṭa
101	11	mūdha	mūḍha
104	4	tatpūrvātāmiva	tatpūrvatāmiva
117	22	Vijayanati	Vijayavatî
117	25	स	च
118	29	irresible	irresistible
120	12	preciptous	precipitous
121	15	misic	music
121	17	Mridargas	Mridangas
122	2	jalagubhiḥ	jalagurubhiḥ
122	11	world	word
122	19	sarajasatāsatāpava-nerapāṃ	sai ajasatamavane -rapāṃ
122	30	vibahbau	vibabhau
124	10	जानुनु	जामुनु
126	29	दमालो	दयालो

128	21	virnal	vernal
130	1	नवनिहितेप्यं	नवनिहितेष्य
130	4	madhusurabhini	madhusurabhiṇi
130	7	hodding	holding
131	8	the poet of	the poet
131	9	the state	the state of
131	10	(Indriya) our	(Indriya) of our
131	10	(rāpa)	(rūpa)
131	12	Bhairavi	Bhāravi
131	30	yattadanîṃ	yattadānim̩
132	12	the the	the wives of the
133	1	gucchayuthikasu	gucchayuthikāsu
137	14	cirmti	ciramati
137	30	मुपतु	मुपैतु
138	13	napyate	nāpyate
141	9	sathaḣ'	saṭhaḣ'
141	14	dharosthama	dharoṣṭhama
141	15	lajjayās aḣ'	lajjayā saḣ'
141	18	asa	as
143	14	tathapi	tathāpi
161	7	bhogānbhôgnai	bhogānbhogāni
161	16	mūdhā	mūḍhā
163	11	pîdā	pîḍā
163	25	thier	this
164	5	night-fold	eightfold
165	17	स्वप्नोमान्मत्वा	स्वप्नोपमान्मत्वा
167	7	nirpekṣa	nirapekṣa
167	29	क्षुभितोवदन्व	क्षुभितोदन्व
171	3	rajna	rājna
191	2	nayanavinimesa	nayanavinimeṣa
192	19	Nā	Na
201	17	convery	convey
201	22	तुहिनाराशि	तुहिनराशि
203	12	vrita	vritra
204	29	mamaraditi	mamaradîti
207	33	sheme	scheme
208	6	liew	lieu
208	16	soice miva	voice of Śiva
208	19	Dviśataḣ	Dviṣataḣ